Income Support for the Unemployed

Issues and Options

**WORLD BANK
REGIONAL AND
SECTORAL STUDIES**

Income Support for the Unemployed

Issues and Options

Milan Vodopivec

THE WORLD BANK
Washington, D.C.

ISBN 0-8213-5761-1

Cover photo: Jure Eržen

Library of Congress Cataloging-in-Publication Data has been applied for.

Contents

Preface vii

Acknowledgments ix

1. Introduction 1

2. Conceptual Issues 5
    Objectives of Income Support Programs for the Unemployed 7
    Accounting for Interactions among Social Risk
        Management Mechanisms 8
    Establishing Evaluation Criteria 14
    Why Should the Public Sector Provide Unemployment Insurance? 17
    Who Should Receive Unemployment Income Support? 19
    Summary 21

3. Review of Income Support Programs
        for the Unemployed 25
    Typology and Description of Main Income Support Programs 25
    The Incidence of Income Support Programs for the Unemployed 52
    Concluding Remarks 62
    Annex 3.1   Determinants of Social Insurance Programs
        for the Unemployed 63

4. Performance of Income Support Programs:
        Theoretical Aspects and Empirical Evidence 65
    Income Protection Effects 66
    Efficiency Effects 81
    Suitability to Confront Different Shocks 104

Resistance to Political Risk 111
Concluding Remarks.. 117
Annex 4.1   Efficiency Effects of Income Support Programs 118

5. **Design and Implementation Criteria: Exploring**
    Country-Specific Conditions... 131
    Interactions with Labor Market Institutions and Shocks 131
    Administrative Capacity for Program Implementation 133
    Characteristics of Unemployment 137
    Size of the Informal Sector 138
    Prevalence and Pattern of Interhousehold Transfers 139
    Nonsocial Insurance and Self-Protection.. 141
    The Nature of Shocks.. 145
    Cultural and Political Factors 146
    Concluding Remarks 151

6. **Improving Income Support Programs for the**
    Unemployed in Developing Countries... 153
    Choosing the Right Program 153
    Designing Unemployment Insurance 177
    Improving Income Protection of the Informal Sector 180
    Concluding Remarks 183

References.. 187

Index... 209

Preface

In May 2003 I was asked to help the Sri Lankan government introduce an unemployment insurance program. The task was daunting: never had I encountered a country at such a low level of economic development, with so large an informal sector and such weak administrative capacity, embark upon such an effort. Yet as I learned, providing unemployment insurance was the only politically acceptable way for Sri Lankan policymakers to reform another badly performing labor market institution: severance pay.

This is an example of the difficult choices and tradeoffs developing countries face in providing income support against unemployment risk. Industrial countries offer such support primarily by providing social insurance. When is a developing country ready to introduce such a program? How should the blueprints for programs in place in industrial countries be modified to meet the circumstances of developing countries, including the different characteristics of unemployed workers and the abundant employment opportunities in the informal sector? How should the tradeoffs between different types of public income support programs be evaluated? What should the mix be between public and private risk management arrangements? How should the income protection and efficiency effects of different programs be balanced? Can income protection come only at the cost of efficiency?

I tackle these questions by evaluating different unemployment support programs and assessing their applicability in developing and transition countries. I combine and reconcile theoretical insights with empirical evidence, paying due attention to country-specific circumstances. I identify the strengths and weaknesses of each program, as well as point out circumstances that are conducive to the success of each. I hope that the book will provide useful information and advice for policymakers throughout developing and transition countries and that it will arouse interest among academicians and others interested in income support for the unemployed.

Writing this book proved to be a fascinating undertaking, not least because the approaches countries have taken are so diverse and because new, innovative, and sometimes controversial programs (such as unemployment insurance savings accounts) are being introduced. With increasing recognition that protecting workers is more productive than protecting jobs, income support for the unemployed has gained in importance, and promising new, attractive solutions may be forthcoming.

Acknowledgments

This book is part of a larger effort of the Labor Market group of the Human Development Network to understand better and synthesize the effects of labor market policies and programs. The author has many intellectual debts to acknowledge. Special gratitude is owed to Robert Holzmann, who provided the impetus for this work, as well as invaluable general guidance; to the reviewers of the World Bank's Editorial Committee for rich, careful, and insightful comments; and to Dhushyanth Raju for excellent research assistance. I also benefited from written comments from Gordon Betcherman, Peter Fredriksson, Indermit Gill, Luis Guasch, Bertil Holmlund, and Jan van Ours, as well as from fruitful discussions with Alan Abrahart, Christine Allision, Mavricija Batič, Jacob Benus, Tito Boeri, Rocio Castro, Wendy Cunningham, Amit Dar, John Earle, Jude Esguerra, Cresenta Fernando, Indermit Gill, Margaret Grosch, John Haltiwanger, Hugo Hopenhayn, Jai-Joon Hur, Arvo Kuddo, Hartmut Lehman, William Maloney, John Micklewright, Gyula Nagy, Philip O'Keefe, Christopher O'Leary, Peter Orazem, Michael Orszag, Carmen Pages, Robert Palacios, Robert Pavosevich, Sonja Pirher, Martin Rama, Mansoora Rashid, Michelle Ribaud, Elizabeth Ruppert, Michal Rutkowski, Stefano Scarpetta, Kalanidhi Subbarao, Jan Svejnar, Hong Tan, Kathy Terrell, Wayne Vroman, David Warren, and Jungyoll Yun.

1

Introduction

Unemployment is becoming an increasingly pressing problem in many parts of the world. Macroeconomic crises and increased globalization have put more workers at risk of job loss in Latin America and, more recently, in East Asia. In an effort to transform themselves into market economies, former socialist countries have faced the enormous task of efficiently reallocating workers and jobs across sectors and firms, which has led to unemployment and poverty of large proportions. In Europe economic growth has declined and unemployment risen since the 1970s. Particularly worrisome is the rise in the share of the long-term unemployed.

Given these trends, the task of helping the unemployed has gained importance and attracted the interest of policymakers. Because job loss entails the loss of income, providing effective income support is a prime concern and a necessary component of assistance to the unemployed, be it in the form of a pure transfer or through jobs created by public programs.[1] But other aspects must also be considered. It is important to consider how to increase the employability of the unemployed, that is, their capacity to search for jobs and to match skills with vacancies. Adverse labor supply incentives created by income transfers also need to be studied and addressed. And the risk of unemployment needs to be reduced, both by designing appropriate income support programs and by increasing employment opportunities.

While the task of increasing employment opportunities reaches far beyond labor market policies and programs, important links between an economy's capacity to create jobs job and income support programs—and social protection systems in general—should not be overlooked. Indeed, income support programs for the unemployed should be developed in line with a broader conceptual framework that lays out the complex linkages between institutions and policies in a systematic and comprehensive way. This book relies on such a comprehensive framework, developed by the World Bank (2001a). By formulating various strategies to manage social risk, the framework provides the analytical foundations for formulating social protection approaches and policies.

The purpose of this book is to provide guidelines for countries wishing to introduce or improve income support programs for the unemployed.

The book focuses on five such programs: unemployment insurance, unemployment assistance, unemployment insurance savings accounts (UISAs), severance pay, and public works. To arrive at guidelines, the book summarizes the evidence on the performance of different types of programs in four areas: how well they protect the incomes of the unemployed, how they affect efficiency, how able they are to confront different types of shocks, and how resistant they are to political interference. Based on this evaluation, the suitability of particular programs for developing and transition countries is assessed, taking account of countries' specific circumstances, chief among them labor market and other institutions, the capacity needed to administer income support programs, the size of the informal sector, and the prevalence of private transfers.

While the book provides a global perspective and reviews programs in countries around the world, its relevance and lessons are geared toward transition countries and middle-income developing countries. Although these countries may offer various income support programs (most often severance pay and public works), the unemployed remain inadequately protected: coverage is limited, programs may suffer from nonperformance, and the programs may impose heavy litigation costs and significant inefficiencies. As these countries develop, the issue of improving public income support programs—particularly by introducing social insurance—inevitably emerges. Indeed, many transition countries have recently introduced unemployment insurance programs, and some middle-income developing countries are contemplating doing so. For these countries, this book will provide valuable guidance by evaluating the choices and tradeoffs between various income support programs. In many low-income countries, social insurance–type programs are not a likely option in the foreseeable future. Some of the issues addressed in the book will thus not be relevant for these countries.

The book's main conclusions can be summarized as follows:

- *Unemployment insurance* enables a high degree of consumption smoothing, performs well under various types of shocks, and acts as an automatic macroeconomic stabilizer, but it creates reemployment disincentives and wage pressures, which increase the equilibrium unemployment rate and make unemployment persistent. Because its successful performance depends on conditions that are typically lacking in developing and transition countries, the case for introducing unemployment insurance in these countries is less compelling than it is in industrial countries.
- *Unemployment assistance* allows more effective targeting than unemployment insurance, but it may not produce savings and it offers a lower level of protection for high-income workers, imposes larger administrative costs, and suffers from similar employment disincentives. Its applicability is thus limited, perhaps to countries with relatively developed administrative capacity and a small informal sector.
- *Unemployment insurance savings accounts* are a potentially interesting option. By internalizing the costs of unemployment benefits, UISAs ameliorate the moral hazard inherent in traditional unemployment

insurance and thus improve reemployment incentives—an important advantage given the weak monitoring capacity of developing countries. By integrating the accounts with social insurance—thus circumventing the main weakness of not pooling risk among individuals—UISAs may improve work incentives while in principle offering income protection comparable to traditional unemployment insurance. UISAs also have the potential to attract informal sector workers. By allowing individuals to borrow from their accounts, some versions of integrated accounts introduce problems of their own, however, creating incentives to withdraw from the formal sector in order to avoid repaying the debt. Because the program has been largely untested, further investigation of its effects and design parameters, including piloting of the program, is needed.

- *Severance pay* is an important program, because it is available in many developing and transition countries, but it offers few advantages. To improve its protection and efficiency effects, countries may consider streamlining severance pay programs and reducing their costs if they are too generous. A more radical reform could introduce prefunding, to improve nonperformance and reduce labor market rigidities.
- *Public works* programs are effective in reaching the poor, have good targeting properties and substantial capacity to redistribute income from the rich to the poor, are able to attract informal sector workers and provide flexible and fast response to shocks, and are administratively less demanding than other public income support programs. Despite weaknesses—high nonwage costs, the likely countercyclical pattern of funding, and, in some countries, stigmatization of participants—public works programs are suitable for developing countries, particularly as a complementary program.

The book is organized as follows. Chapter 2 examines the conceptual issues that arise in evaluating and designing income support programs for the unemployed. It describes their objectives and discusses the need to evaluate them in a broader, social risk management framework that allows for various interactions. Based on this framework, two sets of evaluation criteria are developed, which are used to assess the applicability of various programs to developing and transition countries. Performance criteria evaluate the income protection and efficiency effects of these programs; design and implementation criteria evaluate how different programs fit the specific circumstances of developing and transition countries. Chapter 2 also explains why unemployment insurance is usually provided as part of social insurance and addresses definitional and measurement issues of unemployment. It notes the historic conditions responsible for the emergence of unemployment and draws implications about the suitability of transferring unemployment support programs from industrial countries to developing and transition countries.

Chapter 3 describes key income support programs for the unemployed and describes their stylized design features. It emphasizes the richness of the approaches and the complexity of the programs, highlighting important features that should be considered when introducing or improving such programs. It also analyzes the incidence of the main types of income support programs for the unemployed throughout the world. It shows that industrial countries base their income protection on social insurance but also provide other unemployment support programs, while some low-income countries have no special programs for the unemployed. The chapter also shows that parameters of a particular income support program differ sharply across countries, contributing to differences in coverage and the degree of protection provided.

Chapter 4 evaluates the performance of the selected income support programs, based on a review of theoretical predictions and empirical evidence. It focuses not only on income protection effects but also on efficiency effects and the ability of such programs to confront various types of economic shocks and resist political risk. It shows that, through various channels and due to complex interactions, these programs generate a wide variety of effects, some intended and some unintended, some anticipated and some unanticipated. It also shows that no program outperforms all others: one program may offer superior insurance properties, but it may create labor market disincentives and generate an "entitlement mentality" that makes reform of the program difficult.

When introducing or improving income support programs, countries should also account for country-specific circumstances, because they crucially determine how well a program fits a particular country. Chapter 5 is therefore devoted to the circumstances prevailing in developing and transition countries. It reviews their key institutional and labor market features, as well as the capacity needed to administer such programs. It shows that these countries may deviate significantly from the typical labor market and other institutional features under which income support programs function in industrial countries and that developing countries may also lack the capabilities necessary for the smooth and effective administration of some programs. Chapter 5 also shows that the desirability of alternative income support programs depends crucially on the interactions of these programs with other social risk management mechanisms and that these interactions may be very different in developing and transition countries.

Building on the discussion of previous chapters, Chapter 6 evaluates alternative income support programs and provides tentative guidelines for improving these programs in developing and transition countries. Drawing on the previously established performance effects, the chapter describes the strengths and weaknesses of each type of income support program and points to country-specific circumstances that are particularly conducive to the performance of each. It also examines some important design features of unemployment insurance and options for improving income support for informal sector workers.

Note

1. An important recent contribution to the analysis of policy options for income support for the unemployed, focusing on the Latin American context, is by de Ferranti and others (2000).

2

Conceptual Issues

Faced with the risk of unemployment, individuals choose among a variety of risk management mechanisms. Some try to get a good education or enter jobs that are known to be stable, in order to reduce the risk of becoming unemployed. Others may accumulate real or financial assets or participate in unemployment insurance programs, in order to have financial means at hand if unemployment occurs. Yet others may rely on private transfers of cash, food, and clothing; draw down financial or real assets; participate in public works or public training; or receive social assistance, in order to cushion the loss of earnings associated with job loss.

How should the desirability of such mechanisms be judged from the viewpoint of society? Successful smoothing of consumption is important, but so are other considerations. Do public programs displace other mechanisms, formal or informal? Do they affect job search effort and the type of post-unemployment job? How successful are they in reaching the hardest-hit segments of the population and the very poor? What are the tradeoffs between pure income transfers and programs that combine transfers with other requirements—and opportunities—such as public works or training? How can the loss of human capital associated with prolonged unemployment spells be prevented?

This chapter provides the conceptual underpinnings of the approach the book takes in evaluating income support programs for the unemployed and describes the rationale for public interventions. The starting point—and the recurrent theme of the book—is the recognition that public income support programs for the unemployed are just a subset of social risk management mechanisms. It is of utmost importance, therefore, to look at the system of social risk management in its entirety, in order to consider links among its components and assess the repercussions of introducing new public programs on other mechanisms. The richness of the mechanisms and strategies available to individuals, families, and communities is staggering. To be tractable, theoretical models must thus focus on specific aspects of income support. The robustness of their conclusions must therefore be verified to insure that they are applicable under the circumstances prevailing in a particular country. So, too, must empirical findings obtained in industrial countries be checked to make sure that they hold under the circumstances prevailing in developing and transition countries.

Because of the complexity of interactions and the lack of generality of theoretical results, as well as the dearth of empirical studies on income support programs in developing and transition countries, the book developed two sets of criteria with which to judge the desirability of income support programs in a particular country. The first set consists of performance criteria, the second of design and implementation criteria. Performance criteria relate to the effects of income support programs predicted by theoretical models and validated by empirical studies. These criteria evaluate programs not only based on how effectively they provide income protection but also based on how they affect efficiency, how suitable they are to confront different types of shocks, and how resilient they are to political risk.

When transferring the experience of one country to another, policymakers need to take account of "initial conditions"—the particular features of the country in question. This is particularly important given that theoretical models are built on many simplifying assumptions and that empirical studies have been conducted largely on industrial countries, where conditions may be very different from those in developing and transition countries. The second set of criteria, the design and implementation criteria, therefore include country-specific features, such as the nature of labor market institutions, the administrative capacity of the country to deliver specific programs, the characteristics of the unemployed, and the size of the informal sector. The degree of informality of the economy determines how many people can take advantage of formal sector programs (such as unemployment insurance and severance pay); the administrative capacity of the economy is a good predictor of the success of programs that require strong monitoring or information capacity.

This chapter also provides the rationale for public provision of unemployment insurance as part of social insurance, while continuing to apply the social risk management framework. Markets provide insurance only under certain circumstances—most notably, in the absence of informational asymmetries and the presence of certain characteristics of the risk—circumstances that are violated in the case of unemployment insurance. Hence there is room for government interventions, which usually consist of mandating membership or providing insurance through the public sector. The chapter also examines the interrelation between unemployment insurance and development of the labor market, emphasizing that unemployment is a special social construct that emerges only in industrial societies and that its emergence, in turn, creates demand for social insurance.

The chapter is organized as follows. After describing the objectives of income support programs for the unemployed—compensating for lost wages, stabilizing employment, helping the unemployed obtain better jobs more quickly—the chapter places income support programs in the context of social risk management. The interaction with other risk management mechanisms—informal and formal, private and public—has an important bearing on the success of these programs and hence on their desirability. Although theoretical modeling of such interactions provides significant insights, the fact that it simplifies these interactions and imposes other constraints means that can provide only limited recommendations on policy. The suitability of alternative income support programs is therefore evaluated using an approach that combines performance evaluation criteria (stressing income protection and efficiency aspects, as well as suitability to confront shocks and resistance to political interference) with design and implementation criteria (stressing countries' specific conditions). (In subsequent chapters, these analytical instruments are used to evaluate various income support programs and assess their desirability for developing and transition countries.) The chapter concludes by describing the rationale for public provision of unemployment insurance and discussing the appropriateness of income support programs for developing and transition countries.

Objectives of Income Support Programs for the Unemployed

From the viewpoint of the individual, the objective of income support programs for the unemployed is precisely that implied by their name—compensation for income loss due to unemployment. Such programs provide income protection to workers by partly replacing their lost wages with social insurance payments (under unemployment insurance and unemployment assistance as well as under some variants of unemployment insurance savings accounts), lump-sum payments upon separation (severance pay), or wages obtained from publicly generated employment (public works). Such payments help cushion the reduction in consumption in the wake of job loss—that is, they smooth consumption—and may also help alleviate poverty.

To varying degrees, other objectives also figure prominently, particularly if these programs are viewed from a broader, societal perspective. These additional objectives, which relate to both efficiency and fairness, include the following:

- *Unemployment insurance*: Stabilizing employment and preventing unemployment by discouraging layoffs and restoring purchasing power, encouraging workers to acquire new skills, providing workers with the means to conduct more extensive and more effective job searches, redistributing income from high- to low-wage earners, and increasing output and efficiency (by promoting restructuring of enterprises or encouraging workers to accept higher wage and thus higher-productivity, but also riskier, jobs, for example).
- *Unemployment assistance*: Similar to the objectives of unemployment insurance, but because unemployment assistance is a means-tested program, the emphasis is on poverty reduction rather than consumption smoothing.

- *Unemployment insurance savings accounts*: Similar to the objectives of unemployment insurance. Because the program design encourages work incentives, the relative importance attached to these objectives may be different, however. In particular, the program leaves less scope for income redistribution.
- *Severance pay*: Stabilizing employment and preventing unemployment by discouraging layoffs. In voluntary schemes, the objective of the firm is to encourage long-term relationships in order to retain valuable workers, as well as to reduce transactions costs due to the loss of skills and firm-specific knowledge generated by labor turnover.
- *Public works*: Providing goods and services for the poor, maintaining and creating human capital, countering the psychological effects of unemployment, reducing income inequalities and countering social exclusion, and fostering community development and empowerment.

The debate preceding the introduction of unemployment insurance in the United States in the 1930s illustrates the opposing views about the objectives of unemployment insurance. The view that eventually prevailed emphasized consumption smoothing (Blaustein 1993). This view attached great importance to the principle that compensation be provided as a matter of right and not as a means-tested benefit. But two other important schools of thought were prominent. One emphasized preventing unemployment by discouraging layoffs. It claimed that employers should be held responsible for unemployment of their workers by bearing the costs of unemployment compensation, through "experience rating." This view has retained ground in the United States to the present day. The other school of thought promoted faster reemployment, claiming that unemployment insurance programs should not only provide resources to the unemployed but also help them find jobs in other ways.

Some of the stated objectives of these programs may fail to materialize—and may indeed backfire. For example, the stated objective of severance pay of stabilizing employment and preventing unemployment should be contrasted with its widely established effects on employment: while the program does stabilize jobs of incumbent workers, it reduces overall employment rates (see chapter 4). Similarly, although public works are sometimes justified on the grounds that they help the unemployed counter the psychological effects of unemployment, these programs often stigmatize participants, thus reducing their job prospects and hurting their self-image. These examples highlight the importance of accounting for the complex interactions typically at work in providing public income support to the unemployed.

Accounting for Interactions among Social Risk Management Mechanisms

The risk of unemployment is best studied in the context of social risk management, the framework that recognizes that many risk management mechanisms—informal and formal, private and public—exist and interact in many important ways. Recognizing and appropriately accounting for such interactions is critical to selecting and designing the most appropriate public income support programs. As shown below, formal treatment of interactions provides significant insights yet of necessity abstracts from many interactions and simplifies institutional features.

Social Risk Management Framework

Public income support programs are a subset of risk management mechanisms available to the unemployed. These mechanisms can be divided into three categories: those that reduce the risk of unemployment (reduce the probability of becoming unemployed or increase the probability of leaving unemployment if unemployed), those that mitigate that risk (reduce the impact of a future unemployment spell), and those applied in response to the undesirable event (coping mechanisms).[1] Within all three categories, informal and formal mechanisms are usually available. Formal mechanisms include both market-based and public mechanisms (table 2.1).

The social risk management framework enables one to position public income support programs for the unemployed in the context of other mechanisms that may be used to manage the risk of unemployment. Viewing the program in its entirety and considering links among various components is useful when evaluating the performance of public programs or assessing the effects of their introduction. Among the diverse interactions that must be considered are the following:

- *General equilibrium and growth interactions.* The introduction of unemployment insurance may encourage the emergence or expansion of more risky jobs or industries, which conceivably could increase efficiency (Acemoglu and Shimer 1999, 2000). Income support programs may also have dynamic effects, including effects produced by the interaction of unemployment benefits with adverse shocks to the economy. As discussed in chapter 4, these interactions typically slow the reduction of unemployment to the shock and thus contribute to the persistence of unemployment. In contrast, in their role as an automatic macroeconomic stabilizer, unemployment benefits soften the impact of adverse shocks on GDP—but they also restrain expansion when the economy starts growing again.
- *Interactions with private risk management mechanisms.* There is a great variety of such interactions, many having important long-term consequences. For example, participation in a public income support program may increase investments in human capital (such as enabling better education of family members and improving health) and reduce the use of undesirable coping strategies (such as selling cattle essential for providing important nutrients). But public programs— as well as private transfers received by participants—may reduce participants' incentives to save or to enroll in training.

Table 2.1. Formal and Informal Income Support Mechanisms for the Unemployed

Strategy	Informal mechanisms	Formal mechanisms	
		Market based	Public
Risk reduction	• Less risky production • Migration • Proper feeding and weaning practices • Maintainence of good health	• Training • Financial market literacy • Company-based and market-driven labor standards	• Sound macroeconomic policies • Public health policy • **Labor market policies** (including employment protection policies, such as **severance pay**)
Risk mitigation			
Portfolio diversification	• Multiple jobs • Investment in human, physical, and real assets • Investment in social capital (rituals, reciprocal gift-giving)	• Investment in multiple financial assets • Microfinance programs	• Multipillar pension systems • Asset transfers • Protection of property rights • Support for extending financial markets to the poor
Insurance	• Savings (in form of financial or other assets) • Marriage, family • Community arrangements • Sharecrop tenancy	• Old-age annuities • Disability, accident, and other personal insurance • Crop, fire, and other damage insurance	• **Unemployment insurance** • **Unemployment assistance** • **Unemployment insurance savings accounts** • Pensions (including **early retirement**), disability, and sickness insurance
Risk coping	• Selling of real assets • Borrowing from neighbors • Intracommunity transfers and charity • Child labor • Dis-saving in human capital	• Sale of financial assets • Commercial loans	• Social assistance • General subsidies • **Active labor market programs (job-search assistance, training, employment subsidies, public works)** • Social funds

Source: Adapted from World Bank (2001a).

Note: Major public mechanisms used to manage the risk of unemployment are shown in bold.

- *Interactions with other policies and programs.* Important links also exist among public policies and programs themselves. The financing of social insurance typically requires contributions from both employers and employees, thus creating a wedge between the wage received and labor costs. To the extent that this wedge reduces labor demand, the introduction of unemployment insurance contributes to higher unemployment. (The increase in the reservation wage in response to higher unemployment benefits has the same effect.) Similarly, increasing the generosity of severance pay is likely to reduce employment rates and slow labor market flows, particularly from employment to unemployment but also from nonemployment to employment. Thus the introduction of a risk mitigation mechanism (such as social insurance) or a risk reduction mechanism (such as severance pay) may increase the unemployment rate or negatively affect the job creation capacity of an economy, thereby worsening the effectiveness of other risk management mechanisms.

The social risk management framework thus makes clear not only that there are multiple mechanisms for dealing with the risk of unemployment but also that there are complex links and interactions among them. Recognizing—and appropriately accounting for—such interactions is critical if policymakers are to choose and design the most appropriate public income support programs. For example, when a low-income country is considering improving its public income support for the unemployed, it must take diverse and far-reaching implications into account. These range from the impact on individuals' self-protection mechanisms (including changes in the intensity of job search and the propensity to enroll in training) to the effects on labor market outcomes (including the unemployment rate and the intensity of labor market flows) to the capacity to administer a particular program (box 2.1).

Guidance and Limitations of Formal Modeling

One rich source of policy advice is economic theory, which provides insights into the working of income support programs and the implications of such programs for economic policy (see chapter 4).

Ehrlic and Becker (1972) propose a comprehensive insurance theory (box 2.2).[2] They conclude that relatively rare and large losses are better insured through market insurance, while relatively frequent and moderate losses are better insured though self-insurance.

Extending the comprehensive insurance approach, Gill and Ilahi (2000) provide the following insights about the rationale of and guidelines for social policies:

- The lack of insurance offered by the market provides a rationale for its public provision.
- One of the best means of self-protecting is investing in human capital, but doing so provides poor collateral. By subsidizing the acquisition

---

Box 2.1. Recognizing Interactions among Different Risk Management Mechanisms

In dealing with the risk of unemployment, Filipino workers employed in the formal sector rely on severance pay (although it may be difficult to obtain). These workers are better off than informal sector workers, who have little or no protection. It is therefore not surprising that Filipino workers have relied heavily on informal mechanisms to manage unemployment risk, many of which are costly, inefficient, and above all inadequate.

How can public policy be improved to help Filipino workers deal more effectively with unemployment? The social risk management framework suggests that the answer should rest on the following considerations, among others:

- How well does the program fit into existing risk management mechanisms? Would its introduction disrupt existing self-protection mechanisms or displace existing coping mechanisms (such as a program of private transfers, especially for the nonpoor population) that may be more efficient than public programs? Is the program well attuned to the prevailing norms and culture? Can existing institutions be "upgraded" to provide better protection and increased coverage?
- How do the likely beneficiaries compare with other population groups? What are the likely effects of the program on income redistribution and poverty reduction?
- Is the program compatible with other public support mechanisms and policies? Above all, does it promote labor reallocation and job creation as sources of productivity growth?
- How well does the program respond to the country's income shocks, such as economic recessions, structural imbalances caused by liberalization and globalization, and shocks caused by natural calamities?
- Is the program well attuned to local circumstances, so that it functions well? Can it be supported with the existing administrative capacity? Are there mechanisms that allow participants to be selected effectively?

Source: Esguerra, Ogawa, and Vodopivec (2001).

---

of human capital, the government can mitigate the resulting tendency to underinvest.

- Private agents may self-insure using "bad" instruments (using cattle or land as a medium of precautionary saving, for example) because "good" instruments (such as diversified financial assets) are not available.
- The government should foster the development of insurance and financial markets. Strengthening of financial markets should be a central component of social policy, because it can foster self-insurance, market insurance, and self-protection (through prudential regulation of capital markets, for example).

Box 2.2.   Insights from the Theory of Comprehensive Insurance

Ehrlic and Becker (1972) model a utility-maximizing individual deciding how much to spend on three risk management instruments: market insurance, self-insurance, and self-protection. (Individuals insure by transferring income from the good to the bad state; they self-protect by taking actions that reduce the probability of the bad state). They draw several important conclusions:

- Market insurance and self-insurance are substitutes, as are self-insurance and self-protection; market insurance and self-protection may be substitutes or complements. An important implication is that the existence of market or social insurance may not reduce self-protection and thus produce a moral hazard problem. If, for example, more intense job search is rewarded by lowering the unemployment insurance premium, moral hazard is not inevitable. (Note that this assumes that self-protection behavior is detectable.)
- Relatively rare and large losses are better insured through market insurance; relatively frequent and moderate losses are better insured though self-insurance. This conclusion follows from the fact that while the price of market insurance is lower if the probability of loss is lower, the (shadow) price of self-insurance (for example, the cost of precautionary saving) does not vary with the likelihood of loss.
- Individuals enjoy higher welfare when all three instruments are available than when one of them is missing.
- Introducing a social safety net reduces self-protection but not necessarily self-insurance.

The richness and complexity of the issues that arise in the context of social risk management means that formal modeling has only a limited ability to capture all relevant aspects. Three problems in particular stand out. First, formal models simplify interactions among risk management mechanisms and abstract from general equilibrium effects. They focus on limited interactions and thus generate results that apply under specific circumstances. Once richer possibilities of interactions are introduced, they may recast the results in a different light. For example, recent research has shown that allowing interactions between unemployment benefits and the determination of wages—an issue that previous modeling had not taken into account—has important implications for the optimal time schedule of unemployment benefits (Cahuc and Lehmann 2000). Allowing for possibilities of private transfers and the existence of individual savings also affects income support modeling, yet these issues have only recently been considered in formal analysis.

Second, formal modeling imposes restrictive assumptions about the behavior and characteristics of economic agents and their knowledge, sacrificing generality for analytical tractability. For example, theoretical models of labor reallocation that explicitly treat job creation and destruction processes are often analytically intractable, forcing researchers to use calibration models that yield solutions under less general conditions.[3] Simplifications include using specific functional forms of utility and other important economic variables; assuming that individuals are homogeneous or allowing heterogeneity in only one trait; and (unreasonably) assuming what kind of information is available to certain agents (for example, that the government or insurer is able to observe abilities or self-protecting activities of insured workers).

Third, formal modeling disregards important institutional features, including features of income support programs themselves. Atkinson and Micklewright (1991, p. 1706) complain that "the great generality of research reaching conclusions about unemployment compensation has paid scant attention to the institutional details, and some elements have been almost totally ignored.... The importance of the institutional aspects is a matter on which we would like to insist." This argument applies with particular force once policy implications of theoretical models are applied to developing countries or OECD-style programs are transferred to developing countries; in doing so, important institutional features and other social risk management mechanisms may be ignored or neglected. In particular, the whole notion of unemployment in developing countries is very different than in industrial countries. Self-protection as well as informal insurance mechanisms are more prevalent, and initial conditions—administrative capacity, existence of financial markets, prevailing culture—are very different.

To summarize, theoretical modeling offers important, increasingly complex, and refined insights into the working of public income support programs. But such models can provide only partial guidance for policymakers—particularly in crafting policy for developing and transition countries, where the implicit assumptions (such as the existence of suitable institutional capacity and strict enforcement of law and order) often do not apply. Moreover, theoretical modeling of income support programs rarely incorporates long-term considerations such as investment in education or health, which are especially important in developing countries.

Establishing Evaluation Criteria

Given the complexity of interactions, the lack of generality of theoretical results, and the dearth of empirical studies on income support programs in developing and transition countries, how can income support programs for the unemployed be evaluated? Two sets of criteria are used here. The first are performance criteria, which assess how well a program works (how well it protects incomes and what other effects it may have). The second are design and implementation criteria, which assess how well a program fits a particular country (how suitable it is given country-specific conditions). This approach combines and reconciles theoretical insights about the performance of such programs with the empirical evidence and country-specific conditions that affect the applicability of programs to developing and transition countries.

The need for a synthetic approach that provides global perspectives and broad comparisons stems from the pressing and difficult choices faced by developing and transition countries. As shown in chapter 3, almost all industrial countries have unemployment insurance programs, while most other countries do not. As the economies of these countries develop, the question of improving public income support programs will inevitably emerge. Indeed, many countries (for example, all European transition economies, as well as China and Turkey), have recently introduced unemployment insurance programs, and some developing countries, including low-income ones (the Philippines, Sri Lanka, Thailand) are contemplating doing so. For these countries, evaluating the choices and tradeoffs between diverse income support programs—which do not lend themselves easily to rigorous modeling in a unified framework—is crucial.

The basis for distinction and the underlying principle of determination of the two groups of criteria are based on the usual role of variables that represent the criteria in economic investigations. Economic models often treat and formally specify the effects of an income support program (the "dependent" variables) as a function of its design features and initial (country-specific) conditions (sometimes called the "control" variables). Dependent variables of such economic models are assigned the role of performance criteria. These dependent variables typically reflect the effects of the program on income protection, income redistribution, and efficiency. In contrast, the control variables—a subset of right-hand-side variables that account for differences across countries when evaluating programs' cross-country performance—are assigned the role of design and implementation criteria.

Performance Evaluation Criteria

The performance of income support programs for the unemployed is measured by their success in achieving their objectives, as well as by other intended and unintended effects and features. Four subsets of performance criteria are assessed: protection criteria, efficiency criteria, suitability to confront shocks, and resistance to political risk.

Coverage and adequacy of support are examined to determine protection effects. The effects of income support programs on income redistribution are also analyzed, as these programs—intentionally or not—often involve substantial redistribution. A variety of measures are examined to assess efficiency effects, including the intensity of job-search effort, post-unemployment wages, equilibrium labor market outcomes, and effects on programs on output and growth. Suitability to confront economic shocks looks at how suitable different programs are for, say, a country that is frequently plagued by sudden, regionally concentrated shocks due to natural disasters or by long-lasting, covariant shocks. Resistance to political risk emphasizes political economy considerations in providing income support, such as which circumstances are conducive to the introduction of various programs and how to raise support for reforms to improve such programs.

Suitability to confront shocks and resistance to political risk are singled out in order to emphasize their role as indicators or predictors of both efficiency and protection performance. If a program is ill-suited for a particular shock or political risk, it means that it does not offer good protection or involves large efficiency costs. These additional criteria could have been ignored and the effects evaluated by them considered under the respective rubrics of protection and efficiency. They are treated separately in order to emphasize their importance.

Design and Implementation Criteria

Programs do not operate in a vacuum: country-specific circumstances affect their performance and thus determine their suitability to meet the specific needs of a country. In addition to performance criteria, which evaluate income support programs based on their performance under typical conditions (conditions that usually prevail in industrial economies), our approach introduces design and implementation criteria, which reflect specific features of the country under investigation. These features include the following:

- interactions with labor market institutions and shocks
- administrative capacity for program implementation
- characteristics of the unemployed
- size of the informal sector
- prevalence and pattern of interhousehold transfers
- ability of individuals to self-insure and self-protect
- nature of shocks
- cultural and political factors

To illustrate: in a country in which certain regions are often affected by natural disasters, income support programs must be flexible and capable of being quickly deployed in affected areas. Where the informal sector is large, programs must be accessible to the self-employed and other informal sector workers. When a program is chosen, a country's administrative capacity has to be taken into account. Unemployment insurance or assistance requires monitoring of recipients (to ensure compliance to continuing eligibility rules); unemployment assistance relies on means testing. The performance of such programs depends crucially on the administrative capacity to provide quality monitoring and testing. Interactions with other programs and policies are also important. For example, to avoid incentive incompatibility, unemployment insurance savings accounts need to be harmonized with old-age income support programs to preclude scenarios in which the accounts are depleted in anticipation of forbearance and generosity on the part of the pension system. Introducing or increasing the generosity of unemployment benefits may have different effects in an economy with different levels of centralization and coordination of wage bargaining: under fragmented and uncoordinated bargaining, unemployment benefits are more likely to increase wage pressures and hence the equilibrium unemployment rate than under alternative arrangements (see chapter 4). Chapter 5 is devoted to the implications of country-specific circumstances for the choice and design of income support programs.

Why Should the Public Sector Provide Unemployment Insurance?

Some studies cast doubt on the welfare benefits of public programs, because such programs may displace old mechanisms for dealing with unemployment risk. While precise conditions for the introduction of public programs are difficult to pinpoint, experience shows that these programs can provide important benefits. Informal insurance mechanisms may often be ineffective, because the loss of employment is too large a shock and may occur too frequently. As Murdoch (1999) points out, informal insurance (such as reciprocal and other forms of transfers) tends to be least effective when insurance is most needed. Moreover, in poor countries the beneficiaries of private transfers are the elderly; keeping more income for themselves would enable the young—who are often also poor—to obtain more education. Providing formal income support may also improve fairness (many informal insurance mechanisms discriminate against women, for example).

If informal insurance mechanisms are not satisfactory and unemployment insurance is desirable, why does the market not provide it? Unemployment insurance is typically provided publicly as a part of social insurance primarily because of strong information asymmetries—moral hazard and adverse selection problems—that prevent markets from providing such insurance. Moral hazard arises because unemployment insurance reduces self-protection; adverse selection arises because information problems prevent insurers from charging bad risks higher premiums. Public programs are also able to pool resources across larger groups than private insurance could. Correcting for market failures calls not only for regulation—obligatory membership to avoid adverse selection—but also for public provision, to improve the monitoring capacity and financial sustainability of the program.

How does unemployment insurance work? By pooling risk across individuals, insurance shifts resources from a good to a bad state (compensating unemployed workers by collecting contributions from employed workers, for example). By offering a certain outcome, insurance can increase welfare. For a risk-averse individual, expected utility from uncertain outcomes falls short of the utility provided by insurance that eliminates uncertainty and provides certain, unconditional income, as long as the price of the insurance falls within certain limits.[4] Individuals are therefore prepared to pay to reduce the uncertainty, even when expected payout by the insurance company is less than the premium paid.

In addition to the welfare gains produced by reducing uncertainty, insurance can increase efficiency, for several reasons. First, insurance can stimulate the emergence of riskier but more productive jobs and industries

(Acemoglu and Shimer 1999, 2000). Second, insuring transient shocks that reduce individual consumption below a threshold needed to retain productivity can prevent "dynamic poverty traps" that lead to chronic poverty (Ravallion 2003). Third, uninsured risk reduces efficiency through costly production and portfolio choices, such as using outdated but less risky production technologies or holding livestock as a form of precautionary savings (see the example of Indian farmers in Rosenzweig and Wolpin 1993). Fourth, uninsured risk can adversely affect human capital accumulation, as children drop out of school in the wake of an income shock, for example.

Markets may fail to provide insurance, or they may provide it inefficiently. For the market to efficiently provide insurance, the following conditions must prevail:[5]

- Risk pooling among a sufficiently large number of individuals must be possible. Such pooling translates uncertain individual outcomes into relatively certain aggregate outcomes, thanks to the law of large numbers.
- The risks of the individuals insured must be noncorrelated. If the distribution of risk is not correlated, in each period there are a predictable number of individuals who suffer losses and those who do not, enabling a smooth operation of the scheme.
- The probability of the unfavorable event occurring must not be great (otherwise, insurance companies would be unable to survive).
- The probability of an unfavorable event must be known or predictable. This allows the insurance company to set the insurance premium.
- The problems arising from asymmetric information (adverse selection and moral hazard problems) must not be serious.[6]

As the existence of numerous insurance markets suggests, markets often overcome the special problems connected with providing insurance. This is not the case with unemployment insurance: in virtually all countries it is publicly provided as a part of "social insurance," which usually includes old-age, health, and disability insurance as well. Why is this the case?

First, informational problems—adverse selection and moral hazard— have a strong effect on unemployment insurance. Adverse selection arises because insurers cannot determine the unemployment risk with sufficient accuracy (work history is an imperfect and in some cases nonexistent predictor). Because insurance premiums do not reflect an individual's risk, low-risk individuals have an incentive not to insure. An even more difficult problem is created by moral hazard: insured workers may reduce their work effort when employed and their job-search effort when unemployed and receiving unemployment benefits, without the knowledge of the insurance company.

Second, unemployment risks are covariant and thus cannot be diversified by private insurance. A severe recession may dramatically increase the number of claimants and jeopardize the existence of private insurers.

Third, the chance of (re)employment of some groups of unemployed—such as workers close to retirement age living in areas with high unemployment—may be so low that private insurance would not be possible.

Fourth, society can adjust unemployment insurance premiums in order to promote equity (keeping in mind that unemployment insurance premiums cannot be actuarially set because of information problems).

For these reasons, unemployment insurance is typically provided as part of social insurance—a program that mimics market insurance arrangements but deviates from actuarial principles. Workers and their employers pay earnings-related contributions that, upon separation, entitle workers to unemployment benefits according to predetermined eligibility conditions. To deal with informational problems, social insurance employs two mechanisms. To correct for adverse selection, membership is compulsory (if not economywide, then within certain sectors). To address the moral hazard problem (a challenging task not only for private but also for public agencies), in addition to directly monitoring claimant's behavior, it relies on information from other public programs when checking eligibility status of benefit claimants—an option unavailable to private providers. Moreover, to correct for covariance of unemployment risk, the government provides financial backing for the program (when the program's current obligations exceed its current contributions and accumulated reserves).

Who Should Receive Unemployment Income Support?

Unemployment is a special social construct that emerges only in industrial societies. Because unemployment arises from the development of the labor market, income support programs for the unemployed need to be attuned to labor market conditions and the characteristics of unemployed workers.

As Atkinson (1995a) persuasively claims, social insurance is a response by the modern, industrial society to the changing nature of the labor market, above all to the development of a modern employment relationship. In an urban, industrial society, employment becomes discretionary: workers either work or do not work. This development has important implications for unemployment. If workers cannot find a job in wage employment, they are unable to resort to self- or home-production, because they are divorced from ownership of the means of production.[7] Similarly, older and less productive workers in industrial societies stop working altogether once their productivity drops substantially. In contrast, in traditional societies workers continue to be economically active as long as they produce something valuable. The emergence of unemployment and the changing nature of retirement create the need to insure against nonemployment.[8] In other words, social insurance is based on the concepts of unemployment and retirement as specific social constructs.

That the notion of unemployment differs substantially in developing and industrial countries is reflected in measurement problems. The standard International Labour Organization (ILO) definition of unemployment

---

Box 2.3.   ILO Definition of Unemployment

According to the International Labour Organization definition of unemployment, the unemployed include all people above a specified age who, over a
specified reference period, are:

- "without work," that is, are not in paid employment or self-employment
- "currently available for work," that is, are available for paid employment or self-employment during the reference period
- "seeking work," that is, are taking specific steps in a specified recent
  period to seek paid employment or self-employment. The specified
  steps may include registering at a public or private employment
  exchange; applying for jobs with employers; checking at work sites,
  farms, factory gates, markets, or other assembly places; placing or
  answering newspaper advertisements; seeking assistance from friends
  or relatives; looking for land, building, machinery, or equipment to
  establish an enterprise; arranging for financial resources; and applying
  for permits and licenses.

Source: Resolution I of the 13th International Conference of Labour Statisticians,
Geneva, October 1982.

---

applied to developing countries classifies some unemployed as employed
or inactive and some as inactive (box 2.3).

Many workers in developing countries who qualify as employed under
the ILO definition are in fact underemployed, especially in rural areas.[9]
These workers may work fewer hours than they would like or work in low-
productivity jobs and earn low wages. But because they are so poor that
they cannot afford to be without a job, workers in developing countries are
rarely unemployed.

Some unemployed may be classified as inactive. People with a marginal
attachment to the labor force—that is, people who are available for and
desire work but who are not actively seeking it because they perceive,
rightly or wrongly, that no jobs are available—are often considered economically inactive when they should be more appropriately classified as unemployed (such workers are sometimes called "discouraged workers").[10]
Moreover, the conventional application of the term "actively seeking work"
falters in light of the fact that much economic activity occurs through informal employment or self-employment arrangements.

Some employed workers may be classified as inactive. According to the
ILO guidelines, an individual who works at least one hour in a week or who
is temporarily absent from work (because of vacation or illness, for example)
is employed. Those who are out of work but do not meet the ILO criteria of
unemployment are classified as economically inactive. However, some

forms of informal economic activity—including home-based work, typically undertaken by women—may escape this definition of employment. Because such workers are not available for work, they do not qualify as unemployed.

Acknowledging the possible restrictiveness and industrial country bias of its definition, the ILO advises to relax these clauses and formulate criteria suitable to the labor market characteristics of developing countries. Supplemental measures of labor market slack, which may be very important in transition economies and developing countries, include measures of underemployment and discouragement. For example, throughout the 1990s the Philippines had about twice as many underemployed worker as unemployed workers (Esguerra, Ogawa, and Vodopivec 2001). In Bosnia and Herzegovina in 2001, there was one discouraged worker per every 2.5 unemployed workers (World Bank 2002). Reflecting historic conditions, the whole notion of unemployment therefore rests on the characteristics of the society and the labor market.

In developing countries, where unemployment is rare because individuals cannot afford to be unemployed, self-protection (risk reduction) emerges as the dominant strategy.[11] It is therefore desirable that the introduction of public income protection only selectively displaces self-protective and self-insurance mechanisms—that is, that it displaces only expensive and counterproductive mechanisms. That means that underemployment also has to be taken into account. Indeed, the unemployed may not even be the most underprivileged group in the labor market.

Summary

A multitude of mechanisms are available to individuals, families, and communities for dealing with the risk of unemployment. When introducing or reforming public income support programs, policymakers should be concerned with the interactions of these programs with other mechanisms and institutions. Theoretical models offer increasingly refined and in-depth insights into the working of income support programs for the unemployed. But many aspects of these programs do not lend themselves to formal modeling, because the underlying theoretical models cannot be solved analytically. To test the generality of the theoretical models, as well as to determine the effects that are theoretically ambiguous, empirical evidence is therefore called for.

The approach adopted here for evaluating alternative income support programs for the unemployed uses two sets of criteria. One set evaluates the performance of these programs, stressing income protection and efficiency effects. The other set—design and implementation criteria— recognizes wide differences across countries and assesses the specific features countries possess.

This approach raises an important question: what can be learned from the experience of industrial countries that is of value for developing and transition countries, given the differences in institutional context and ability to govern? Industrial countries' experience with income support programs can offer valuable lessons for developing and transition countries—provided that country-specific circumstances are appropriately accounted for. For example, severance pay was found to reduce labor market flows and employment rates and to limit participation of marginal groups in OECD and Latin American countries (Heckman and Pages 2000). Some other findings from OECD countries, such as the "automatic stabilization" effects of unemployment insurance and the effects of monitoring on the duration of the receipt of unemployment benefits, also offer important lessons for developing and transition countries, once the scale of the program has been properly accounted for. The transferability of general equilibrium results—such as interactions between unemployment insurance systems and labor market institutions and policies, including collective bargaining—is more questionable.

Industrial countries also offer valuable guidance on how to adapt income support systems when introducing them in developing countries. For example, monitoring of continuing eligibility for unemployment insurance—which relies on a subjective assessment of recipients' behavior and their labor market status—has proved challenging even for OECD countries, prompting them to adopt various approaches and measures to improve it (see chapter 6). Given the weaker administrative capacity, larger informal sector, and different cultural norms in developing countries, programs there might do well to adapt the standard conditions of continuing eligibility (together with some other parameters of the program) and to drop the subjective assessment of recipients' behavior and status (perhaps as a temporary measure). Unless such changes are made, monitoring is likely to be ineffective, costly, and prone to corruption (for the importance of adapting the lessons learned in OECD countries to the circumstances facing developing and transition countries, see chapter 5).

Notes

1. For a comprehensive framework of social protection based on social risk management, see World Bank (2001a).

2. Besley and Coate (1995) provide another comprehensive approach, offering insights into the design and desirability of selected income maintenance programs, including negative income tax, wage subsidies, and workfare.

3. Davis and Haltiwanger (1999), Hopenhayn and Rogerson (1993), and Mortensen (1994) provide calibrations and simulations of the distortions in the magnitude of reallocation that can occur from various labor market interventions.

4. The net price for the insurance must be less than the difference between the expected income from uncertain outcomes and the certain income obtained by taking insurance (Barr 1990).

5. These are special circumstances that apply to insurance situations. In addition, for market forces to produce efficient outcomes, there must be perfect information, perfect competition, and no market failures. Perfect information requires knowledge of prices, quality, and the future. Perfect competition in product and factor markets calls for economic agents to be price-takers and have equal power.

The main market failures are represented by the presence of public goods, external effects, and increasing returns to scale (Barr 1990).

6. According to Barr (2001), adverse selection arises when the insurer is imperfectly informed about the individual's risk status (that is, when a poor risk can conceal that fact from the insurance company). Moral hazard arises when the insurer cannot monitor the insured's behavior. The insured can therefore influence the insurance company's loss without the knowledge of the insurance company, by affecting either the probability of the insured outcome or the size of the loss.

7. Unemployment is a relatively new phenomenon, emerging for the first time around 1895, in Great Britain, according to Atkinson (1995a).

8. Atkinson (1995a, p. 214) summarizes the origin of social insurance as follows: "The move from the traditional agricultural sector to modern industry may be characterized as that from a lower level of income to one where the wage was higher but subject to the 'catastrophic' hazard of total unemployment. Unemployment emerges as part of the 'modernization' of the economy."

9. According to the ILO, "underemployment exists when a person's employment is inadequate in relation to specified norms of alternative employment account being taken of his or her occupational skill" (Resolution I of the 13th International Conference of Labour Statisticians, Geneva, October 1982).

10. For a discussion of the conceptual issues in defining discouragement and a review of its incidence in industrial countries, see OECD (1995b).

11. As Cox Edwards and Manning (2001, p. 346) note, "The transition from widespread underemployment to open unemployment is in part an income effect. As countries grow and household incomes rise, jobless workers are able to endure periods without work while waiting for a job to open."

3

Review of Income Support Programs for the Unemployed

Countries differ widely in the ways in which they provide income support for the unemployed. The social insurance program for the unemployed with the richest tradition—unemployment insurance—exists predominately in industrial countries. In most transition countries, unemployment insurance was introduced in the early 1990s. In developing countries, unemployment insurance is uncommon, and the unemployed often struggle to make ends meet. Faced with job loss, formal sector workers with permanent contracts may rely on severance pay. But these workers are often in the minority. Little protection is available to workers in nonregular employment and to those working in the informal sector; these workers must often rely on their own means to deal with unemployment. Among the few public programs they can sometimes turn to are training and, above all, public works. Governments often provide public works programs in response to shocks that individuals, households, and communities are ill-equipped to deal with, such as economic recessions and natural calamities.

This chapter reviews how different countries provide income support for the unemployed. It begins with the typology of such programs, distinguishing between income maintenance and active programs. It then describes the features of the most important income support programs—participation rules, eligibility conditions, benefit levels, and sources of financing. It concludes by examining the incidence of these programs around the world. It examines the prevalence of various programs in individual countries, by themselves and in conjunction with other programs, and shows how their prevalence is related to the level of development, geographic position, and unemployment rate.

Typology and Description of Main Income Support Programs

Two main types of public income support programs assist the unemployed: income maintenance programs and active programs (table 3.1). Income maintenance programs determine benefit eligibility based on program

Table 3.1.   Types of Income Support Programs for the Unemployed

Program	Benefit level	Duration	Eligibility	Financing	Main objective
Income maintenance programs					
Defined benefit programs					
Unemployment insurance	Benefits are usually a percentage of past wages, sometimes declining over time	Limited	Conditional on past contributions, no-fault dismissal, availability and willingness to work, and job search	Contributions by employers, employees, or both; often additional financing from general tax revenues	Smooth consumption
Severance pay	Lump-sum payment, generally based on years of service	One-time payment	Laid-off formal sector workers	Paid by the employer (either unfunded or funded through book reserves or insurance contracts)	Link income support and human resource management objectives of the employer
Early retirement	Special program that grants retirement rights several years earlier. Pensions are typically reduced, often at less than the actuarially fair rate.	n.a.	Formal sector workers	Paid by other social security contributors; sometimes partly financed by the employer and state revenues, if pension credits have to be purchased	Reduce overstaffing without directly increasing unemployment

Public sector retrenchment (may include some type of active involvement of workers)	Special program that sheds redundant labor in the public sector through mass layoffs	Limited	Formal sector workers	Employer/government subsidy	Reduce overstaffing in order to meet human resource, efficiency, and political objectives
Defined contribution programs					
Unemployment insurance savings accounts	Replacement rate same as under unemployment insurance	Limited	Conditional on the availability of funds in the individual's account (with optional limited borrowing or public funding)	Contributions of employers, workers, or both deposited in individual accounts and sometimes solidarity account (funded program)	Provide insurance without distorting incentives (strong link between benefits and contributions)
Means-tested programs					
Unemployment assistance	Tops income to a specific threshold for average family income or pays flat amount	Unlimited (if stand-alone) or limited (after unemployment insurance has expired)	Means-tested	From general revenues (or contributions if unemployment insurance has expired)	Reduce poverty, smooth consumption
Social assistance	Tops income to a specific threshold for average family income or flat amount	Unlimited	Means-tested	General revenues	Provide means-tested income support program of last resort

(continued)

Table 3.1. *(continued)*

Program	Benefit level	Duration	Eligibility	Financing	Main objective
Active programs					
Public works	Usually below-market wage	Usually limited	Anyone (self-selection based on wage)	General revenues	Provide income support, goods, and services; empower communities
Training	Stipend and training	Limited	If deemed appropriate by program officials	General revenues	Link income support with investment in human resources
Wage subsidies	Wage-related or flat	Usually limited	Selected categories of unemployed	General revenues	Link income support with job creation

n.a. Not applicable.

participation rules, including the payment of a premium, under unemployment insurance. No offsetting services are performed in exchange for these transfers, although certain actions on the part of recipients are usually required, such as job seeking. Income maintenance programs can be divided into three subgroups: defined benefit programs, defined contribution programs, and means-tested programs. Active programs require that beneficiaries perform certain services or activities (such as participating in public works or training) in exchange for income support or subsidy. These programs are included as income support because they provide income to participants; sometimes this goal is quite explicit in the program design.

This chapter describes the features of the five programs that are the focus of this book: unemployment insurance, unemployment assistance, unemployment insurance savings accounts, severance pay, and public works. For the sake of completeness, it also describes some other programs that provide income support to unemployed workers.

These programs are not mutually exclusive. In many countries unemployment insurance coexists with unemployment assistance, severance pay, and public works. Under particular circumstances, the differences between some programs also become blurred. For example, if unemployment insurance benefits are paid at a flat rate rather than related to earnings, particularly if they are set at a relatively low level, they do not differ much from those provided by unemployment assistance (although the beneficiaries may differ). The level of benefits under unemployment and social assistance may also be similar, but the initial and continuing eligibility criteria are different. Moreover, some programs, particularly recently introduced programs, blend various traditional programs. The new Chilean unemployment insurance program, for example, combines individual savings accounts with social insurance and partly replaces the severance pay program.

Unemployment Insurance

Unemployment insurance is provided as part of social insurance, together with pension and health insurance. The program requires that workers, their employers, or both make contributions, which are used to finance unemployment benefits. While it mimics market insurance, unemployment insurance deviates from actuarial principles by charging premiums that do not reflect individual risks.

In industrial countries, unemployment insurance is the most widely used income protection program for the unemployed (figure 3.1). It is typically mandatory, with the few voluntary programs (in Denmark, Finland, and Sweden, for example) subsidized by the state and resembling the compulsory programs of industrial countries in both function and form (Holmlund 1998).[1] Most mandatory programs cover the majority of employed people, irrespective of occupation or industry. People who are not insured, such as recent university graduates, first-time job seekers, and the self-employed, are sometimes eligible for benefits, while casual workers and domestics are most often not

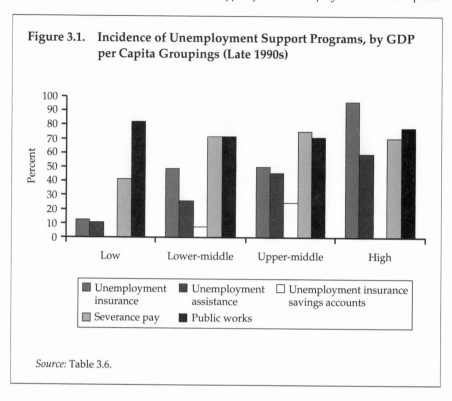

Figure 3.1.   Incidence of Unemployment Support Programs, by GDP
              per Capita Groupings (Late 1990s)

Source: Table 3.6.

(see table 3.2 for stylized features of unemployment insurance by groups of countries). A few programs, particularly those in developing countries, cover only workers in industry and commerce. In order to qualify for unemployment insurance, an individual must satisfy the minimum covered employment or contribution requirement, the most common length being six months in the past year. The cause of dismissal may affect if and when the individual is entitled to benefits. A usual condition for maintaining entitlement to unemployment benefits is that applicants be capable of, available for, and looking for work. Noncompliance with other labor market requirements can also result in the permanent or temporary suspension of benefits.

Benefits are usually a proportion of average earnings over some stipulated period of the recipient's most recent employment spell. Generally, the initial replacement rate is 40–75 percent of average earnings. In some transition countries, benefits are paid as a flat rate (that is, all recipients receive the same amount). Wage or benefit ceilings are used to limit the range of the benefits; benefit floors, typically set at the minimum wage, are also sometimes set. In addition to the basic benefit, some programs provide supplements for dependents. Benefits commonly decline over time and are limited in duration. However, extensions are sometimes given to people with long,

Table 3.2. Stylized Features of Unemployment Insurance Programs, by Groups of Countries

Coverage	Level of benefit	Benefit duration	Initial eligibility conditions	Continuing eligibility conditions	Source of financing
OECD countries[a] Offered by most countries. Majority of programs cover all employed individuals irrespective of sector. In Austria, Germany, and Luxembourg, coverage extends to apprentices and training graduates. Many programs exclude the self-employed, either generally, by occupation groups, or based on other conditions. Austria and Canada exclude public sector employees (voluntary provisions exist for provincial government employees). Ireland, Japan, Portugal, Spain, and the United States exclude domestic or casual workers.	Initial replacement rates are usually 40–75 percent of recent average earnings. Notable exception is Denmark, with 90 percent replacement rate. However, ceilings on wages and maximum benefit provisions limit range. Ireland, France, and the United Kingdom provide flat-rate benefits. Waiting period is 3–7 days. In some countries, in cases of voluntary quitting or dismissal due to misconduct, waiting period is extended by 6 weeks–6 months. Belgium, Germany, and the United Kingdom provide additional flat-rate benefits or additional percentages of average earnings for workers with spouses or children. Most countries, including Belgium, Canada, Denmark, France, the Netherlands, the United Kingdom, and the United States, tax benefits. In some countries, long-term unemployment insurance recipients transit into unemployment assistance.	Most countries limit length of unemployment insurance entitlement. Maximum entitlement period is usually 3–12 months, but in some European countries it is much longer (60 months in France, 48 months in Denmark, 36 months in Norway, and 32 months in Germany); in Belgium benefit duration is unlimited. Benefit duration is sometimes related to factors such as duration of social security contribution payments within a certain period, years of service, and age.	To qualify, a person must usually be employed at least 6 months in past year. Range: 10 weeks in last 52 weeks in Iceland to 540 days in last 24 months in Portugal. All countries require registration at employment office. France and Iceland have residency requirements. Almost all countries deny benefits in cases of voluntary quitting, work stoppage, or refusal of a suitable job offer.	Programs typically require recipient to be able, available, and willing to work, as well as searching for work. Recipients are disqualified if they fail to undergo training, unjustifiably refuse a suitable job offer, or fail to comply with job search requirements. Severity of offense determines period of disqualification (usually 1–4 months). Regularly reporting to employment office is typically required.	Most programs financed by contributions from employers and workers, with equal or higher contribution rates levied on employers. In only a few countries do only employers or only workers contribute (contributions are made only by employers in Iceland, Italy, and the United States; contributions are made only by workers in Luxembourg). Typically, the state covers any deficits that arise. In Italy and Spain, the state provides subsidies. In Italy, Japan, and the United States, the state covers administrative costs. Contribution rates vary significantly across countries. In most, contribution rates are less than 3 percent (but some require contributions of as much as 8 percent).

(continued)

Table 3.2. (continued)

Coverage	Level of benefit	Benefit duration	Initial eligibility conditions	Continuing eligibility conditions	Source of financing
Eastern Europe and Central Asia (transition countries)					
Majority of programs cover employed workers (citizenship or residency required). Coverage by age: usually 16–59 for men and 16–54 for women. In Croatia university or training graduates are also eligible. Domestic and casual workers are usually excluded.	Initial income replacement rates are usually 50–75 percent of recent average wages. Benefits are limited by floors (usually the minimum wage) and ceilings (usually the local, regional, or national average wage). Benefit level sometimes depends on cause of job loss. Some countries (Albania, Poland) provide flat-rate benefits (usually in proportion to minimum or average wage) instead of or in addition to earnings-related benefits. Earnings-related or flat-rate benefits can be graduated over time. Sometimes first-time job seekers receive flat-rate benefits that are lower than minimum wage. Albania, Azerbaijan, the Kyrgyz Republic, the Russian Federation, Ukraine, and Uzbekistan provide supplements for dependants.	Maximum entitlement duration is 6–24 months. In some countries (Azerbaijan, Bulgaria, Croatia, Poland, the Russian Federation, the Slovak Republic, Slovenia), entitlement duration varies depending on length of employment, contribution period, and/or age. University and training graduates have shorter entitlement periods. Some countries provide extensions for people near retirement age.	Minimum past employment requirement ranges from 3 to 12 months. Registration at employment offices required by all countries. In Latvia, Romania, and Ukraine income level must be below minimum wage. In most countries workers are ineligible if they are dismissed because of misconduct.	Programs typically require the recipient to be able, available, and willing to work, as well as searching for work. Recipients are disqualified if they refuse to undergo training. Benefits are reduced, postponed, or terminated if the recipient refuses a suitable job offer or does not comply with labor market requirements (job search, participation in public works or training) or files a fraudulent claim.	Almost all countries require employer contributions; some also require worker contributions. Worker contribution rates range from 0.06 percent (Slovenia) to 1 percent (the Slovak Republic). Employer contributions range from 0.06 percent (Slovenia) to 6 percent (Albania). State subsidies (when needed) or deficit financing is common. In Latvia the state finances unemployment insurance for special groups. In the Slovak Republic the state finances special programs.

Latin America and the Caribbean

Argentina, Barbados, and Brazil provide unemployment insurance. Unemployment insurance legislation was introduced in Venezuela (last amendments in 1991), but the program has yet to be implemented. Argentina and Brazil cover all wage workers. Venezuela excludes domestics and casual workers. Barbados excludes public sector employees and the self-employed.	Income replacement rates are 50–60 percent of recent average wages. In Argentina and Brazil, minimum and maximum benefit limits are proportional to the minimum wage. Waiting period is 3 days in Argentina and Brazil, 60 days in Barbados, and 30 days in Venezuela.	Maximum entitlement period is 3–12 months. In Argentina and Brazil, the length of entitlement depends on the length of employment. In Brazil entitlement durations are increased under special circumstances.	Generally, recipients must have been employed for 6–12 months in some stipulated period of recent employment. In Brazil applicants are ineligible if dismissal due to misconduct, and claimants must lack other means to support self or household. In Argentina applicants cannot receive other social security benefits.	In Argentina and Venezuela, recipients must be able, available, and willing to work. Continuing eligibility in Argentina does not require looking for a job.	Contribution rates range from 0.75 percent to 2 percent, with both employers and employees usually contributing. In Brazil the program is financed by employers, mainly through a business sales tax of 0.65 percent.

(continued)

Table 3.2. *(continued)*

Coverage	Level of benefit	Benefit duration	Initial eligibility conditions	Continuing eligibility conditions	Source of financing
Asia					
China, Iran, Kuwait, the Republic of Korea, Taiwan (China), and Turkey provide unemployment insurance. Coverage differs significantly. Iran excludes the self-employed, voluntarily insured people, and people covered by other provisions. China excludes permanent and contract workers in public sector enterprises and some collective enterprises. The Republic of Korea includes all firms. Taiwan (China) excludes the self-employed and firms with fewer than five workers.	Income replacement rates are 50–60 of recent average wages, except in China, which pays flat-rate benefits below the minimum wage. Iran provides a 10 percent benefit supplement per dependent for up to four dependents. The Republic of Korea offers a reemployment bonus if claimant leaves unemployment before exhausting half of the entitlement. Waiting period in the Republic of Korea and Taiwan (China) is 14 days.	China: 1–2 years, Republic of Korea: 90–240 days, based on age of claimant and length of previous employment (benefits extended in special cases); Taiwan (China): 6 months; Iran: 6–50 months, based on employment length and marital status.	Insured employment requirement: 6 months in Iran, 1 year in China, 6 months in the Republic of Korea, 2 years in Taiwan (China). In the Republic of Korea and Taiwan (China), unemployment must be involuntary. In Iran unemployment cannot be due to misconduct or refusal to accept suitable offer. Registration at employment office required.	Recipients must be able, available, and willing to work and looking for a job. In Turkey the job-search requirement is not effectively enforced.	In China employers contribute 0.6–1.0 percent (rate depends on local government provisions), the state provides subsidies. In Iran employers contribute 3 percent, the state finances deficit. In the Republic of Korea, employers contribute 0.5 percent, workers 0.5 percent. In Taiwan (China), workers contribute 0.2 percent, employers contribute 0.7 percent, and the state covers the cost of administration, by providing 0.1 percent of worker wages and, if needed, transferring resources from other social insurance funds.

Africa

Algeria, Egypt, and South Africa provide unemployment insurance. Coverage differs across countries. In Algeria program covers only laid-off salaried workers from formal sector. Egypt excludes public sector employees, casual workers, and agricultural workers. South Africa excludes domestics and highly paid employees.	Replacement rates are 60 percent of recent average wages in Egypt and 45 percent in South Africa. In Algeria replacement rate is mean of average earnings and national minimum earnings, with a floor of 75 percent of the national minimum earnings. Algeria provides graduated benefits and spousal allowances. Waiting period is 7 days in Egypt and South Africa.	In Algeria duration is 12–36 months, based on length of employment. In Egypt maximum entitlement duration is 16–28 weeks, based on contribution length. In South Africa benefits are paid for 26 weeks.	Algeria: 3 years of covered employment; employer must be current with contributions. Three months of active search required before applying for benefits. Egypt: 6 months. South Africa: 13 weeks in past 52 weeks. Unemployment cannot be due to voluntary separation, misconduct, or, in South Africa, participation in strike.	Must be able, available, and willing to work.	In Algeria employees contribute 1.5 percent, employers 2.5 percent. In Egypt employees contribute 2.0 percent, the state finances deficit. In South Africa employees and employers each contribute 1 percent.

Sources: U.S. Social Security Administration (1999, 2002a, 2002b); Tzannatos and Roddis (1998); OECD (2000a).

[a]Transition countries that are members of OECD are included under transition countries.

continuous employment records or to those near early or regular retirement age. In many countries, it is also possible to move into means-tested unemployment assistance after exhausting unemployment insurance benefits.

Unemployment insurance is typically financed through regular contributions based on wages by employers, workers, or both. The rate paid by employers is usually the same as or higher than that paid by workers. Sometimes, however, workers are not required to make contributions. In the United States, employer contributions depend on the employer's layoff experience—employers who lay off workers more frequently and thus impose heavier financial burden on the program are assigned a higher rate (the practice is known as the "experience rating"). In some countries, the state subsidizes or finances program deficits that arise.

Unemployment Assistance

Unemployment assistance is a means-tested minimum income granted to working-age individuals who are unemployed and do not have the necessary financial resources to maintain a minimum standard of living for themselves and their families. Australia provides means-tested unemployment benefits through two back-to-back programs. The Job Search Allowance is offered for a maximum duration of 12 months. If necessary, it is followed by the NewStart Allowance, which is offered indefinitely.

Self-standing unemployment assistance programs currently exist in few countries, notably Australia, Hong Kong (China), and New Zealand among high-income countries and Serbia and Montenegro and Tunisia among middle-income countries. In all other countries that offer unemployment assistance, the program functions in tandem with unemployment insurance and is available upon expiration of eligibility for unemployment insurance to unemployed people who pass the means test (Vroman 2002).

Like unemployment insurance, unemployment assistance programs require that applicants be capable of, available for, and looking for work (see table 3.3 for stylized features of unemployment assistance by groups of countries). Claims are reviewed at regular intervals to assess job-seeking intensity and to determine changes in household circumstances that may require a change in the benefit level. In some countries, eligibility for unemployment assistance is not conditional on previous employment or contribution history. However, in most countries, unemployment assistance is an extension of unemployment insurance offered to the long-term unemployed who have satisfied some minimum length of employment and do not have the economic means to support their households. The two primary groups that receive unemployment assistance are people who have exhausted their unemployment insurance entitlement and people who are ineligible for unemployment insurance because of insufficient employment records. Some countries penalize applicants whose unemployment was voluntary by limiting the length of unemployment assistance entitlement or extending the waiting period.

Table 3.3. Stylized Features of Unemployment Assistance Programs, by Groups of Countries

Coverage	Level of benefit	Benefit duration	Initial eligibility conditions	Continuing eligibility conditions	Source of financing
OECD countries					
Present in about half of member countries (to those who exhausted benefits under unemployment insurance programs). Only Australia and New Zealand have self-standing unemployment assistance programs. Available to all unemployed workers, irrespective of sector or occupation.	Benefits are flat rate. Typically, benefit level depends on marital status and number of dependents. Some countries have threshold income levels, above which benefits are reduced or eliminated. Special provisions usually exist for the older unemployed. Sometimes special provisions also granted to younger people. Generally, no waiting periods. However, waiting period sometimes applied to applicants not transiting from unemployment insurance (3 days in Ireland, 5 days in Sweden).	Unlimited, as long as conditions are fulfilled. Exceptions include the Netherlands (2 years), Spain (6–18 months), and Sweden (5 months). In Portugal duration depends on age and whether or not claimant has exhausted unemployment insurance benefits (duration is longer for those who have).	Typically, recipients must satisfy means test (household income and assets test, which excludes state assistance, such as family and housing benefits). Generally offered irrespective of employment or contribution history. Exceptions include the Netherlands (4 years of employment in 5 years preceding unemployment), Portugal (6 months of contributory employment in the year preceding unemployment), and France (5 years of employment in 10 years preceding unemployment). In some countries employment or contribution conditions apply only to unemployment assistance applicants ineligible for unemployment insurance (Germany, for example, has a 6-month requirement). In some countries, such as Austria, unemployment assistance available only to people who have exhausted their unemployment insurance benefits. In Australia if unemployment is voluntary, due to labor dispute, or refusal of suitable job offer, benefits are reduced and limited or waiting period is extended to 8 weeks.	Programs usually require claimant to be unemployed, able and available for work, and actively seeking work. Eligibility conditions must be satisfied throughout the period of receipt (periodic checks conducted).	Stand-alone programs: government financed through general tax revenues. Unemployment assistance in tandem with unemployment insurance: same financing as unemployment insurance.

(continued)

Table 3.3. (continued)

Coverage	Level of benefit	Benefit duration	Initial eligibility conditions	Continuing eligibility conditions	Source of financing
Eastern Europe and Central Asia (transition countries)					
In tandem with unemployment insurance, programs in place in Bulgaria, Hungary, Romania, the Slovak Republic, and Slovenia. Serbia and Montenegro has a stand-alone unemployment assistance program. Estonia also had a stand-alone program in the 1990s; in 2002, it introduced a new unemployment insurance-type of program, which took effect in January 2003. In all countries with programs, all salaried workers are covered. Special provisions exist for recent graduates and discharged military officers.	Means-tested minimum assistance at flat rates. Benefit level usually depends on marital status, number of dependents, household size, and age of children. Receipt of other social assistance usually does not affect benefit level, but casual earnings are deducted.	Entitlement length is 3–18 months, sometimes shorter for certain groups, such as recent graduates. In Estonia duration extended if claimant is near retirement, has 3 or more children, or income is below the poverty line.	Must satisfy means test (household income and assets test). In stand-alone programs, assistance may be provided irrespective of employment or contribution history; when provided in tandem with unemployment insurance, it is typically available for unemployed people who have exhausted their unemployment insurance entitlements. Must be registered as unemployed.	Regular visits to the employment offices required. Must continue to satisfy household income (and assets) test. Claimant must be able, available, and willing to work and looking for job. Refusal of training or acceptable job offer results in termination of benefit. Eligibility conditions must be satisfied throughout the period of unemployment assistance receipt.	Stand-alone programs: government financed through general tax revenues. Unemployment assistance in tandem with unemployment insurance: same financing source as unemployment insurance.

Asia Hong Kong (China)	Means-tested, flat-rate benefits based on marital status and presence of dependents.	No limit.	Beneficiaries must actively seek paid employment and participate in other programs if so requested.	Government financed through general tax revenues.
Africa Available in Mauritius and Tunisia. In Tunisia all nonagricultural salaried workers covered under National Social Security Fund.	In Mauritius means-tested income available to household heads after 30 days of registered unemployment. In Tunisia benefits are minimum wage in industry and commerce.	Tunisia: 3 months	In Tunisia recipients must have contributed to the fund for 12 quarters, must be registered as unemployed, and capable of work. Recipients must be involuntarily unemployed, have dependents, and have no other source of income.	Government financed through general tax revenues.

Sources: U.S. Social Security Administration (1999, 2002a, 2002b); Boeri and Edwards (1998); OECD (1995a).

Note: Blank cells = not applicable.

Benefits are usually in cash but can be in kind as well. Cash benefits are typically paid as a flat rate at some officially stipulated level (usually a guaranteed minimum income at a uniform level), with possible supplements for certain groups. Means- or income-testing is conducted not only on the financial resources of the applicant but also on those of the applicant's spouse and other adult members of the household. The level of benefits can vary based on household income and the recipient's marital status, the number of dependents, and the ages of the recipient's children. Benefits are periodically adjusted for inflation and sometimes offered indefinitely, as long as the recipient satisfies the eligibility conditions. The duration of benefits is sometimes limited for recent graduates and other groups and extended for claimants near early or regular retirement age.

Unemployment assistance is typically financed by governments through general tax revenues. In countries with dual unemployment insurance/assistance programs, the source of financing (contributions by employers and workers) is usually the same for both programs.

Unemployment Insurance Savings Accounts

Unemployment insurance savings accounts (UISAs) are a relatively new program, although Brazil has used them since the 1960s. More recently, several other Latin American countries (Argentina, Chile, Colombia, Ecuador, Panama, Peru, Uruguay, and Venezuela) have introduced UISAs (Heckman and Pages 2000).

UISAs function as follows. Employers deposit some specified fraction of each worker's earnings in a special individual savings account on a regular basis (see table 3.4 for the stylized features of UISAs). In Chile workers are also required to make regular contributions to their accounts. Upon separation—and in most countries, regardless of the reason for separation—workers can make withdrawals from their savings accounts as they deem fit (some programs allow access before separation, for health, education, and housing). In Brazil workers can access their accounts only in the case of involuntary separation, and employers are required to make an additional payment of 40 percent of the account balance (plus interest) to the individual. In all countries, positive account balances are added to old-age pensions at retirement.

Under some proposals unemployed workers would be able to draw benefits monthly, as under traditional unemployment insurance, and the government would lend money to accounts in which the balance fell below zero (Cortazar 1996; Feldstein and Altman 1998). Chile introduced a program similar to this—combining social insurance and self-insurance—at the end of 2002. Under that program, the unemployed first draw benefits from their individual accounts. Upon depletion—and subject to the usual unemployment insurance eligibility conditions—they then draw from the solidarity fund (see chapter 6).

Table 3.4. Stylized Features of Unemployment Insurance Savings Account Programs

Coverage	Level of benefit	Eligibility conditions	Sources of financing
In Brazil, Chile, Colombia, Ecuador, Panama, Peru, and Venezuela, all private sector workers are covered. In Uruguay, only workers in industry and commerce are covered. Argentina covers only construction workers.	Amount accumulated in account (deposits plus interest earned) paid either as a lump sum or in monthly payments, subject to continuing eligibility. In Chile benefits are paid monthly and the level is linked to past earnings, with a declining schedule. Resources are drawn first from individual's account and upon depletion from the solidarity account. In Brazil, if worker is dismissed "without just cause" (including separations for economic reasons), employer must pay additional 40 percent.	Upon separation, regardless of the reason of separation, except in Brazil, where workers are eligible only if dismissed. Some programs allow access for other reasons as well (health, education, housing). In Chile withdrawals from individual accounts are triggered by separation from employer, regardless of reason, and from the common fund by insufficient resources in individual accounts if the claimant satisfies the usual conditions of continuing eligibility under unemployment insurance, but withdrawals are limited to two withdrawals every five years. In Ecuador and Uruguay unemployment benefits are provided as part of comprehensive insurance, subject to usual eligibility conditions under unemployment insurance.	Employer and employee contributions, deposited in workers' individual savings accounts. In Chile contributions are split between individual accounts and a common, solidarity account, as they are in Uruguay, where unemployment benefits are provided as part of comprehensive insurance (a mixed social-private insurance program that covers old age, disability, death, sickness, maternity benefits, family allowances and unemployment). In Uruguay workers contribute 15 percent of earnings. About half is paid to the common fund; the balance, less a 3 percent administrative fee, is paid to an individual account. Employers contribute 12.5 percent, with the government financing the deficit if necessary.

Source: Acevedo and Eskenazi (2003); Heckman and Pages (2000); Lipsett (1999); and Mazza (1999).

Several types of UISA programs can be distinguished: a pure UISA program, in which withdrawals are strictly limited by the UISA's balance (that is, the balance on an individual's UISA must always be nonnegative); the UISA-cum-borrowing, in which, within predetermined limits, individuals can borrow from their UISAs; and the UISA-cum-solidarity-fund, in which upon depletion of their own accounts, individuals may receive payments from the solidarity fund. The second and third programs combine self-insurance with public insurance (in the UISA-cum-borrowing, workers can leave the program with negative terminal balances, which must be covered by other workers). A pure UISA program is identical to a prefunded severance pay program.

Severance Pay

Severance pay refers to lump-sum payments made to discharged workers either voluntarily by employers (through collective agreements or as part of firm policy) or as mandated by governments. Such payments are made following both individual and collective dismissals, usually with no special dispensations for collective dismissals. Coverage is generally broad, encompassing both white- and blue-collar workers (see table 3.5 for the stylized features of severance pay programs). However, in some countries, severance pay is provided only in some sectors or only in firms above certain sizes (this practice is more common in developing countries). Severance pay is typically provided to individuals who are discharged due to redundancy; employees dismissed due to gross misconduct are generally not eligible. Minimum years of service requirements are also sometimes used to limit eligibility.

Severance benefits typically increase with years of service with the employer, with each year of service often rewarded by one-half to one month's pay. More complex formulae exist in which workers with long records of service, older workers, or both are entitled to more generous severance pay than other employees. In some countries, the generosity of severance benefits may differ for white- and blue-collar workers, permanent and fixed-term workers, and workers covered by collective agreements and workers who are not.

Severance pay is usually financed by employers. However, in some countries, the government provides financial assistance, particularly for large-scale restructuring operations that involve worker retrenchment in mass layoffs.

Public Works

Generally introduced as a temporary measure in response to economic and natural shocks, public works programs (also known as "workfare") provide low-wage employment opportunities—that is, participants must work to obtain benefits. Bangladesh and India have used public works programs to provide relief during famines and droughts as well as to attenuate seasonal

Table 3.5. Stylized Features of Severance Pay Programs, by Groups of Countries

Coverage	Level of benefit	Eligibility conditions	Sources of financing
OECD countries			
Scandinavia			
Except for white collar workers in Denmark and long-serving, older employees affected by restructuring in Finland, no legislated severance pay for individual or collective dismissal. Severance pay sometimes provided through collective agreements in private sector.	Denmark (white collar): 12+ years of service: 1 month's pay; 15+ years: 2 months' pay; 18+ years: 3 months' pay. Finland: age 45+, years of service 5+: 1–2 months' pay	Separation due to personal reasons or economic redundancy. Minimum years of service: 12 in Denmark, 5 in Finland.	Employer financed. Firms sometimes receive state assistance.
Western Europe			
Mandatory programs covering all workers exist in many countries. Germany, the Netherlands, and Switzerland have no legislated severance pay for individual or collective dismissals (exceptions for special cases), but severance pay is often part of collective agreements or social compensation plans. Except in Belgium, where severance pay is provided only for collective dismissal, no special regulations for collective dismissals.	Benefit formula varies significantly. France: 10 percent of monthly pay per year of service plus an additional 6.7 percent of monthly pay after 10 years. Ireland: 1 week's pay plus half a week's pay per year of service under age 41 plus 1 week's pay per year of service over age 41 (subject to a certain maximum). United Kingdom: 5 weeks' pay per year of service (age 18–21), 10 weeks' pay per year of service (age 22–44), 15 weeks' pay per year of service (age 41–65).	Separation due to personal reasons or economic redundancy. Minimum years of service: 3 in Austria, 2 in Ireland, and 2 in the United Kingdom.	Employer financed. Firms sometimes receive state assistance.

(continued)

Table 3.5. *(continued)*

Coverage	Level of benefit	Eligibility conditions	Sources of financing
Southern Europe			
In Greece, Italy, Portugal, Spain, and Turkey, legislated severance pay exists for both individual and collective dismissals. All workers covered.	Standard formula is 1 month per year of service. Collective agreements in Italy and Turkey can increase benefits. In Greece severance pay reduced if advance notice given, and white-collar workers receive more generous severance pay than other workers. In Spain fixed-term contract workers receive less generous severance pay.	Minimum years of service: 5 in Greece, 1 in Turkey: 1. Separation must not be due to own fault.	Employer financed. Firms sometimes receive state assistance.
Non-European countries			
Australia provides severance pay for redundant workers only. Some areas of Canada provide legislated severance pay for individual and collective dismissals; no special regulations for collective dismissal. In some countries, severance pay provided as part of collective agreements or as firm practice; no mandated severance pay in the United States.	Benefits vary significantly across Australia (for redundant workers), from 4 weeks for less than 2 years of service to 8 weeks for more than 4 years of service. Common firm practice in Japan is 1 month's pay per year of service, less for voluntary quits and more for layoffs. Common firm practice for redundant workers in New Zealand is 6 weeks' pay for first year of service, 2 weeks' pay for each additional year. In Canada federal legislation provides 2 days' pay per year of service, with minimum of 5 days.	Separation due to personal reasons or economic redundancy. One year minimum years of service in Australia and Canada (federal).	Employer financed. Firms sometimes receive state assistance.

East Europe and Central Asia (transition countries)

Most countries mandate severance pay covering all workers. In Poland legislated benefits provide only for collective dismissals. In the Czech Republic and Hungary, legislated benefits for individual and collective dismissal; no special regulations for collective dismissal.	Level of benefits strongly varies. Bulgaria provides 1 month's pay regardless of years of service. In Poland benefits range from 1 month's pay for less than 10 years of service to 3 monthly wages for 20+ years of service. Croatia and Slovenia provide roughly 1 month's pay for two years of service.	Dismissal due to personal reasons or economic redundancy. Condition of minimum years of service applies.	Employer financed. Firms sometimes receive state assistance.

Latin America and the Caribbean

Argentina, Barbados, Belize, Bolivia, Chile, Colombia, Ecuador, Mexico, Nicaragua, Panama, Peru, Venezuela, and Uruguay mandate severance pay. All workers (public and private sectors) are usually covered.	Level of compensation typically very high (one month's pay per year of service). In Peru it is even higher—1.5 months' pay per year of service. In some countries, employers are required to make additional payment as seniority premium (sometimes through individual accounts).	Dismissal for unjustified reasons (economic difficulties of a firm are not considered just cause). In the Caribbean, severance pay is offered to workers made redundant due to labor adjustment. In Belize, Bolivia, Chile, and Nicaragua, severance pay is offered for voluntary quits as well.	Employer financed.

(continued)

Table 3.5. *(continued)*

Coverage	Level of benefit	Eligibility conditions	Sources of financing
Asia			
Covers formal sector workers, sometimes in firms above certain size (firms with more than 20 employees in Pakistan, firms with more than 15 employees in Sri Lanka).	Bangladesh: casual workers: 14 days' pay per year of service; permanent workers: 1 month's pay per year of service. India: 15 days' average pay per year of service. Indonesia: 1 month's pay per year of service, double if redundancy is due to economic reasons or dismissal is due to unjust cause. Malaysia: 10–20 days' pay per year of service; merit allowances may double severance pay. Pakistan: 30 days' pay per year of service. Sri Lanka: law requires authorization of the Commissioner of Labor, who also decides about compensation, which can be as high as 6 months' wages per year of service.	Malaysia: at least 12 months of continuous service.	Employer financed.
Africa			
Covers formal sector workers, often in firms above certain size.	Libya: 100 percent of earnings up to 6 months.	Minimum months of continuous service: 60 in Botswana, 3 in Tanzania.	Employer financed.

Sources: Cox Edwards and Manning (2001); Islam and others (2001); Mansor and others (2001); Mazza (1999); OECD (1999b); U.S. Social Security Administration (1999, 2002a, 2002b).

dips in income (Ravallion 1991). These programs usually employ unskilled manual workers for short durations on projects such as construction and maintenance of roads and irrigation infrastructure, reforestation, and soil conservation. Because providing employment to poor people is valued per se, these programs are designed to be more labor-intensive than commercial projects. Subbarao (2003) reports that in most road construction projects, the cost of labor ranges from 40 to 50 percent of total cost; in road or drainage maintenance projects and in soil conservation and reforestation projects, it ranges from 70 to 80 percent. In some well-known examples, such as the Maharashtra Employment Guarantee Scheme in India, the wage bill represented 60–70 percent of total cost. In Argentina's Trabajar program it ranged from 30 to 70 percent. Public works programs allow for significant control of participation. Program rules may favor certain groups, such as discouraged workers or the long-term unemployed.

Remuneration for public works is typically paid on a piece-rate or time-rate basis, in cash, in kind (usually in the form of food aid), or in some combination of the two. In principle, program wages are set at a low level—around prevailing market wages or statutory minimum wages for unskilled labor—in order to attract only the poor. Setting the remuneration rate low also reduces the likelihood that the program displaces alternative low-wage local employment, and it encourages participants to seek more remunerative employment outside the program. But some cross-country evidence shows that when the minimum wage was higher than the prevailing market wage and the program wage could not be set below the minimum wage, substantial numbers of nonpoor workers were attracted into the program (Subbarao 2003). Such was the case in Kenya, where the program wage was set at the minimum wage, which exceeded the prevailing wage, and in the Philippines, where the program pay consisted of cash wages equal to the minimum wage plus substantial food aid. In Argentina and Chile, the program wage rates were maintained below the minimum wage, which facilitated self-selection among the poor.

Setting public works wages below comparable local wages often proves difficult. In South Africa—where trade unions have a long history of struggles for higher wages and better working conditions—changing union-won labor standards was controversial and became a political issue. Adato and Haddad (2001) report that although trade unions accepted the principle of exempting public works from these standards, labor disputes over wages were common throughout the country. Questions were raised about the minimum acceptable wage rate for a public works program, how to resolve disputes with formal contractors who paid higher wages, and how to set working conditions and benefits. Adato and Haddad report that of 101 projects investigated, 39 had strikes or labor disputes, of which 27 increased wages. Nonetheless, nearly 80 percent of the projects set wages below the districtwide wage rates, a result Adato and Haddad attribute to the successful dialogue between project steering committees and participants.[2]

The duration of participation varies significantly across programs. The average duration of participation is 15–30 days a year in India's nationwide Jawahar Rojgar Yojana program and 100 days a year in the Maharashtra Employment Guarantee Scheme. The average duration of participation is about five months in Argentina's Trabajar program and five to six months in jobs created by social investment funds in Latin and Central American countries (Subbarao 2003).

Public works programs are generally financed by the government through general tax revenues. They are sometimes funded by nongovernmental organizations or international donors. The Maharashtra Employment Guarantee Scheme is financed primarily by special taxes, which fall disproportionately on the nonpoor, and partly by general tax revenues (Ravallion 1991).

An innovative alternative to the traditional "top down" approach of public works that also creates employment opportunities, often for the poor, are social funds. These are agencies that finance small-scale projects in poor communities. To ensure that truly valuable projects are selected, communities identify and partly finance projects themselves. The social fund approach was first introduced in Bolivia in 1987 and has gained popularity since then. It has fostered cooperation among local actors, provided valuable products and services to vulnerable segments of population, and engaged the poor in implementing projects (Rawlings, Sherburne-Benz, and Van Domelen 2002).

Other Programs

Other programs described below also help unemployed workers reduce the risk of unemployment (work sharing and early retirement), help them cope with the risk of unemployment (social assistance and short-time compensation), or combine various risk management strategies (public sector retrenchment programs).

SOCIAL ASSISTANCE. Social assistance benefits are targeted not at the unemployed but at the poor generally. They are available mostly in industrial countries. These programs provide a range of cash and in-kind benefits on a means-tested basis to applicants with insufficient resources to maintain a minimum standard of living, as officially determined. Benefits are typically provided indefinitely, subject to periodic checks to determine the eligibility status of the claimant. In countries in which unemployment assistance is unavailable, social assistance programs are often the next destination for the poor unemployed who lose unemployment insurance eligibility. As with unemployment insurance and unemployment assistance, most social assistance programs require that recipients be capable of, available for, and looking for work and that they comply with other applicable labor market requirements (training, public works participation, and so forth). Benefits

---

Box 3.1. Temporary Assistance for Needy Families in the United States

Enacted in 1996 to replace the Aid to Families with Dependent Children (AFDC) and Job Opportunities and Basic Skills Training (JOBS) programs, the Temporary Assistance for Needy Families (TANF) program provides means-tested cash assistance to families in economic need. Under TANF states are allotted a block grant from the federal government and are responsible for designing and administering their own programs. Two key features of the TANF program are its stringent work requirements and the limited duration of benefits.

Under the TANF block grant, with a few exceptions (people who are ill or incapacitated, 60 years of age or older, pregnant, or caring for a young child), claimants must work or participate in some work-related activity (vocational training, community service) as soon as they are able to or after 24 months of benefit receipt, whichever comes first. In fact, some states require TANF applicants to begin looking for a job before applying for assistance. In most states, the minimum number of work hours required for single adults without children is 25 hours a week. Up to six weeks of job search (four weeks if consecutive) count toward the work requirement. Failure to meet program work requirements can result in a reduction or termination of benefits.

In most states claimants can receive TANF for a maximum lifetime duration of 60 months. Some states have adopted shorter durations (Georgia: 48 months; Idaho: 24 months). States can relax their time limits for up to 20 percent of claimants for various reasons, as determined by them. States may also temporarily or permanently reduce benefits, impose limits on the duration of benefits over some specified period of time, or establish waiting periods between benefit receipt spells.

Source: Rowe (2000).

---

are generally temporarily or permanently terminated in cases of noncompliance (see box 3.1).

In most countries, social assistance benefits are provided at a flat rate at a low level (below the average earnings of unskilled industrial workers) in order to encourage employment. The composition and type of household, the number of income earners in the household, housing costs, and other characteristics are also sometimes taken into account in determining benefits.

Social assistance is generally financed by the government through general tax revenues. These programs are sometimes administered at the national level; more often they are administered locally.

EARLY RETIREMENT PROGRAMS. In contrast to programs that compensate the unemployed for temporary income loss, early retirement programs facilitate the early withdrawal of older workers from the labor force. These programs were introduced in industrial countries in the late 1960s in response to increasing unemployment and the deterioration of reemployment prospects for older unemployed workers. More recently, they have been introduced in some transition countries.

There are several types of early retirement programs. Under some programs, older unemployed workers are entitled to early receipt of full or, more often, reduced pension benefits (Blöndal and Scarpetta 1997). Other programs enable older workers to avoid unemployment altogether. Under these programs, workers with sufficiently long periods of contributions into the pension fund can retire early and receive pensions at full or reduced value. In the United States and Canada, for example, individuals can retire early, but with their pensions actuarially reduced. In many countries, early retirement pensions at full value are offered to people employed in hazardous workplaces or arduous work.

Other early retirement programs include job release programs, which allow older workers to retire early and receive full pension benefits (or a special allowance), conditional on employers replacing the early retiree with a younger unemployed worker. Some countries, including Denmark, Germany, and the Netherlands, have used disability pensions to encourage early retirement (such efforts are less common today than they once were). Under these programs, older unemployed people with even minor infirmities are entitled to full disability pensions until they retire if suitable jobs are hard to find. In several OECD countries, the conditions for drawing unemployment insurance benefits are relaxed for older unemployed workers, who are allowed to receive benefits until they retire.

In addition to public programs, employers use private pension plans to facilitate early retirement. In Germany and the Netherlands, for example, under negotiated "social" plans, employers are required to "top up" the unemployment insurance benefits received by older redundant workers up to the level of previous net earnings.

WORK SHARING. Work sharing is aimed at enabling employers to retain skilled workers and workers to avoid layoffs associated with temporary economic downturns. Under such arrangements, workers agree to reduce their working time and to accept a cut or proportional reduction in wages. Usually undertaken at the firm or sectoral level on a voluntary basis, work-sharing seeks primarily to preserve jobs during difficult economic times. With recovery, normal working hours and wages are usually restored.

Mandatory work-sharing is sometimes imposed by governments to create jobs. This type of measure takes the form of reductions in working time, limits on overtime, increases in the duration of leave, and other strategies. Some mandated work-sharing programs, such as Canada's program, have also been undertaken in the context of public sector downsizing. Work-sharing programs are most prevalent in Western Europe. They have been used on a limited scale in North America. They are uncommon elsewhere.

SHORT-TIME COMPENSATION. Short-time compensation permits employers to reduce the number of work hours of workers with proportional cuts in wages. Under this mechanism, the lost wages of affected workers are partially compensated using unemployment insurance benefits. These programs are well-established and widespread in Western Europe (Germany, the Netherlands, Sweden, the United Kingdom, and elsewhere). In the United States and Canada, such programs first appeared in the mid-1970s. As of the mid-1990s, 17 U.S. states had introduced short-time compensation programs. These programs do not exist in developing countries.

The structure of benefits, eligibility conditions, financing, and administration of short-time compensation programs vary greatly across countries. In the United States workers who reduce their work hours receive unemployment insurance benefits pro-rated for the hours lost due to work-sharing. Benefit duration varies from state to state but is usually limited to 20–30 weeks. The employer; the relevant union or unions, if present; and the state must agree on the work-sharing plan. Employers are also required to show that at least 10–20 percent of the workforce is affected. Some states limit benefit receipt to 40–50 percent of the workforce (Abraham and Houseman 1993).

PUBLIC SECTOR RETRENCHMENT PROGRAMS. Overstaffing, excessively high wages, generous benefits, and gross inefficiencies characterize the public sectors of many countries. To address these issues, labor retrenchment programs have increasingly become an integral part of public sector reforms. These programs can take various forms. They can be voluntary or involuntary, standard or tailor-made. They may or may not include active labor market programs.

In a review of 41 public sector retrenchment programs in 37 countries, Haltiwanger and Singh (1999) find that program design is closely associated with the underlying causes of retrenchment. Where retrenchment was perceived as a one-time event to address issues such as ghost workers or low worker productivity, compensation typically consisted of severance pay and enhanced pensions, and the retrenchment programs were voluntary in nature. In contrast, where retrenchment was perceived as part of a radical transformation of the public sector, including a restructuring of the labor market, as in transition countries, severance pay and enhanced pensions were accompanied by worker safety net measures, such as unemployment benefits, job placement services, and worker retraining. In addition, the programs more often included a mandatory component. Severance pay was the most common instrument (used in 68 percent of projects), followed by enhanced safety nets (63 percent) and enhanced pensions (29 percent). Haltiwanger and Singh also find that for every $1 spent on severance pay, an additional $1.20 was spent on enhancing safety nets and $2.20 on enhancing pensions.

For political reasons, voluntary retrenchment programs have become increasingly popular (Rama 1999). Standard voluntary retrenchment programs, offering benefits based primarily on years of experience, may lead to severe adverse selection problems, because the most productive workers often have superior labor market opportunities outside the public sector. Tailor-made programs may increase the efficiency of downsizing by disclosing worker characteristics. The use of confidential individual bids for exit compensation, with safeguards to prevent collusion, can be one procedure that leads to such disclosures (Jeon and Laffont 1999). Unproductive workers tend to be those with the highest bids, as they stand to lose the most from separation. For state-owned enterprises in Egypt, Asaad (1999) finds that a tailor-made program could reduce total compensation by 31 percent compared with a standard program and that a severance pay program that provides higher payments to long-tenured workers is likely to overpay them.

Because determining the right menu to be offered in tailor-made programs may be difficult, Rama (1999) recommends using other, simpler procedures as well. One such procedure that is considered more cost-effective than others is determining ("indexing") severance pay by estimating welfare losses arising from the worker's separation. Severance pay can be indexed to a wide selection of observable worker attributes, including present wages, job security, gender, years of service, expected duration of unemployment, and prevailing wages the separating worker can expect to earn in the private sector.

When is the decision to downsize justified? Managers can look at the financial return—the impact of downsizing on the consolidated government budget (positive financial returns occur when the net present value of reduced wage and benefit expenditures exceeds the net present value of the retrenchment costs). But they should also consider economic returns—the increase in output and welfare arising from improved allocation of labor and the lower level of taxes—although many of the relevant private and social costs and benefits are difficult to quantify.

The Incidence of Income Support Programs for the Unemployed

How are public income support programs spread across countries at different income levels? Not surprisingly, developing countries, particularly low-income ones, offer much weaker protection against unemployment risk than industrial countries. The primary means of providing income protection in industrial countries is social insurance (backed by social assistance as the program of last resort), but other income support programs are also widely used, including severance pay and public works (figure 3.1). In contrast, low-income countries primarily use public works programs, which are modest in scale, and severance pay, which reaches only selected formal sector workers. Middle-income countries rely on a somewhat richer choice, with some combining severance pay (which is considerably more prevalent than in low-income countries), public works, and social insurance programs. (A formal econometric analysis of the determinants of the incidence of unemployment insurance and assistance programs appears in the annex to this chapter.)

Income Support Programs for the Unemployed in Low-Income Countries

In low-income countries, public support to the unemployed consists almost exclusively of public works and severance pay programs (figure 3.1, table 3.6). The most prevalent program is public works, available in more

Table 3.6. Incidence of Unemployment Support Programs around the World

	Unemployment insurance		Unemployment assistance		Unemployment insurance savings accounts			Severance pay	Public works		Reference variables	
	Replacement rate	Maximum duration (months)	Replacement rate	Maximum duration (months)	Replacement rate	Maximum duration (months)	Contribution rate (employer and employee obligations) (percent)	Benefits after 20 years of service (months' pay)	Participation rate (percent)	Expenditure as percent GDP	Unemployment rate (percent)	Share of informal employment (percent)
Low-income countries												
Afghanistan										..	..	..
Angola										..	..	..
Armenia	$4–$7 per month	12								..	22.9	26.7
Azerbaijan	70 percent	6								..	1.0	..
Bangladesh								2.0	0.2	..	2.5	..
Benin								4.0		..		65.0
Burkina Faso								9.3		..		..
Burundi										..	2.2	..
Cambodia								6.75		..		..
Cameroon										..		..
Central African Rep.										..		..
Chad	Flat (below minimum wage)	12–24										
China								20.0		..	3.0	21.9
Congo, Rep. of										..	..	..
Congo, Dem. Rep. of										..	..	..
Côte d'Ivoire								6.8		..	..	..
Ethiopia								9.3	1.0	..	11.9	
Gambia, The									0.1	..		72.3
Ghana										..		..
Guinea										..		..
Haiti								8.0	1.8	..	3.7	..
Honduras								6.0	2.1	..		50.4
India								9.0	2.2	..	5.2	37.4
Indonesia								10.0	0.0	..		40.8
Kenya								1.0		..		40.0
Kyrgyz Republic	100–150 percent of minimum wage	6								..	..	..
Laos												

(continued)

Table 3.6. (continued)

	Unemployment insurance		Unemployment assistance		Unemployment insurance savings accounts			Severance pay	Public works		Reference variables	
	Replacement rate	Maximum duration (months)	Replacement rate	Maximum duration (months)	Replacement rate	Maximum duration (months)	Contribution rate (employer and employee obligations) (percent)	Benefits after 20 years of service (months' pay)	Participation rate (percent)	Expenditure as percent GDP	Unemployment rate (percent)	Share of informal employment (percent)
Liberia											..	..
Madagascar									..	..	..	57.5
Malawi									..	..	..	51.7
Mali									0.1	..	..	36.0
Mauritania		..							..	..	28.9	..
Moldova	50–60 percent of average wage							2.0	..	..	6.1	..
Mongolia								1.0	..	..	5.7	11.5
Mozambique								28.5	..	..	..	72.5
Myanmar											..	..
Nepal								20	..	..	1.1	..
Nicaragua								20.0	1.1	..	14.6	..
Niger								6.8	0.2	..	7.8	..
Nigeria									..	..	..	48.9
Korea, Democratic People's Rep. of								20.0	..	..	..	..
Pakistan								20.0	0.1	..	5.7	60.0
Rwanda									..	..	..	..
Senegal									0.5	..	..	62.4
Sierra Leone								1.0	..	..	..	..
Somalia									..	..	..	..
Sudan									..	..	..	..
Tajikistan									..	..	..	..
Tanzania									..	..	..	42.2
Togo								12.0	..	..	..	..
Turkmenistan	Limit of 3 months' wages											
Uganda									..	..	7.4	56.4
Vietnam								3.0	..	..	..	..
Yemen									..	..	11.5	..
Zambia									..	..	15.0	..
Zimbabwe									..	..	6.5	33.9

Lower middle-income countries

Country										
Albania	Flat	12–18				10.0	::	::	15.8	::
Algeria	75–300 percent of base	12–36					::	::	28.3	::
Belarus	50–70 percent	6.5				3.0	:	:	2.7	:
Bolivia	30–40 percent	3–12				20.0	6.8	:	3.9	51.3
Bosnia and Herzegovina						6.7	::	:	::	:
Bulgaria	60 percent	4–12				1.0	::	0.0	14.8	63.0
Colombia	Flat	3		Lump sum	Employer: 9.3 Worker: 0	26.8	::	::	13.6	53.8
Costa Rica						8.0	6.2	::	5.7	:
Cuba										:
Dominican Republic						15.3			16.1	52.0
Ecuador				Lump sum	Employer: 8 Worker: 0	20.0	::	::	12.8	58.8
Egypt, Arab Rep. of	60 percent	4–7					1.3	::	21.3	64.2
El Salvador							0.6	::	7.7	:
Georgia	Flat	6				1.0	::	::	11.9	36.7
Guatemala						20.0	::	::	::	::
Iran	Flat (55 percent of national average wage)	6–50				20.0	::	::	::	::
Iraq										
Jamaica									16.0	::
Jordan							::	::	15.0	::
Kazakhstan						20.0			12.7	40.0
Latvia	90 percent	6				1.0	::	::	16.0	::
Lithuania	50 percent	6				1.0	::	::	15.0	::
Macedonia	40–50 percent	24				24.0	::	::	33.4	::
Morocco						10.0	::	::	19.8	::
Papua New Guinea									:	::
Paraguay				Lump sum					8.2	::
Peru					Employer: 8 Worker: 0	12.0	0.8	0.0	7.6	54.6
Philippines	50–55 percent		30 percent				0.0	::	8.6	30.6
Romania	45–75 percent	9	18			20.0	::	::	6.8	42.7
Russian Federation						1.0	::	::	11.5	42.2
South Africa	45 percent	6				5.0	::	::	21.2	::
Sri Lanka						20.0	::	::	11.3	31.3
Swaziland									::	::
Syria						17.5			::	::

(continued)

Table 3.6. *(continued)*

	Unemployment insurance		Unemployment assistance		Unemployment insurance savings accounts			Severance pay	Public works		Reference variables	
	Replacement rate	Maximum duration (months)	Replacement rate	Maximum duration (months)	Replacement rate	Maximum duration (months)	Contribution rate (employer and employee obligations) (percent)	Benefits after 20 years of service (months' pay)	Participation rate (percent)	Expenditure as percent GDP	Unemployment rate (percent)	Share of informal employment (percent)
Thailand								10.0	..	..	1.9	..
Tunisia	35–60 percent		Minimum wage	3				3.0	..	..	..	57.1
Ukraine		12	75 percent of minimum wage	6				1.0	..	..	9.1	..
Uzbekistan	50 percent	6						2.0	..	..	0.4	..
Yugoslavia			70 percent	3–30				4.0	..	..	..	..
Upper middle-income countries												
Argentina	60 percent	4–12			Lump sum (available only in construction)		Employer: 12 (8 after first year) Worker: 0	10.0	6.4	..	15.9	..
Botswana	50 percent	6–11						3.0	10.2	..	21.5	..
Brazil					Lump sum (+40 percent if not dismissed for "just cause")		Employer: 8 Worker: 0	6.0	..	..	7.9	49.2
Chile	60–80 percent				30–50 percent	5	Employer: 2.4 Worker: 0.6	11.0	7.7	..	6.5	40.0
Croatia	40–50 percent	2.5–10						10.0	..	..	11.2	70.0
Czech Republic			Flat (16 percent of average wage in 2001)	..				2.0	0.2	0.0	5.6	..
Estonia		6	Flat (7.3 percent of average wage in 2001)	6				4.0	..	0.0	10.2	..
Gabon											..	..
Hungary	65 percent	9–12	Flat	9				5.0	2.2	0.2	8.7	..
Lebanon								10.0	..	..	8.6	..
Libya								12.0	..	..	..	..
Malaysia									..	..	2.9	..
Mauritius								17.4	4.4	..	9.8	..
Mexico									..	0.5	3.7	..
Oman									..	..	..	..
Panama					Lump sum			5.0	0.7	..	13.4	..

Poland	Flat (23 percent of average wage in 2001)	6–18				0.7	0.1	12.0	:
Saudi Arabia					17.5			:	:
Slovak Republic	45–50 percent	6–9	Flat		2.0	:	0.0	13.0	:
Republic of Korea	50 percent	3–8	50 percent		20.0	5.2	:	3.9	:
Trinidad and Tobago				6				15.1	:
Turkey	50 percent	6–10			20.0	:	:	6.9	:
Uruguay	50 percent		Employer: 15 Worker: 12.5 (comprehensive insurance)		6.0			10.5	:
Venezuela	60 percent	3–6	Lump-sum		9.0	0.3	0.1	11.9	:
High-income countries									
Australia	41–99 percent of average wage in 2001			No limit	2.0	0.3	0.1	7.9	6.4
Austria	55 percent of net earnings	5–18	51 percent of net earnings	6 (extendable)	9.0	:	0.0	4.9	16.0
Belgium	44–60 percent	No limit			1.3	3.2	0.5	9.1	:
Canada	55 percent	11			3.0	0.1	0.1	8.8	4.4
Denmark	90 percent	12–48			1.0	0.8	0.2	5.9	15.4
Finland	Up to 90 percent	16.5	Flat	No limit		2.0	0.3	12.9	:
France	57–75 percent	4–60	53 percent of net earnings	No limit	2.0	1.5	0.2	11.9	9.0
Germany	60 percent of net earnings	6–32		No limit		1.6	0.3	9.0	22.0
Greece	40–50 percent	4–9		No limit	5.8			9.8	:
Hong Kong (China)	$165–$231 per month in 2002			No limit	2.0			3.8	:
Ireland	Flat (13 percent of average wage in 2001)	15		No limit	2.5	3.7	0.6	9.6	:
Israel	40–80 percent of average wage	4.5/year			20.0	:	:	7.7	:
Italy	40–80 percent	6–27			18.0	:	0.0	11.5	39.0
Japan	60–80 percent	10			20.0			3.8	:
Kuwait	$250–$680 per month (in 2002)	12						:	:
Netherlands	70 percent	6–60	Flat (70 percent of minimum wage)	24		0.3	0.4	5.4	:

(continued)

Table 3.6. *(continued)*

	Unemployment insurance		Unemployment assistance		Unemployment insurance savings accounts			Severance pay	Public works		Reference variables	
	Replacement rate	Maximum duration (months)	Replacement rate	Maximum duration (months)	Replacement rate	Maximum duration (months)	Contribution rate (employer and employee obligations) (percent)	Benefits after 20 years of service (months' pay)	Participation rate (percent)	Expenditure as percent GDP	Unemploy-ment rate (percent)	Share of informal employment (percent)
New Zealand			15–40 percent of average wage in 2001	No limit				11.0	0.9	0.0	6.7	..
Norway	73 percent	18–36							0.1	0.0	4.0	..
Portugal	65 percent	12–30	Flat (80 percent of minimum wage)	12–30				20.0	0.8	0.1	6.2	..
Singapore								20.0			3.2	..
Slovenia	60–70 percent	3–24	Flat (80 percent of minimum wage)	15				10.0	1.1	0.1	7.4	31.0
Spain	60–70 percent	24	Flat	6–18				12.0	1.4	0.1	20.0	21.9
Sweden	75 percent	10	Flat	5					2.7	0.4	8.8	19.8
Switzerland	70 percent	5–17							0.0	0.2	3.4	..
Taiwan	60 percent	6						7.0			2.8	..
United Kingdom	Flat (41 percent of average wage in 2001)	6	Flat	No limit				5.0	0.1	..	6.5	..
United States	50 percent	6.5–10							0.1	0.0	5.0	..

Sources: Unemployment insurance, unemployment assistance: U.S Social Security Administration (1999, 2002a, 2002b); OECD (1999a); Vodopivec, Wörgötter, and Raju (2003). *Unemployment insurance savings accounts:* Acevedo and Eskenazi (2003); Heckman and Pages (2000); Lipsett (1999); and Mazza (1999). *Severance payments:* Botero and others (2002); OECD (1999b). *Public works:* World Bank's databases on public works and social funds projects, available at www1.worldbank.org/sp/safetynets and wbln0018.worldbank.org/HDNet/HDdocs.nsf/socialfunds/; Betcherman and Islam (2001); Beegle, Frankenberg, and Thomas (1999); Marquez (1999); OECD (1999b); and Subbarao (1997, 2003). *Unemployment:* ILO (2001); World Bank (2003). *Share of informal employment:* Botero and others (2002).

Notes: Blank cell = not applicable; .. = not available.

Included are countries covered in U.S. Social Security Administration (1999) with populations of 1 million or more. *Unemployment insurance and unemployment assistance:* Reference period for countries in Europe and East Asia and the Pacific is 2002; for all other countries reference period is 1999. Replacement rates are percentage of gross wage unless specified otherwise. Benefit levels in dollars are benefits in local currency converted into dollars at average yearly exchange rates. For Algeria, base is average monthly salary plus monthly national guaranteed minimum salary divided by 2. *Severance pay:* Reference period is 1999. Benefits refer to months of salary paid to dismissed employee with 20 years of service. For Sri Lanka figure is an estimate (see box 6.6). *Public works:* For developing and transition countries, includes social funds. Reference period is the 1990s and 2000–02 (yearly average or single year). Participation rate is defined as 100 × the number of participants divided by the labor force. *Unemployment rates:* Five-year averages for 1995–99 (if single year, numbers appear in italics) and refer to one of the years during 1995–2000). *Share of informal employment:* Estimates of the share of the labor force employed in the unofficial economy in the capital city as a percent of the official labor. Reference period is late 1990s. Figures are based on surveys and, for some countries, econometric estimates.

than 80 percent of these countries. Strikingly, however, the participation rate in public works in low-income countries is smaller than in all other income groups. The average participation rate of middle-income countries is 3.2 percent—four times the 0.8 percent rate in low-income countries. This gap in participation rates may reflect the weak institutional capacity—and perhaps financing—of low-income countries.

Severance pay programs are available in less than half of low-income countries. Because they have large informal sectors (for the group of low-income countries with severance pay programs, the average share of informal employment is 42.3 percent), severance pay programs leave out significant proportions of the labor force. Moreover, as discussed in chapter 4, legal entitlement to severance pay often does not guarantee its payment. Social insurance programs are nonexistent, except in China and a few other transition countries, and they cover only (subgroups) of formal workers.

Overall, then, except for few formal sector workers, the unemployed in low-income countries are provided with little public income protection. Among low-income countries one out of six countries offers no public support programs, and 60 percent offer only a single program, usually public works (figure 3.2).

Income Support Programs for the Unemployed in Middle-Income Countries

Middle-income countries offer a larger set of programs. Severance pay, available in more than 70 percent of middle-income countries, is the most prevalent program (figure 3.1, table 3.6). About two-thirds of middle-income countries also offer public works programs. These countries use public works programs more intensely than low-income countries. Middle-income countries also offer social insurance and unemployment insurance savings accounts, either as self-standing programs, as in Chile, or in combination with unemployment insurance, as in Brazil and Argentina. By combining severance pay and public works with social insurance, these countries offer more diverse and more effective income protection than low-income countries. Still, about 13 percent of middle-income countries offer no public income support program, and only about half of middle-income countries offer more than two types of programs (figure 3.2).

Income Support Programs for the Unemployed in High-Income Countries

High-income countries provide income protection primarily through social insurance, in the form of unemployment insurance, unemployment assistance, or both. Indeed, virtually all high-income countries offer at least one of these two programs, and nearly half offer both (figure 3.1, table 3.6). The single exception is Singapore, the only affluent country that does not have a social insurance program to cover unemployment risk. More than a third of high-income countries provide unemployment benefits indefinitely, subject to satisfying continuing eligibility conditions. The remaining countries in

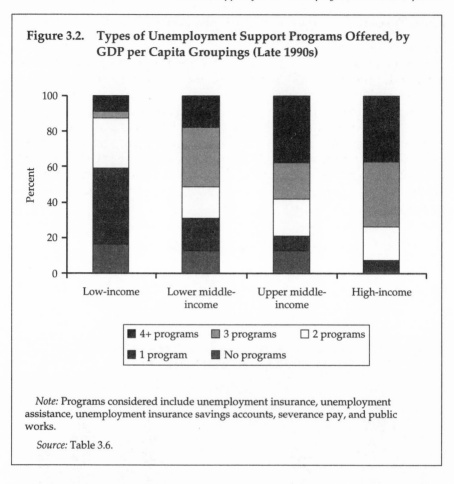

Figure 3.2.   Types of Unemployment Support Programs Offered, by GDP per Capita Groupings (Late 1990s)

Note: Programs considered include unemployment insurance, unemployment assistance, unemployment insurance savings accounts, severance pay, and public works.

Source: Table 3.6.

this group effectively match such protection by complementing social insurance with other programs, primarily social assistance, that provide individuals, including the unemployed, with benefits for an unlimited period of time (benefits are usually less generous than unemployment benefits). High-income countries also use other income support programs, including severance pay and public works. More than three-quarters of these countries offer three or more types of programs, and just 7 percent only one (figure 3.2). Interestingly, public works seem to cater to different population groups and serve different objectives than in developing countries. In high-income countries, the emphasis seems to be less on poverty relief and more on helping the disadvantaged and long-term unemployed remain tied to the labor market and avoid marginalization. No high-income country uses unemployment insurance savings accounts to protect against unemployment. The recent reform of Austrian severance pay may be paving the way for such a method, however (see box 6.7).

Income Support Programs for the Unemployed across Regions

The incidence of income support programs also varies systematically across geographic regions. While the pattern is obviously heavily influenced by the level of development, several patterns emerge. First, social insurance is common in the OECD countries and in European transition countries, but it is very rare elsewhere (figure 3.3). Mandatory severance pay is widespread in all regions—particularly in European transition countries and in Latin America—except Africa. Unemployment insurance savings accounts are used only in Latin America. Public works programs are the most evenly distributed across all regions. Interestingly, although public works programs are the most widely used type of income support in Africa, their incidence is higher in other regions (except in Asia).

Income Support Programs for the Unemployed across Countries

Explaining why some countries use some programs and others use different ones is beyond the scope of this book. Based on table 3.6 and on an

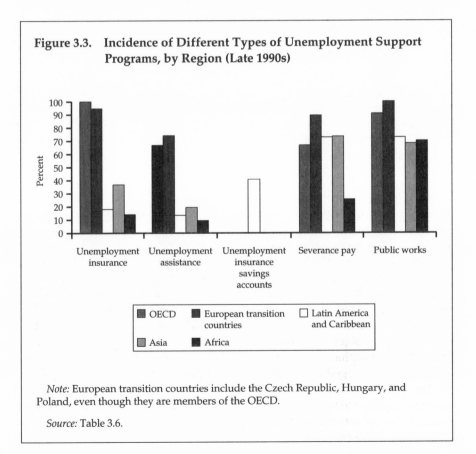

Figure 3.3. Incidence of Different Types of Unemployment Support Programs, by Region (Late 1990s)

Note: European transition countries include the Czech Republic, Hungary, and Poland, even though they are members of the OECD.

Source: Table 3.6.

Box 3.2.   Trade Unions and the Introduction of Social Insurance

The presence of organized labor seems to foster the introduction of social insurance, as suggested by the cases of Algeria and Brazil. During the early 1990s, Algeria was in a difficult economic situation, brought about by depressed world prices for oil, its principal export. As a result, in 1994 the government initiated reforms of public enterprises that included mass layoffs from distended industries. As part of the reforms, the requirement that unions had to approve layoffs for economic reasons on a case by case basis was dropped. In consultation with unions, however, the government simultaneously introduced an unemployment benefit program, so that in addition to severance pay, laid-off workers were eligible for social insurance benefits.

The 1986 Cruzado Plan introduced universal unemployment insurance in Brazil. There is no consensus regarding the forces that contributed to its emergence. One theory states that it was provided in response to increased union pressure demanding the implementation of the program, which had been promised earlier. An alternative theory identifies the primary motivating factor as the growing public dissatisfaction arising from urban population pressures and economic instability. Yet a third theory suggests that unemployment insurance was included in the plan in return for less favorable labor clauses.

Source: Ruppert (1999) and Cunningham (2000).

---

econometric analysis of the incidence of social insurance systems (see annex), however, some observations can be made. First, the incidence of social insurance is correlated with the level of development. Second, econometric testing suggests that people's ability to affect the political decision-making process is important for introducing social insurance programs (for illustrations of such a process, see box 3.2). Third, there is no correlation between the unemployment rate and the incidence of various programs across countries (corresponding correlation coefficients computed from data presented in table 3.6 are insignificant).

Concluding Remarks

Countries use very different approaches in providing income support to the unemployed. Industrial countries base their income protection on social insurance and rely on multiple programs. Some developing countries, particularly low-income countries, offer no special programs for the unemployed. Moreover, the parameters of income support programs differ sharply across countries, contributing to differences in coverage and the degree of protection provided. Even countries that are geographically proximate and at similar levels of economic development often choose quite different welfare regimes, as the diversity of regimes across Europe suggests (Gough 2000).

How can such a diversity of approaches be explained? The "one size fits all" rule does not apply for a variety of reasons. Countries choose and design programs that fit their specific circumstances and needs. Special interest groups and political economy considerations also seem to be important. Different programs have different distributive and efficiency objectives and effects. For example, reaching the chronic poor requires one type of program, providing income-smoothing for skilled workers requires another.

One implication of these findings is that in reforming their programs, countries may well follow different transition paths and their programs may never converge. Even economies with similar technologies and preferences can reach very different, stable equilibria regarding the level of unemployment insurance. For example, in explaining differences in unemployment insurance programs in Western Europe and the United States, Hassler, Zilbotti, and Mora (1999) argue that the interaction of skill specificity and preferences reinforces differences in initial skill distributions of a society to generate one equilibrium with high unemployment, low turnover, and a high level of insurance and another with low unemployment, high turnover, and a low level of insurance.

Annex 3.1 Determinants of Social Insurance Programs for the Unemployed

This annex uses econometric techniques to empirically test the determinants of the incidence of social insurance. It stipulates that the incidence of social insurance (unemployment insurance, unemployment assistance, or dual programs in which both are offered) depends on the vulnerability of a country to unemployment risk (on the demand side) and the ability of the public to influence government decisionmaking in favor of the public provision of unemployment benefits (on the supply side).

Because neither factor is easy to measure, proxy variables are used. On the demand side, the size of the urban population is used as a proxy for the level of a country's vulnerability. The ability of the urban population to absorb shocks is lower, because its ability to self-protect and to cope with unemployment is likely to be limited, due to the covariant nature of unemployment shocks (that is, the fact that a shock affecting one individual will also affect others).[3] On the supply side, a variable indicating whether or not a country has ratified the International Labour Organization's freedom of association convention (the right of workers and employers to freely establish associations or organizations) is used as a proxy for the public's ability to affect the political decisionmaking process. The level of per capita GDP is also included among possible determinants, to reflect the capacity of an economy to redistribute income, as social insurance programs may entail redistribution from the rich to the poor.

The results show that the likelihood of a country possessing a social insurance program is indeed positively and significantly related to the ratification of the freedom of association convention (table A3.1).[4] The percent of the labor force that is included in trade unions is also positively associated

Table A3.1. Determinants of the Incidence of Social Insurance Programs for the Unemployed (probit estimates, standard errors in parentheses)

Independent variable	Specification	
	Equation 1	*Equation 2*
GDP per capita, PPP	0.052*	0.081**
(in thousands of current dollars)	(0.023)	(0.028)
Urban population (percent of total)	0.021**	0.011
	(0.007)	(0.009)
Signed the ILO Freedom of		1.05**
Association Convention	--	(0.314)
Constant	−1.791**	−2.12**
	(0.333)	(0.506)
Sample size	160	114
Log likelihood	−82.7	−56.5

Sources: Presence of Social Insurance: U.S. Social Security Administration (1999); *Signed ILO Freedom of Association Convention:* Rama and Artecona (2000). *All other data:* World Bank (2003).

Note: Social insurance includes unemployment insurance, unemployment assistance, and dual programs in which both unemployment insurance and assistance are provided.

*Significant at 5 percent level.
**Significant at 1 percent level.
-- = variable not included in equation.

with the presence of social insurance. This result (not reported) is in line with the casual evidence about the role of trade unions in the emergence of unemployment insurance in Algeria and Brazil (box 3.2). The percent of the population that is urban is positively associated with the incidence of social insurance, but the variable loses significance once the ratification variable is included in the regression. As expected, the results confirm the link between per capita GNP and the presence of social insurance.

Notes

1. Although unemployment insurance in Sweden is administered by trade unions, it can be considered a public program whose administration has been taken over by the private sector, because more than 90 percent of the funding is public, the program is extensively regulated, and individuals not covered are eligible for tax-financed, noncontributory benefits (Barr 2001).

2. Interestingly, the ratio of project to local-market wages was lower in projects with substantial community participation than in projects with no community participation (Hoddinott and others 2001). Such an outcome was presumably perceived as more equitable, as lowering the wage meant that more people had the opportunity to work.

3. Horton and Mazumdar (2001) report that during the recent crisis in Thailand, many recent migrants to urban areas returned to their regions of origin and agriculture.

4. The results may be subject to reversed causality and thus should be taken as preliminary.

4

Performance of Income Support Programs: Theoretical Aspects and Empirical Evidence

This chapter reviews the evidence on the performance of various income support programs for the unemployed. It evaluates the protection and efficiency effects of these programs, examines how suitable they are for confronting various types of shocks, and assesses how resistant they are to political risk. The discussion focuses on programs whose main objective is to provide compensation for the loss of earnings due to unemployment: unemployment insurance, unemployment assistance, severance pay, unemployment insurance savings accounts, and public works. Selective outcomes of some other programs (social assistance and early retirement) are also reviewed.

Three caveats about the pitfalls of such a task need to be mentioned. First, many income support programs tend to be very complex, because design parameters interact in numerous ways. In evaluating the performance of these programs, it is critical to appropriately account for their design parameters (the program's "architecture"), as well as for the degree of enforcement of the programs' rules (Atkinson and Micklewright 1991). Differences in the design of income support programs may help explain not only variations in their coverage but also other effects these programs have on different labor market outcomes (the incidence of part-time workers, the share of women and the long-term unemployed among the unemployed, the duration of unemployment, to name just a few). Long duration of insured unemployment, for example, may be attributable not only to low labor demand but also to a generous replacement rate, long maximum duration periods for benefit collection, lax monitoring of job search, ineffective job-search assistance, and eligibility rules that attract workers with weak labor force attachment and poor motivation. Similarly, a high share of women among benefit recipients may be attributable to low relative demand for women's labor, but it may also reflect program rules that extend benefits to mothers until children reach a certain age, as the rules in Estonia did during the 1990s.

Second, programs cannot be evaluated separately from other important institutional features of the economy. In conjunction with structural parameters of income support programs, a host of institutional and other features—primarily those affecting the performance of the labor market, such as labor legislation and collective bargaining arrangements—as well as labor market conditions have to be considered in order to more accurately determine the effects of income support programs. For example, an increase in the intensity of job-search monitoring may well produce different results depending on the rate of unemployment. Similarly, the effects of experience rating on layoffs depend largely on the strictness of employment protection legislation—if such legislation is in place, the additional effects of experience rating may be small. Unemployment benefit programs are also affected by wage-setting arrangements: under flexible wage arrangements, more adjustment is likely to be achieved through real wage reductions than through employment reductions. In contrast, more rigid wage determination may prompt more employment adjustment and larger inflows to insured unemployment; in turn, higher costs of unemployment benefits stifle job creation and contribute to higher unemployment, particularly for marginal groups of workers (Aghion and Blanchard 1994; Layard, Nickell, and Jackman 1991). Recognizing such effects, the analysis below notes whether the effects are of a partial or a general equilibrium nature.

Third, simultaneous programs and policies can have offsetting or reinforcing effects. For example, the employment effects of liberalization of fixed-term work depend not only on job protection of regular jobs but also on whether fixed-term workers qualify for unemployment benefits. Similarly, increasing monitoring of job search may not help reduce the duration of covered unemployment if monitoring of informal employment remains lax. Moreover, the effects of the generosity of the unemployment benefit program may well depend on a host of labor market policies—from wage-setting behavior and minimum wage regulations to employment protection legislation—that influence the job creation capacity of the economy and thus the demand side of the market. For example, Orzsag and Snower (1998) argue that the positive effects of lower benefits on the intensity of job search are reinforced by tax cuts that induce employers to hire more workers (this speaks in favor of broader reforms, which tend to be more effective and politically more acceptable [see below]). Changing only one program may not produce the desired effects. In line with the interdependency of social risk management mechanisms emphasized in chapter 2, policymakers should therefore judge the effects of a program in the context of the entire economic program rather than in isolation.

Income Protection Effects

The main objective of income support programs for the unemployed is to compensate workers for the loss of income when they become unemployed. Three interrelated aspects—coverage, adequacy, and redistribution—are examined. Particular attention is paid to unemployment benefits programs in transition countries, most of them introduced in the beginning of the 1990s, for which substantial empirical analysis was conducted using household expenditures surveys.

Coverage

Most workers in industrial countries are protected by several income support programs (see table 3.6). As described in chapter 3, most unemployment insurance programs are government mandated and cover all employees; many exclude the self-employed and some other groups, such as agricultural workers and household workers. Coverage by legislated severance pay also tends to be widespread. All industrial countries also offer social assistance programs that provide assistance of last resort. In most countries these programs are open-ended in duration. Industrial countries also offer other types of income support programs (early retirement, public works, training, employment subsidies), which are usually targeted to specific groups.

In transition countries, unemployment insurance covers most of the labor force, and workers are also usually eligible for severance pay. Unemployment benefits represented an important source of income in these countries in the mid-1990s (table 4.1). As many as 78 percent of households in Hungary and 65 percent of households in Poland with at least one unemployed worker received unemployment benefits; the share in other countries was lower, particularly in Estonia and Latvia, where just 17–19 percent of such households received unemployment benefits. Interestingly, among households with at least one unemployed member, the receipt of unemployment benefits was less prevalent among poor households, except in Estonia (table 4.1).

In contrast, workers in developing countries are covered by few, if any, public income maintenance programs. Unemployment insurance is available in only a small number of developing countries, and it does not always cover all workers in the formal sector. For example, only about 60 percent of all wage workers in the Republic of Korea were covered in 1999, four years after the program's introduction (Hur 2001). Moreover, although most Latin American and East Asian countries mandate severance pay, these programs only benefit formal sector workers. In all countries, workers in the informal sector are therefore much more exposed to unemployment risk than formal sector workers.[1] They are excluded from programs that require payment of social security contributions, and typically there are few other public programs in which they can participate.

Because of a large informal sector, unemployment insurance and legislated severance pay tend to cover only a part of the workforce in developing countries (see table 3.6 for the prevalence of informal sector employment across countries). In 2003 less than a third of the workforce was covered by unemployment insurance in the Republic of Korea (see chapter 6) and only

Table 4.1. Poverty-Related Effects of Unemployment Benefits in Transition Economies, Mid-1990s

Item	Bulgaria[a] All hh.	Estonia All hh.	Estonia Hh. with unemp.	Hungary All hh.	Hungary Hh. with unemp.	Latvia All hh.	Latvia Hh. with unemp.	Poland All hh.	Poland Hh. with unemp.	Slovak Republic All hh.	Slovak Republic Hh. with unemp.	Slovenia All hh.	Slovenia Hh. with unemp.
Coverage (percent)													
Share of households that receive unemployment benefits	4.2	1.9	18.7	16.2	77.5	2.1	17.4	9.3	64.7	7.8	24.4	8.1	42.7
Share of poor households that receive unemployment benefits[b]	10.6	5.1	20.8	32.5	64.5	5.2	13.0	15.6	51.6	17.8	32.1	13.8	34.6
Targeting (share of unemployment benefits budget received by each group)													
Poor households	38.9	46.3	46.3	12.8	12.8	19.7	19.7	18.5	18.5	9.9	9.9	19.8	19.8
Households drawn from poverty by unemployment benefits	12.2	11.6	11.6	38.2	38.2	33.2	33.2	34.4	34.4	25.6	25.6	25.1	25.1
Households above the poverty threshold even if they did not receive unemployment benefits	48.9	42.1	42.1	49.0	49.0	47.1	47.1	47.2	47.2	64.5	64.5	55.1	55.1
Average share of unemployment benefits in total household income (percent)													
All households	0.6	0.4	4.1	4.2	19.9	0.8	6.3	3.2	22.3	0.7	2.1	2.1	11.3
Households receiving the benefit	13.0	21.9	21.9	25.7	25.7	36.2	36.2	34.5	34.5	8.5	8.5	26.4	26.4

Poverty reduction brought about
by receipt of unemployment
benefits

Percent of hypothetically poor (prebenefit headcount)[c]	3.3	1.3	4.7	40.0	53.3	4.0	9.2	20.6	44.7	21.6	31.2	8.0	15.7
Percent of total population	0.6	0.3	1.8	5.2	19.7	0.6	3.8	3.5	19.2	1.1	3.0	1.3	5.8
Memorandum items													
Poverty headcount	17.6	18.6	37.4	7.8	17.3	14.3	37.3	13.6	23.7	3.8	6.6	15.2	31.4
Percent of households that have an unemployed member	—	10.4	100.0	20.9	100.0	12.3	100.0	14.4	100.0	32.1	100.0	18.9	100.0
Poverty gap[d]	3.4	3.4	—	0.9	—	2.0	—	1.9	—	0.17	—	2.6	—

Source: Calculated based on Household Expenditure and Income Data for Transitional Economies (www.worldbank.org/research/transition/house.htm). Slovenian data provided by the Slovenian Statistical Office. Survey year: Bulgaria, 1995; Hungary, 1993; Latvia, 1997; Poland, 1993; Slovak Republic, 1993; Slovenia, 1997–98. Sample size: Bulgaria, 2,466; Hungary, 8,105; Latvia, 7,690; Poland, 16,051; Slovak Republic, 2,129; Slovenia, 2,577. Survey weights used where appropriate.

Note: Unemployment benefits include unemployment insurance and unemployment assistance.

— Not available

a. Data do not allow identification of unemployed household members.
b. The poor are households (and individuals living in them) whose income per equivalent adult is below the poverty line. The poverty line is defined as 60 percent of the median of the distribution of income per equivalent adult. The number of equivalent adults is obtained by using the OECD weighing program: 1 for the first adult in the household, 0.7 for each subsequent adult, and 0.5 for each child under the age of 15.
c. The hypothetically poor are households with pre-unemployment-benefit income per equivalent adult below the poverty line.
d. The poverty gap is the share of income that, if distributed among poor households, would bring them out of poverty, based on total household income.

40 percent of urban workers in Brazil were covered. Unemployment insurance savings accounts covered 47 percent of urban workers in Colombia (de Ferranti and others 2000). MacIsaac and Rama (2000) estimate that only about 20 percent of private sector workers in Peru are legally entitled to severance pay, most of them wealthier workers. Coverage is so low because many private sector workers are self-employed or work in household enterprises, and many salaried workers do not have the minimum seniority needed to qualify for severance pay.

But under severance pay, coverage—and thus legal entitlement—does not guarantee the actual receipt of the benefit. This is the so-called nonperformance problem of severance pay. For example, in Peru only about half of workers who are legally entitled to severance pay are estimated to receive benefits if dismissed (payment is more likely if the worker has a written contract and works in a larger, unionized firm that pays social security contributions) (MacIsaac and Rama 2000). In Slovenia in 1994–2002, employers denied severance pay to more than 5 percent of the workforce and total claims for unpaid severance pay reported by workers to the public guarantee fund in the late 1990s amounted to about 0.2 percent of GDP per year (Vodopivec and Madzar 2003). Vodopivec and Madzar also report that in 2000, unpaid claims amounted to more than one-third of total severance pay provisions. Understandably, many workers turn to the courts, imposing heavy litigation costs. Nonperformance of severance pay is related to limited risk-pooling, coupled with the nonfunded nature of the program and the fact that the liabilities often arise when the firm is least capable of paying them.

There is also a more subtle point about the effects of severance pay on the coverage. The generosity of severance payments limits the access of particular groups of workers to jobs, thus preventing them from being covered by formal income support programs. Blanchard (2000) shows that an increase in firing costs leads to higher unemployment of marginal groups of workers because of their inferior access to jobs. The productivity of these workers before hiring is not easily revealed, and therefore their probability of being hired in the presence of increased firing costs is lower. Indeed, an OECD study (1999b) finds that stricter employment protection legislation reduces employment among prime-age women, young people, and older workers, thus rendering them more susceptible to unemployment risk. Kugler and Saint-Paul (2000) show that higher firing costs increase discrimination against unemployed workers, because they increase the costs associated with hiring a bad worker. Moreover, in the presence of higher severance costs for older workers, separation decisions may be biased against young workers. In other words, high firing costs contribute to the emergence of dual labor markets made up of well-protected formal sector workers (who tend to be predominantly prime-age males) and much less protected informal sector workers and the unemployed. In line with these findings, Besley and Burgess (2004) show that pro-worker legislation may work against the poor in developing countries (see below).

Unemployed workers may also qualify for other income support programs. Unemployment assistance is available in some transition countries after beneficiaries exhaust unemployment insurance benefits, as are early retirement programs. Social assistance is rarely available in developing countries; if it is, it is often provided on a one-time basis. Workers may also benefit from public sector retrenchment programs. In the absence of social assistance, public works programs provide assistance of last resort, although such programs are often not available to all potential beneficiaries. In Mexico training is used as a form of assistance of last resort (30 percent of the unemployed receive some training [de Ferranti and others 2000]). Recently, other innovative programs have emerged, including unemployment insurance savings accounts and social funds. In response to economic crisis, countries may also introduce temporary programs, such as the Emergency Loan Facility available to displaced workers in the Philippines, where workers obtain loans contingent on their previous payments into the social security fund (Esguerra, Ogawa, and Vodopivec 2001).

Among the programs available to informal sector workers, public works programs are probably the most important. Many developing countries, particularly those in South Asia, have longstanding traditions of such programs. Public works programs can generate significant employment (see chapter 3). Interestingly, the participation rate in public works (including social funds) is highest among upper middle- and lower middle-income groups and lowest for high-income and low-income countries (see table 3.6).

Adequacy of Support

Replacement rates and the entitlement duration of unemployment benefit programs as well as the consumption-smoothing, and poverty-reduction effects of income support programs are examined to gauge the elusive concept of adequacy of support.

REPLACEMENT RATES AND ENTITLEMENT DURATION OF UNEMPLOYMENT BENEFITS. Replacement rates differ widely across countries. In most industrial countries they are 40–75 percent. In the Nordic countries they are even higher (the replacement rate in Denmark is 90 percent; see table 3.6). In the United States a broad consensus has emerged that an adequate income replacement rate is 50 percent (O'Leary 1997). The replacement rates in developing and transition countries are mostly in the range of 45–70 percent, although there are notable exceptions. In the late 1990s through 2003, for example, Estonia offered flat-rate benefits of less than 10 percent of the average wage (Vodopivec, Wörgötter, and Raju 2003).

The range of the maximum entitlement duration of benefits is also very large. In industrial countries it ranges from six months to indefinite. In developing and transition countries, it ranges from 6 months to 24 months (with some extensions close to retirement age).

A summary measure—the net (after-tax) replacement rate—that combines income received from various programs confirms the generous nature of income protection in industrial countries. On average OECD countries offer more than 60 percent of expected earnings in work; some countries (Denmark, Finland, the Netherlands, Sweden, and Switzerland) offer more than 80 percent (Martin and Grubb 2001).[2] The United States, which provides net replacement of just 34 percent, and Greece, with a net replacement rate of just over 10 percent, are at the bottom among OECD countries.

Given the wide differences in the replacement rate and the entitlement duration, a better comparison of adequacy is obtained by combining the two measures in an "index of generosity." The index of generosity is defined as the product of the replacement rate and the share of benefit recipients in the total number of unemployed times 100. It equals the cost of unemployment benefits per percentage point of unemployment (Vroman 2002). By this measure, on average unemployment benefit programs in transition countries lag significantly behind benefits in OECD countries, but there are substantial variations within the two groups of countries (see Vroman 2002 for OECD countries and Vodopivec, Wörgötter, and Raju 2003 for transition countries). Among European transition countries in the 1990s, the most generous unemployment benefits were provided in Slovenia and Hungary (and in Poland until 1996); the least generous were in Estonia.

CONSUMPTION-SMOOTHING EFFECTS. Research on industrial countries (primarily the United States) suggests that unemployment benefits smooth consumption. Hamermesh and Slesnick (1995) find that the welfare of benefit recipient households was on average only 3–8 percent lower than the welfare of otherwise identical households. Gruber (1997a) finds that in the absence of unemployment insurance, average consumption expenditures would fall by 22 percent.

Only a few studies examine the consumption-smoothing effects of income support programs in developing countries. MacIssac and Rama (2000) report that per capita consumption fell 10–20 percent following unemployment in Peru. But they find that the receipt of severance pay more than outweighed this effect of unemployment, so that per capita consumption of the unemployed who received severance pay was higher than otherwise similar workers who were employed. This result suggests that severance pay was overly generous. Kugler (2002) shows that withdrawals from unemployment insurance savings accounts in Colombia increased consumption by nonemployed household heads. Interestingly, mandated severance pay programs appear to be least generous in low-income and high-income countries. In these countries, severance pay for a worker with 20 years of service is equivalent to about 9 months of wages—less than the 10.8 months in lower middle-income countries and the 9.4 months in upper middle-income countries (table 3.6).

POVERTY-REDUCTION EFFECTS. Evidence suggests that public works and, somewhat surprisingly, unemployment benefits can strongly reduce poverty and that the indirect effects of severance pay on poverty can be strongly negative.

In the mid-1990s unemployment benefit programs contributed substantially to poverty reduction in European transition countries—an unexpected finding given that reducing poverty is not one of the stated goals of unemployment benefits. The effects were strongest in Hungary and Poland. In Hungary poverty among the unemployed fell more than 50 percent; in Poland it declined 45 percent (table 4.1).[3] In Hungary 5.2 percent of the total population was drawn out of poverty by unemployment benefits; in Poland the figure was 3.5 percent. Benefits reduced poverty among the unemployed in other countries as well, albeit less significantly. Poverty fell 31 percent in the Slovak Republic, 16 percent in Slovenia, 9 percent in Latvia, and 5 percent in Estonia (table 4.1).

These strong effects reflect both the favorable distributive properties of unemployment benefit programs and the small poverty gap in these countries. A large share of households received unemployment benefits, and the benefits were sizable. The average share of benefits in household income was largest in Hungary (4.2 percent), followed by Poland (3.2 percent)—the two countries in which poverty reduction was greatest. The shares in other countries were much smaller, with the smallest in Estonia, the country with the most modest poverty-reduction effects. Benefits were also well targeted: in every country but the Slovak Republic and Slovenia, more than half of benefits went to the poor or to those who were pulled out of poverty by the benefits. (The largest share of unemployment benefits received by the poor was in Estonia, but few people there were drawn out of poverty because of the modest size of the benefits.) Strong poverty-reduction effects were also greatly facilitated by a relatively small poverty gap—in Bulgaria and Estonia, the countries with the smallest poverty-reduction effects, the poverty gap was largest in both absolute terms and in comparison with unemployment benefits.

The poverty-reduction performance of unemployment benefit programs in transition countries is unlikely to be matched in developing countries. In transition countries, unemployment insurance programs have covered virtually all workers from the time the programs were introduced. Coverage in developing countries is much more limited. Moreover, covered workers already have the advantage of working in the formal sector and thus usually belong to a relatively prosperous population group (in the Republic of Korea, for example, eight years after its introduction unemployment insurance covered less than one-third of the workforce; see chapter 6).

The scope for reducing poverty through public works also appears to be large. Subbarao and others (1997) report that evaluations of public works programs reveal significant improvements in participants' economic circumstances. Evidence shows that participants in India's Maharashtra Employment Guarantee Scheme (MEGS) have higher annual incomes than nonparticipants, with wages from the program contributing significantly to total income. Datt and Ravallion (1994) estimate that the severity of poverty declined from 5 percent to 3.2 percent as a result of MEGS. One reason why the program achieved such significant poverty reduction was the low cost of participation—the program was structured to minimize earnings forgone from other sources as a result of participation. Although public works programs have had some success in preventing the exacerbation of impoverishment, due to the temporary nature of most of these programs, their impact on poverty is often transitory. As for social funds, Rawlings, Sherburne-Benz, and Van Domelen (2002) report that these programs have benefited more poor than nonpoor. They show that the poor and the extremely poor have been more than proportionally represented among beneficiaries.

Other direct evidence on the effects of public works on poverty reduction is scant, partly because calculations require accounting for forgone income by participants. But the results of two other studies are suggestive. Von Braun, Teklu, and Webb (1991) report that public works programs for food security in Bangladesh improved dietary intake for all participating groups relative to control groups (they emphasize that such nutrition benefits of public works depend on the project design and cannot be taken for granted). In their study of Argentina's Trabajar program, Ravallion and others (2001) report income losses of 75 percent of gross wages in the first six months after separation and slightly less than half in the subsequent six months.

There is also an interesting insight about the overall long-term effects on poverty of pro-poor labor legislation, a crucial element of which is regulation about employment protection and severance pay in particular. Besley and Burgess (2002) find that not only did pro-worker legislation in India not redress the unfavorable unbalance between capital and labor, it actually increased poverty. Their estimates show that had no pro-worker or pro-firm legislation been passed since 1958, poverty in 1990 would have been only 90 percent of the actual rate in the Indian state of West Bengal (the state with the most pro-worker legislation) and 110 percent of the actual rate in Andhra Pradesh (the state with the most pro-employer legislation). These effects are produced by changes in manufacturing employment and output brought about by changes in legislation.

As for other programs, family assistance programs have been shown to protect families from poverty in industrial countries. Subbarao and others (1997) show that in OECD countries, social insurance benefits reduced household poverty by 7–93 percent. Other means-tested programs show a similar range of impact. Evidence for non–OECD countries has been harder to come by, but the impact on poverty has been considered weak due to meager public spending on such provisions, the low levels and short durations of benefits, and poor targeting.

Income Redistribution

Do different programs have different effects on income redistribution? The evidence derived from the incidence of benefits and beneficiaries for different programs shows that by far the most progressive programs are public works and training: among the poorest 20 percent of households, 79 percent participate in public works and 70 percent participate in training (table 4.2).

Table 4.2. Beneficiaries and Distribution of Benefits of Unemployment Support Programs, Mid-1990s

Support program	Ranked by prebenefit income per person					Ranked by postbenefit income per person				
	Poorest quintile	Second-poorest	Middle	Second-richest	Richest quintile	Poorest quintile	Second-poorest	Middle	Second-richest	Richest quintile
Unemployment insurance										
Brazil	11.4	26.5	20.5	27.0	14.6	—	—	—	—	—
Bulgaria	59.0	16.7	7.7	10.3	6.3	48.9	19.3	12.9	7.4	11.5
Estonia	61.0	13.9	8.3	10.9	5.8	52.0	16.5	11.1	14.0	6.4
Only households with unemployed	37.9	18.8	15.1	11.5	16.7	31.4	11.8	24.3	12.7	19.8
Hungary	67.8	14.6	9.8	5.0	2.9	37.4	24.1	17.6	13.0	8.0
Only households with unemployed	31.0	22.6	18.7	15.0	12.8	16.6	21.1	21.6	21.2	19.5
Latvia	64.9	9.0	13.3	7.7	5.1	29.1	15.7	16.6	18.6	20.0
Only households with unemployed	37.0	15.2	17.7	16.6	13.6	9.1	11.7	14.1	27.5	37.6
Poland	64.6	19.2	9.7	4.0	2.6	35.1	28.1	20.1	11.4	5.3
Only households with unemployed	29.4	21.1	18.4	16.8	14.3	16.3	20.0	20.9	22.3	20.5
Slovak Republic	53.7	15.6	14.8	8.5	7.5	34.0	26.1	15.2	11.5	13.3
Only households with unemployed	44.7	12.3	13.1	14.0	16.0	25.8	16.1	20.2	13.1	24.8
Slovenia	49.0	24.9	14.2	8.1	3.9	27.5	18.8	26.3	18.7	8.7
Only households with unemployed	28.2	17.3	17.8	18.1	18.6	11.5	15.1	15.2	25.5	32.8

(continued)

Table 4.2. (continued)

Support program	Ranked by prebenefit income per person					Ranked by postbenefit income per person				
	Poorest quintile	Second-poorest	Middle	Second-richest	Richest quintile	Poorest quintile	Second-poorest	Middle	Second-richest	Richest quintile
Unemployment insurance savings accounts										
Colombia	0	4.3	0	19.1	76.6	—	—	—	—	—
Severance pay										
Peru	4.7	9.5	28.6	33.3	23.8	—	—	—	—	—
Public works										
Argentina	78.6	15.3	3.5	2.1	0.4	—	—	—	—	—
Training										
Mexico	69.9	15.5	8.1	5.0	1.5	—	—	—	—	—

Source: Same as table 4.1 for transition countries; de Ferranti and others (2000) for Latin American countries.

Note: The table presents the share of benefits received by quintile for transition countries and the share of beneficiaries in the population group for Latin American countries. For transition countries, unemployment insurance benefits include both unemployment insurance and unemployment assistance, and income per equivalent adult is used (see table 4.1 for equivalency scale).

— Not available.

Given that both programs are financed from general revenues, the net benefits of these programs accrue to the poor. Except for unemployment insurance, the data refer to single countries only, so conclusions are preliminary.

The strong potential of public works for redistribution is shown by the program's targeting performance. Subbarao (2003) reports that nearly 100 percent of public works participants in Chile and 60–70 percent in India (both in the nationwide program and in the Maharashtra Employment Guarantee Scheme) were poor. Based on an analysis of 101 national public works projects in South Africa, Haddad and Adato (2001) conclude that the vast majority of public works programs considerably outperform hypothetical benchmarks consisting of untargeted transfers, under fairly robust assumptions. Social funds also have a moderate progressive impact on redistribution. In Honduras, for example, the poorest decile of the population received 19 percent of the program's benefits, the poorest quintile received 32 percent, and the poorest two quintiles received 51 percent (Rawlings, Sherburne-Benz, and Van Domelen 2002).

This does not mean that the targeting method used for public works—self-selection based on working in the program—outperforms other social safety net programs that use different targeting methods. Coady, Grosch, and Hoddinott (2002) compare the effectiveness of various targeting methods. After studying the performance of 67 programs, they conclude that no method provides clear advantages.[4] Although a public works program (Argentina's Trabajar) received the best score for its targeting performance, three public works programs ranked among the 10 worst programs. Coady, Grosch, and Hoddinott also find considerable evidence that it is the implementation of the program, rather than the method of targeting, that is key to successful targeting.[5]

The redistribution of income implied by unemployment benefits is also strongly progressive in all of the transition countries studied (table 4.2). When all households are included, the share of benefits received by the bottom 40 percent of households is very large, ranging from 69 percent in the Slovak Republic to 82 percent in Hungary. The conclusion that unemployment benefits are effective in improving recipients' relative income is reinforced by evidence that the incidence of benefits is progressive when distribution is based on prebenefit income and regressive when based on postbenefit income (considering distributions of households with at least one unemployed member). The exceptions are Estonia and the Slovak Republic, the countries with the smallest share of unemployment benefits in household incomes, where the small scale of transfers did not make a difference in the postbenefit distribution.

The strong redistributive performance of unemployment benefits in transition countries may be the result of circumstances—such as nearly universal unemployment benefit coverage—that are not present in developing countries. Brazil's unemployment benefit program has a neutral effect on the redistribution of income (table 4.2). And unemployment benefits have not been an important tool for income redistribution in industrial countries:

unemployment benefits are progressive in about half of OECD countries and neutral in the other half (Forster 2000). Nonetheless, the evidence presented here suggests that under specific circumstances, unemployment insurance and assistance programs offer substantial scope for income redistribution—particularly if the fact that redistributive effects tend to be accentuated by the program financing rules (unemployment insurance contribution) is taken into account.

Participants in both the Colombian unemployment insurance savings account program and the Peruvian severance pay program belong mostly to the richest segments of the population (this pattern is not an inherent property of these programs, but it is probably typical for low-income countries) (table 4.2). Although the direct distributive effect of these programs may be limited, some efficiency properties of these programs may have distributive effects. Severance pay, for example, hinders access to jobs by disadvantaged groups (see above). By contributing to labor market dualism, it increases the advantage of already privileged formal sector workers, thus increasing inequalities in society.

What are the predicted distributive effects of introducing unemployment insurance savings accounts (UISAs)? The program can in principle provide the same income protection as traditional unemployment insurance programs, possibly with fewer adverse incentives (see next section). Switching from an unemployment insurance program to an UISA program, however, does have distributive consequences, because the benefits are financed in different ways. Simulations suggest that the distributive effects for the United States are likely to be small—and regressive. Feldstein and Altman (1998) find that individuals in all quintiles gain slightly, and individuals in the bottom quintile lose slightly (the fact that these estimates do not take account behavioral responses to the changed program most likely means that they understate the distributive effects). Similar simulations for Estonia show that the income redistribution achieved by UISAs is substantially less than that achieved under unemployment insurance and that UISAs allow for more redistribution when unemployment is high and unemployment benefits are more generous (Vodopivec and Rejec 2002). Under some designs, however, UISAs can be made more progressive, provided that the government subsidizes the accounts of low-income workers.

Summary of Income Protection Effects

COVERAGE. In comparison with their counterparts in industrial economies, formal sector workers in developing countries face a much more limited choice of income support programs for the unemployed (table 4.3). For example, the most prevalent form of insurance against unemployment in Latin America is severance pay, but not all formal sector workers are legally entitled to this benefit. Moreover, even those who are entitled to benefits often do not receive severance pay when dismissed.

Table 4.3. Summary of Protection Effects of Income Support Programs for the Unemployed

Support program	Coverage	Adequacy	Effects on income redistribution
Unemployment insurance/ unemployment assistance	• In industrial and most transition countries , coverage is broad, although self-employed, agricultural, and household workers excluded. • In most developing countries, program is not available or available only to segments of formal sector workers.	• In industrial economies, consumption level of claimants is fairly well preserved; in most transition countries, benefits are less generous. • In transition countries, benefits strongly reduce poverty; effects depend on country-specific circumstances.	• Progressive (in transition countries and some industrial countries) or neutral.
Unemployment insurance savings accounts	• Available to some formal sector workers.	• Evidence is inconclusive.	• In its pure form, redistributive effects are eliminated by design. • Program participants are concentrated among the rich in Columbia. • Simulation results for Estonia and the United States suggest that redistributive effects are likely to be small.

(continued)

Table 4.3. (continued)

Support program	Coverage	Adequacy	Effects on income redistribution
Severance pay	• Available to some formal sector workers but not always actually provided, despite legal entitlement. • Hinders access to formal sector jobs by disadvantaged groups.	• Little evidence • In Peru consumption per capita of unemployed who receive severance pay is higher than otherwise similar workers who are employed.	• Little evidence. • Program participants in Peru are concentrated among the rich. • By contributing to labor market dualism, severance pay increases the advantage of already privileged formal sector workers, thus increasing inequalities in society.
Public works	• In principle, program is available to all (self-selection based on wages); in reality, jobs are often rationed. • Average participation rates of public works in the 1990s: 0.8 percent of labor force in low-income, 2.6 percent in lower middle-income, 4.2 percent in upper middle-income, and 1.2 percent in high-income countries.	• Strong effects on poverty reduction.	• Strongly progressive.

Source: Derived from discussion in the text and table 3.6.

Workers in the informal sector are the least protected, excluded from all programs in which eligibility is conditional on social security contributions. Their options are thus limited to a subset of formal programs (such as public works) and, increasingly, to innovative programs offered by self-help organizations.

ADEQUACY OF SUPPORT. Replacement rates and entitlement duration of unemployment benefits vary widely in industrial economies, but benefits are more generous than in transition countries. Abundant evidence shows that unemployment benefits are effective in smoothing consumption in industrial economies. There is little evidence of such effects for either unemployment benefits or other income support programs in developing or transition countries. Public works seems to be most effective in reducing poverty in developing countries. The effects of unemployment insurance may also be sizable.

INCOME REDISTRIBUTION. The most progressive programs are public works and training, but unemployment insurance and assistance programs of transition countries are also strongly progressive. Program implementation seems to be more important than the method of targeting in determining the redistributive properties of the program. By design the UISA program in its pure form offers no redistribution; only under the variations of the program are individuals who deplete the savings in their accounts entitled to transfers from the public purse (see chapter 6). Severance pay seems to increase the advantage of already privileged formal sector workers, contributing to labor market dualism.

Efficiency Effects

What are the efficiency effects of unemployment support programs? How do they affect unemployment and labor force participation, unemployment, and output and growth? For each type of income support program, this section considers three effects:

- *Unemployment and labor force participation.* By changing the opportunity cost of leisure and through a variety of other channels, unemployment support programs are often hypothesized to affect unemployment, employment, and labor force participation. The effects on job-search intensity, post-unemployment wages, labor supply of other family members, and the promotion of regular versus informal jobs are also examined.
- *Persistence of unemployment.* Recent research points to the importance of the interaction of unemployment benefit programs with adverse shocks, so the effects of benefit programs on the persistence of unemployment are considered in their own right.
- *Output and growth.* Income support programs may interfere with allocation and reallocation decisions, affecting output and growth.

Recent research on worker and job flows shows that reallocation contributes significantly to aggregate productivity growth. In the U.S. manufacturing sector, the reallocation of outputs and inputs away from less productive to more productive businesses accounts for about half of total factor productivity growth (Davis and Haltiwanger 1999). Effects on facilitating restructuring of enterprises are also considered.

Unemployment Insurance

Benefits influence unemployment by affecting job-search intensity and wage bargaining. These effects are theoretically ambiguous, but empirical studies—both micro and macro—overwhelmingly show a positive effect on equilibrium unemployment. Effects on employment and labor force participation are less clear cut. In addition, by interacting with shocks, benefits contribute to the persistence of unemployment. Benefits may also affect output and growth—by influencing the pace of enterprise restructuring and the intensity of layoffs, for example.

EFFECTS ON UNEMPLOYMENT AND LABOR FORCE PARTICIPATION. Undoubtedly the most researched effects of unemployment insurance are the effects on unemployment. Benefits affect unemployment through two main channels. First, they influence job-search effort and the reservation wage of recipients—with theoretically ambiguous effects on efficiency. As described in the annex to this chapter, models can be constructed that predict that benefits prolong unemployment spells (by emphasizing the fact that leisure becomes more attractive, for example) or shorten them (by stressing that more resources enable more effective job search, for example). Second, unemployment benefits improve the bargaining position of workers, which leads to higher wages—and hence to a higher equilibrium unemployment (Blanchard 1999).

In light of these theoretical ambiguities, empirical studies are of particular relevance. By and large, they show that unemployment benefits increase unemployment. Summarizing the evidence, Calmfors and Holmlund (2000, p. 145) argue that "there is considerable support for the hypothesis that lower benefit levels and shorter entitlement periods associated with unemployment insurance reduce unemployment." Decker (1997) reaches a similar conclusion for the United States. As shown in the annex, many studies of individual countries based on microdata find that both a higher level and a longer duration of benefits increase unemployment (for the evidence on OECD economies, see table 4.4; for the evidence on transition countries, see table 4.5).[6] Most cross-country studies directly investigating the relationship between equilibrium unemployment and the generosity of the benefits corroborate such findings (Layard, Nickell, and Jackman 1991; Elmeskov, Martin, and Scarpetta 1998; Nickell and Layard 1999; Haltiwanger, Scarpetta, and Vodopivec 2003). Some studies find insignificant effects of

Table 4.4. Incentive Effects of Unemployment Insurance in OECD Countries

Study	Data	Model/methodology	Findings
Marston (1975)	Household survey of people in Pennsylvania who exhausted their benefits 1966–67	Empirical hazard	• Unemployment insurance program causes an increase in unemployment of 0.2–0.3 percent of the labor force. • Weekly escape rates rise dramatically, from 1.1 percent just before exhaustion to 13.4 percent just afterward.
Lancaster (1979)	United Kingdom 1973; survey data for registered unemployed	Proportional hazard, alternative specifications, including Weibull	• Unemployment spell increases significantly with age, unemployment rate, and benefit level. • Benefit elasticity is 0.43–0.60. • A 10 percent rise in benefit level increases duration by 1 week if duration was 17 weeks (benefit elasticity is 0.6).
Moffit and Nicholson (1982)	United States 1974–77; benefit recipients eligible for federal supplemental benefits extension	Regression, static labor-leisure choice model	• A 10 percent increase in replacement rate increases average unemployment spell by 1.5–2.3 weeks for males, 1.3–1.7 weeks for females.
Moffit (1985)	United States 1983; continuous wage and benefit history file for 13 states	Nonparametric proportional hazard, alternative specifications	• A 10 percent increase in weekly benefit level increases unemployment duration by about 1.5 week (benefit elasticity is 0.36). • A one-week increase in benefit duration increases unemployment duration by one day (duration elasticity is 0.16).
Narendranathan, Nickell, and Stern (1985)	United Kingdom 1978–79; survey and administrative data for benefit recipients	Weibull model, alternative specifications	• Benefit elasticity is 0.28–0.36. • Benefit effect declines with duration for first six months. After six months, benefit effect becomes negligible.

(continued)

Table 4.4. *(continued)*

Study	Data	Model/methodology	Findings
Ham and Rea (1987)	Canada 1975–80; sample includes males (18–64) from Canadian Employment and Immigration Labor Force File	Discrete time duration model, alternative specifications	• Exit rates first decline (until 24th week) and then rise, with a spike near benefit exhaustion.
Meyer (1990)	United States 1983; continuous wage and benefit history file for 12 states. Male unemployment insurance recipients under the age of 55	Semiparametric proportional hazard, alternative specifications	• A 10 percent increase in benefit level increases duration by 1.5 weeks (benefit elasticity is 0.88). • Exit rates vary over benefit duration, first declining, then remaining steady, then sharply increasing near benefit exhaustion. Exit rates triple during six weeks before benefit exhaustion.
Carling and others (1996)	Sweden 1991	Semiparametric proportional hazard	• Exit rate increases sharply close to benefit exhaustion. • Job-finding rates increase by 170 percent in three weeks before benefit exhaustion.
Nickell (1979)	United Kingdom 1971–72; unemployed males from 1971–72 General Household Survey	Logit, alternative specifications	• Negative duration dependence for first 20 weeks of spell (benefit elasticity is 0.84–0.95), negligible effect thereafter. • Benefit elasticity is 0.8–0.9.
Katz and Meyer (1990)	United States 1983; male unemployment insurance recipients from continuous wage and benefit history file for 12 states	Semiparametric proportional hazard, alternative specifications	• Potential benefit duration elasticity: 0.36–0.44 at 26 weeks, 0.48–0.5 at 36 weeks. • Exit rates rise sharply before benefit exhaustion; exit rates decrease from 26 to 12 weeks until benefit exhaustion.

Table 4.5. Incentive Effects of Unemployment Insurance in Transition Countries

Country/study	Data	Model/methodology	Findings
Bulgaria Jones and Kotzeva (1998)	Aggregate data from Ministry of Labor, household surveys, labor office registers 1993–96	Survivor functions, binary logit	• Exit rate to employment increases markedly between 18th and 26th month of the spell (after social assistance benefits are exhausted). • Survival functions for social assistance recipients and nonrecipients indicate "waiting behavior" by recipients.
Cazes and Scarpetta (1998)	Administrative data on entry to registered unemployed, 1991–93	Empirical hazard function, piecewise constant hazard function	• Exit probability toward end of entitlement period increases dramatically. Benefit recipients exit unemployment more slowly than nonrecipients, but many leave to inactivity, especially in backward areas.
Kotzeva, Mircheva, and Wörgötter (1996)	Registered unemployed, December 1992–July 1994	Binomial logit	• Recipients of unemployment insurance are significantly less likely to take a job.
Czech Republic Ham, Svejnar and Terrell (1998)	Registered unemployed, October 1991–March 1992	Hazard model	• Elasticity of duration with respect to increase in replacement rate: 0.34. Elasticity of duration with respect to increase in duration of benefit: 0.44.
Estonia Vodopivec, Wörgötter, and Raju (2003)	Labor force survey 1991–95	Empirical hazard function	• Exit to employment significantly increases around the point of benefit exhaustion.

(continued)

85

Table 4.5. *(continued)*

Country/study	Data	Model/methodology	Findings
Hungary			
Micklewright and Nagy (1998)	Unemployment insurance register; follow-up surveys March–April 1994	Nonparametric and parametric proportional hazard, discrete time-duration model	• High proportion of unemployment insurance recipients remain until benefit exhaustion. Exit rates are characterized by a large spike in the period immediately after benefit exhaustion: job-exit hazard increases six- to eightfold compared with the period before exhaustion.
Poland			
Adamchik (1999)	Labor force surveys 1994–96	Proportional hazard	• Negative effect of the receipt of benefits on probability of exit to a job; dramatic increase in hazard as benefit is about to expire.
Puhani (1996)	Labor force surveys 1992–94	Hazard model; Weibull model, different specifications	• Entitlement to unemployment benefits significantly prolongs duration of unemployment. Magnitude of effect remains roughly the same after unemployment insurance reform that reduced potential length of the entitlement.
Steiner and Kwiatkowski (1995) (cited in Kwiatkowski 1998)	Labor force surveys 1992–93	Multinomial logit	• Unemployment insurance recipients have lower exit rates than nonrecipients, particularly with respect to exit rate from unemployment to inactivity.
Boeri and Steiner (1996)	Administrative data 1990–93	Hazard	• Exit rates increase as entitlement duration approaches exhaustion, especially in the capital. For males, increased flow is to employment; for females it is to inactivity. • Exit rate to inactivity increased markedly in month after benefit exhaustion.

Study	Data	Method	Results
Gora (1996) (cited in Kwiatkowski 1998)	Labor force surveys 1992–93	Binomial logit	• Unemployment insurance recipients have lower exit rate to employment than nonrecipients.
Cazes and Scarpetta (1998)	Administrative data on entry to registered unemployed, 1990–93	Empirical hazard function, piece-wise constant hazard function	• Exit probability related to maximum length of unemployment benefits entitlement. Unemployment benefit recipients exit unemployment much more slowly than nonrecipients, but many leave to inactivity rather than to employment, especially in backward areas.
Romania			
Earle and Pauna (1998)	Labor force survey, administrative sources 1993–96	Hazard model	• Receipt of benefits increases probability of leaving unemployment (no disincentive effects).
Slovak Republic			
Lubyova and van Ours (1999)	Labor force surveys 1994–96	Proportional hazard	• Little evidence of disincentive effects.
Ham, Svejnar, and Terrell (1998)	Registered unemployed, October 1991–March 1992	Hazard mode	• Elasticity of duration with respect to increase in replacement rate: 0.06; increase in duration of benefit: 0.41.
Slovenia			
Vodopivec (1995)	Administrative sources 1990–92	Semiparametric proportional hazard	• Strong waiting effect: exit to employment significantly increases just before benefit exhaustion.

Box 4.1.   How Large Are the Employment Disincentive Effects of Unemployment Insurance?

The disincentive effects of unemployment insurance are measured by the benefit elasticity (the elasticity of the duration of unemployment with respect to the benefit replacement rate) and the duration elasticity (the elasticity of the duration of unemployment with respect to the potential duration of benefits).

According to Layard, Nickell, and Jackman (1991), the benefit elasticity ranges from 0.2 to 0.9, depending on the state of the labor market and the country concerned (a 0.6 elasticity means that in response to a 10 percent increase in the replacement rate, the duration of an unemployment spell increases by one week, when an average duration of the receipt before the increase of the replacement rate is 17 weeks). According to Katz and Meyer (1990), the duration elasticity in the United States is 0.4–0.5 (a one-week increase in the potential entitlement duration of unemployment benefits is associated with a one- to one-and-a-half–day increase in the average unemployment spell of recipients).

Katz and Meyer (1990) estimate that increases in potential benefit duration have much larger adverse incentive effects on unemployment than do changes in unemployment benefit that leave benefit expenditures unchanged. They suggest that a longer duration of benefits explains about 10–30 percent of the difference in mean unemployment spell duration between the United States and the United Kingdom.

Source: Layard, Nickell, and Jackman (1991); Katz and Meyer (1990).

---

unemployment insurance on unemployment, but most observers agree that the evidence on positive effects is more compelling.

The evidence based on microstudies is particularly credible.[7] Many studies, in both industrial countries and transition countries, find a positive elasticity of unemployment with respect to the level and duration of benefits (box 4.1). Moreover, disincentives created by unemployment benefits show up clearly in a spike in the probability of exit from unemployment just before benefit exhaustion. And unemployment insurance experiments in the United States also provide strong evidence of moral hazard: unemployed people who were offered a bonus for rapid reemployment significantly reduced their unemployment spells, without affecting their reemployment earnings.

Several other results related to the effects of benefits on unemployment should be mentioned. First, direct evidence on the intensity of job search by benefit claimants is scarce and inconclusive. Second, there is no compelling evidence that unemployment benefits, by subsidizing job search, facilitate better job matches, as indicated, for example, by the level of post-unemployment wages. While several studies from the 1970s confirmed such effects, newer studies show weak or negligible effects. Third, there is no conclusive evidence that benefits facilitate entry into regular jobs. In fact, Cunningham (2000) shows that by relaxing a liquidity constraint, an increase in the generosity of unemployment insurance in Brazil led to increased participation in the self-employment sector. Fourth, empirical studies confirm theoretical predictions that more generous replacement rates suppress the labor supply of other family members. (See annex for details on these results.)

Higher taxes on labor, including unemployment benefit contributions, significantly increase unemployment (Nickell and Layard 1999; Daveri and Tabellini 2000; Haltiwanger, Scarpetta, and Vodopivec 2003). By creating a wedge between the costs of labor and the real consumption wage, labor taxes reduce the demand for labor and (if demand for labor is not perfectly inelastic) employment, increasing unemployment. Nickell and Layard (1999) report that a 5 percentage point decrease in the aggregate tax wage (which includes payroll, income, and consumption taxes) would reduce the unemployment rate by 13 percent (for example, from 8 percent to 7 percent).[8] They also argue that different types of taxes have the same effect on unemployment. Elmeskov, Martin, and Scarpetta (1998) show that there are significant interactions between taxation and collective bargaining arrangements and that the effects of the tax wedge are less pronounced in both highly centralized and decentralized countries. This result is consistent with the hump-shaped effect of wage-bargaining programs on unemployment reported by Calmfors and Drifill (1988).

Does it matter whether employers or workers pay contributions for unemployment insurance? In essence, no. Who bears the tax depends primarily on the elasticity of demand for and supply of labor (de Ferranti and others 2000). Even if employers are nominally paying the contributions, they may be able to shift the burden to workers; the more elastic the supply of labor, the more they can do so. But wage-setting mechanisms seem to matter here. To the extent that wages are prevented from adjusting, taxation may have a more pronounced effect on employment (and hence on unemployment) than flexible wage-setting. Moreover, there may also be a signaling effect: if workers are paying contributions, they will be more aware of the costs and less likely to support generous programs (World Bank 1994).

The effects of unemployment benefits on labor force participation have not been adequately researched. In the context of developing countries, Ravallion's (2003) argument—that uninsured transient shocks that reduce individual consumption below a threshold needed to retain productivity force individuals to drop out of the labor force—is particularly relevant, but empirical evidence on the effect is scant. For industrial countries, Atkinson and Micklewright (1991) report studies that find that specific groups are attracted into the labor force by the entitlement to unemployment insurance. According to the OECD's jobs study (1994), the availability of benefits seems to be positively correlated with the unemployment rate of women and older workers. But the entitlement effect has little effect on employment of these groups, as increases in unemployment are attributable to reductions in inactivity. For the United States, Clark and Summers (1982) estimate that benefits

increase the labor force participation rate by increasing both the unemployment and the employment rate. In contrast, Nickell and Layard
(1999) find that the effects on the increase in unemployment and labor force
participation cancel each other out, with no net effect on employment.

EFFECTS ON PERSISTENCE OF UNEMPLOYMENT. Another efficiency aspect re-
lates to the capacity of the economy to reduce unemployment to the equilibrium level in the wake of an adverse shock. Theoretical models show
that benefits slow the adjustment to such a shock.

Theoretical models predict that economies with unemployment benefits
experience greater and more prolonged unemployment following a transient shock. Ljungqvist and Sargent (1997) develop a model to study the
dynamics of two economies—one with an unemployment insurance program and one without—when a transient economic shock is introduced. The
economy without unemployment insurance recovers more rapidly, as reservation wages adjust more quickly and job-search intensity is greater. The
economies also respond differently to "economic turbulence." Unemployment in the economy without unemployment insurance remains more or
less constant, while the economy with unemployment insurance experiences a large increase in unemployment, as more workers experience significant skill losses. Millard's (1997) modeling exercise finds that a transient
productivity shock leads to prolonged unemployment when replacement
rates are high.

The interaction of institutions with adverse shocks helps explain the rise
in European unemployment in the past several decades. Until recently, one
of the stumbling blocks for proving that institutions (particularly unemployment insurance) have affected aggregate unemployment had been the
lack of empirical support for such a link in explaining the increase in European unemployment. Since the same institutions existed when unemployment was much lower, changes in these instructions alone cannot explain
the persistent rise in the average unemployment rate.

Blanchard and Wolfers (2000) and Blanchard (1999) explain the rise in
European unemployment by showing that the impact of a shock on the persistence of unemployment can be amplified by a more generous unemployment insurance program and higher employment protection (including
more generous severance pay). More generous unemployment insurance
and employment protection change the nature of unemployment, increasing
the average duration of unemployment and the number of the long-term
unemployed. Blanchard and Wolfers argue that the long-term unemployed
who are not searching for a job do not matter for wage formation, because
they do not exert enough pressure on wage moderation. They therefore slow
the adjustment of unemployment after an adverse shock. According to
Blanchard and Wolfers, this effect works through two channels: duration
dependence (less intense job-search activity and the loss of skills due to the
prolonged duration of unemployment) and marginalization (risky workers

are less likely to be hired, due to higher expected firing costs in the presence of employment protection).

Fehn, Berthold, and Thode (2000) provide another explanation. They show that institutional shocks contribute to high unemployment by encouraging the long-term substitution of labor with capital. Daveri and Tabellini (2000) point to the rise in labor costs and the cost of a generous European welfare state in general. And Caballero and Hammour (2000) argue that the main culprit is poor institutions that have given too much power to labor, which has been able to profit disproportionally in comparison with capital from gains arising from joint production.

EFFECTS ON OUTPUT AND GROWTH. Unemployment benefits may also affect output (by attracting workers to risky but highly productive jobs, for example) and growth (by affecting the pace of job creation, for example). They may also affect growth by stimulating enterprise restructuring and the intensity of layoffs (here experience rating is likely to play a role). Benefits may also affect the cyclical pattern of growth by acting as an automatic stabilizer.

The effects of unemployment insurance on output and growth have not been adequately researched, let alone quantified. The predictions of theoretical models about the effects on output are conflicting. On the one hand, the general equilibrium modeling of Acemoglu and Shimer (1999, 2000) suggests that unemployment insurance helps the economy produce more output by contributing to the creation of high-quality, high-wage jobs with greater unemployment risk. Similarly, Hassler, Zilbotti, and Mora (1999) argue that more generous benefits help workers obtain and retain specialized skills, which may enhance efficiency. Particularly in the context of developing countries, one may also argue that insured risk may increase output and growth through better production and portfolio choices (Rosenzweig and Wolpin 1993) and increased human capital accumulation (for example, by reducing drop-out rates from schooling). On the other hand, Attanasio and Rios-Rull (2000) show that government-mandated programs may crowd out private insurance programs and thus reduce the efficiency of the economy.

One channel through which unemployment insurance may affect growth is by encouraging labor reallocation and, in particular, the restructuring of enterprises. While partial equilibrium results indeed suggest this is the case, general equilibrium models may not support such conclusions. Considerable empirical evidence on the United States suggests that the availability of benefits strongly increases the probability of temporary layoffs (Clark and Summers 1982; Feldstein 1978; Topel 1983), although benefits have little effect on the probability of quitting or being permanently laid off. In other words, when making decisions about temporary layoffs, employers take into account the availability of unemployment insurance. Similarly, restructuring programs that provide workers with sufficiently generous compensation are successful in the sense that they facilitate the downsizing of an enterprise to a desirable level, although some may suffer from rehiring problems (Haltiwanger and Singh 1999).

These partial equilibrium results do not necessarily carry over to the general equilibrium framework. Blanchard's (1997) theoretical modeling does not support the argument that restructuring could be facilitated by more generous unemployment benefits (see annex). In the context of a job creation/job destruction model, Mortensen (1994) finds that an increase in the replacement rate of unemployment insurance reduces job creation and thus aggregate output. (Because his computations fail to account for the insurance value of the unemployment insurance program, the welfare consequences are not clear.) The overall potential of income support programs in spurring enterprise restructuring is therefore likely to be limited.[9]

In the context of enterprise restructuring, what effect does experience rating have? By imposing additional costs on employers, experience rating curbs layoffs and thus increases employment (Feldstein 1976). But this is a partial equilibrium result. In a more complex model, Burdett and Wright (1989) show that the effect on employment is ambiguous—that by increasing labor costs, experience rating reduces the number of workers the firm is willing to hire. In a similar vein, Mortensen's (1994) model of job creation and job destruction shows that the transition of the current U.S. program to one of full experience rating would discourage layoffs, but only by a relatively small amount. Because job creation would be adversely affected, the net effect, according to Mortensen, would be "a small although probably insignificant increase in the unemployment rate" (p. 206). The effects of experience rating thus appear primarily as a reduction in inflows to and outflows from unemployment, not as an increase in employment.[10] Experience rating is more important when employment protection is low, as it is in the United States. In Europe employment protection legislation takes over the role of experience rating, with similar effects on labor market flows and employment.

Another aspect of unemployment benefits programs that may affect growth is the taxation of labor. Summarizing the literature, Nickell and Layard (1999) conclude that total labor taxes (which include payroll, income, and consumption taxes) may negatively affect the growth rate but that the result is not robust. For Europe (where unions are strong but not coordinated), Daveri and Tabellini (2000) find that the distorting effects of labor taxes are larger than those produced by either capital or consumption taxes. They claim that higher labor taxes (which exclude consumption taxes) were shifted to higher real wages, which led firms to substitute labor with capital, slowing growth and investment. By reducing the wedge between wages and the cost of labor to employers, they claim, general taxation is more conducive to job creation and growth than financing based on contributions.

Does unemployment insurance act as an automatic stabilizer? Unemployment benefits soften the impact of adverse shocks on GDP and restrain expansion when the economy starts growing again. Theoretical modeling by von Furstenburg (1976) shows that benefit expenditures and taxes work in opposite directions to moderate economic contractions and expansions.

During downturns, unemployment insurance benefit payments increase and unemployment insurance taxes fall; the net injection of purchasing power moderates the severity of the contraction. During upturns, unemployment insurance taxes increase and unemployment insurance benefits decrease, restraining the expansion.

The evidence seems to show that unemployment insurance reduces GDP losses during downturns by 10–15 percent. Dungan and Murphy (1995) find that the Canadian unemployment insurance program reduced the decline in GDP by 13–14 percent during the 1983–84 and 1990–91 recessions. For the United States, Chimerine, Black, and Coffey (1999) find that unemployment insurance reduced the loss in real GDP by about 15 percent during recessions. Other researchers find that the effect of unemployment insurance is weaker. Hamermesh (1992) cites studies indicating that unemployment insurance reduced the magnitude of cyclical output fluctuations by no more than 10 percent. Dunson, Maurice, and Dwyer (1991) find that the effectiveness of the U.S. unemployment insurance program as a countercyclical macroeconomic stabilizer has diminished over time.

To summarize, unemployment benefits thus increase the duration of unemployment spells of recipients (evidence from single-country studies), and contribute to higher equilibrium unemployment (evidence from cross-country studies), although the magnitude of such effects has not been firmly established. Benefits also contribute to the persistence of unemployment. Less research has been conducted on the effects on restructuring and growth, which are probably not very significant. The evidence on some other effects, such as the effects of benefits on post-unemployment wages, is inconclusive.

Why, despite the wealth of studies, has no consensus been reached on these issues? First, many theoretical and empirical results are of a partial equilibrium nature, and these results may or may not be validated in a general equilibrium framework. Second, many institutional and program features provide rich possibilities for interaction, and only a subset of these features is usually incorporated in a general equilibrium model. Omitting relevant aspects may account for the different results generated by different models. Third, some of the empirical estimates are country specific, and no corrections have been made to account for country differences. While most studies find a positive relationship between benefits and the duration of unemployment spells of recipients, estimates of the magnitude of these effects vary. Quite likely, some of the differences in magnitudes across countries could be attributed to differences in the effectiveness of monitoring and enforcement of job search. If job-search requirements and work tests are strictly enforced and benefits withdrawn when job offers are rejected, the generosity of benefits is less important and moral hazard problems are less pronounced. For a given level of benefits, the stricter the monitoring the fewer disincentives benefits create. The recorded incidence of benefit sanctions varies greatly across OECD countries, and such sanctions have a fairly large impact on individual rates of exit from unemployment (OECD 2000a). Monitoring and enforcement features of benefit programs, which are hard to measure, have been inadequately controlled for in empirical research on disincentive effects of unemployment benefits, contributing to differences in estimates across countries.

Unemployment Assistance

With benefits contingent on the family income (and assets) of the unemployed individual, unemployment assistance is susceptible to several types of disincentive problems. First, the program may encourage longer unemployment spells, because, other things equal, the largest payments are received by people with zero earnings; a lower wage rate or fewer hours worked increases payments. Second, payment of unemployment assistance benefits to an unemployed family member may influence labor supply decisions of other family members. If one of the spouses is unemployed, the other may be less likely to work, since his or her earnings could either make the family ineligible for benefits or reduce the size of the payment. Third, knowing that they qualify for unemployment assistance benefits, workers have an incentive to quit and become unemployed. Fourth, young people may claim to be unemployed in order to collect benefits when they are not seriously searching for work or engaged in training.

Vroman (2002) reports that less research has been conducted on the disincentive problems related to unemployment assistance than on those related to unemployment insurance. His analysis of the Australian unemployment assistance program suggests that a lower income guarantee would probably result in shorter spells of unemployment (although no hard evidence is presented). Suggestive of incentive problems are frequent changes in policies aimed at promoting employment among benefit recipients (box 4.2). Vroman also points to another body of literature that is relevant in this context: the analysis of the work disincentives of social assistance programs. Those studies conclude that high effective marginal tax rates (related to phasing out benefits when family income exceeds the maximum allowable for the receipt of full benefits and taxing the earnings and income of the family), as well as poverty traps deter social assistance recipients from working. Studies of Slovakia and Poland show that the presence of an unemployed spouse lowers the probability of exit from unemployment to employment (see annex). Vroman also reports that part of the reason why Australia changed to a more individualized unemployment assistance program in 1995 was its desire to encourage work among family members (often wives) in families in which one member is unemployed.

Unemployment Insurance Saving Accounts

THEORETICAL PREDICTIONS. The main rationale and key advantage of a UISA program over traditional unemployment insurance is its potential for improving the incentives of employed workers and job seekers while providing the same protection as traditional unemployment insurance. As several theoretical articles show, UISAs would radically change workers' incentives

---

Box 4.2.   Activation among Recipients of Unemployment Assistance in Australia

Australia has launched a variety of initiatives to promote activation among recipients of unemployment assistance. These initiatives include adjustments in the way a suitable job is defined and the work search requirement administered.

Before the large increase in unemployment in the mid-1970s, workers could not refuse "suitable work" while retaining entitlement to benefits. With a sharp increase in the unemployment-vacancy ratio, "suitable work" was redefined. Guidelines were broadened in 1976 to require acceptance of work in line with local job availability, even if it meant a reduction in wages, status, or both. By 1989 this definition had been modified to require acceptance of casual, part-time, or temporary work.

Work search requirements have also become more formal, and evidence of active search has been emphasized. Changes effective in 1991 required both the short-term and the long-term unemployed to satisfy an activity test. For individuals who have been unemployed less than 12 months, the activity test includes active work search or participation in labor market or vocational training. The long-term unemployed must participate in an activity arrangement (which could include unpaid volunteer work) that is tailored to individual circumstances. Other changes in the activity test became effective in 1995, when increased emphasis was placed on the early identification of recipients who were likely to be unemployed long term.

Source: Vroman (2002).

(Orszag and Snower 2002; Orszag and others 1999). By internalizing the costs of unemployment benefits, UISAs avoid the moral hazard inherent in traditional unemployment insurance. They thus have the potential to substantially decrease overall unemployment and, by lowering payroll taxes, increase wages. Orszag and Snower (1997) show that UISAs reduce unemployment by increasing both the on-the-job effort of employed workers and the job-search effort of unemployed workers. Orszag and others (1999) recommend a comprehensive versus a piecemeal approach when introducing UISAs. They warn that a potential complementarity problem exists if the account is not set up for multiple uses. Under traditional unemployment insurance, workers who have built up substantial resources in their pension accounts have the incentive to withdraw from the labor force and claim unemployment benefits until they retire. Setting up an integrated savings account reduces such incentives.

One important caveat about the feasibility of UISAs applies, however. UISAs eliminate the pooling of resources across individuals, relying instead on the incomparably more restrictive intertemporal pooling of the resources of a single individual. If, by making modest contributions from their earnings, a significant proportion of workers cannot save enough during their productive life to draw on their accumulated savings during their unemployment spells, a UISA program will not be viable. In other words, if unemployment is concentrated among a group of workers, these workers may not be able to finance their unemployment benefits through their own savings (and there may be a large group of workers who would never use their savings accounts to draw unemployment benefits). Under such circumstances, the UISA system would be irrelevant as an alternative to the traditional unemployment insurance system.

EMPIRICAL EVIDENCE. UISAs are still largely uncharted territory. It is thus premature to evaluate this program.

In the only empirical studies of UISAs, Kugler (1999, 2002) examines the effects of the 1990 conversion of Colombia's severance pay program into a funded severance pay with individual accounts. She finds that the lion's share of the costs of the transfer that firms make to individual workers' accounts (75–87 percent) shows up as a reduction in wages. She also finds that, in accordance with theoretical predictions, the conversion increased both firing and hiring (see more on her findings in chapter 6). Her work does not shed light on the effects of UISAs on job-search incentives.

No other rigorous empirical work has been done on the effects of UISA programs, although some researchers report problems with the Brazilian Fundo de Garantia do Tempo de Servico program (box 4.3). More research, as well as piloting, is needed to determine whether the problems with the Brazilian program can be avoided.

Box 4.3.   Incentive Problems with Individualized Severance Funds in Brazil

Because of difficulties monitoring eligibility conditions of traditional unemployment insurance, Brazil introduced a variant of the UISA called the FGTS (Fundo de Garantia do Tempo de Servico) in 1966. Eight percent of wages are deposited into an individual account. If dismissed, the worker receives the resources accumulated in the account; if the dismissal is without cause, the employer must pay an additional 40 percent of the balance.

While the program avoids the problem of job-search disincentives of unemployment insurance, it creates incentive and other problems of its own. The program creates perverse incentives for workers to precipitate a firing in order to be able to access the funds in the savings account. It is estimated that the program increases labor turnover rates by 30 percent. The program also creates additional litigation costs incurred in determining whether or not the cause for dismissal is just.

Source: Amadeo, Gill, and Neri (2002).

In the absence of suitable real-world practices, Feldstein and Altman (1998) simulate the working of a UISA program for the United States. The protection provided by unemployment benefits is the same as under the current program, but it is financed through UISAs, to which individuals are required to contribute 4 percent of their wages. Their simulations show that over a 25-year period, only a small proportion of workers (5–7 percent) end their working lives with negative balances (these estimates are conservative, because they do not account for behavioral responses to changes in incentives) and that the cost to taxpayers is reduced by more than 60 percent. Feldstein and Altman thus conclude that, for the United States, the UISA program represents a viable alternative to the standard unemployment insurance program.

Simulations by Vodopivec and Rejec (2002) show that UISAs are also viable in a transition country (Estonia). Using a methodology similar to that of Feldstein and Altman and permitting borrowing from UISAs, they find that 8–27 percent of workers end their active lives with negative cumulative balance on their UISA account, and 35–54 percent of workers experience negative balances on their UISA account at least once during their working lives (the lower numbers refer to the low-unemployment and the higher to the high-unemployment scenarios).

Severance Pay

THEORETICAL PREDICTIONS. Severance pay is associated with both potential efficiency gains and potential efficiency losses (for an excellent review of both theoretical and empirical effects, see Addison and Teixeira 2001). Among the gains, severance pay may promote longer-lasting employment relationships and thus improve employers' incentives to provide training, thereby increasing the current productivity of workers as well as their future employability. Moreover, longer-lasting employment instills trust, cooperation, and loyalty between the employer and workers, and it encourages team spirit among workers, which may increase productive efficiency and reduce the resistance of workers to the introduction of new technologies (OECD 1999b). Such effects may be particularly strong under severance pay programs that are introduced voluntarily.

Among the costs, severance pay is recognized as a source of labor market "sclerosis," reducing the intensity of labor market flows, particularly to and from unemployment. As Blanchard (2000) shows, severance pay increases firing costs and thus reduces the probability of exit from employment to unemployment, but at the same time it imposes additional costs on employers and thus hinders job creation. (The predicted effects of severance pay on unemployment are therefore ambiguous.) Blanchard's model also shows that severance pay contributes to labor market dualism. Calmfors and Holmlund (2000) note that high firing costs slow the pace of structural change, by reducing the incentives of employers to introduce new technologies.

EMPIRICAL EVIDENCE. No direct empirical evidence based on firm-level data appears to exist on the positive effects of severance pay on firm productivity. Nickell and Layard (1999) find a positive effect of employment protection on aggregate growth, but the effect disappears once differences in the level of productivity across countries are controlled for. Moreover, it is not clear which circumstances and interactions may be instrumental for such effects.[11]

Considerable evidence exists on the negative effects of mandatory severance pay. Several studies show that strict employment protection reduces employment. Lazear (1990) finds that severance pay reduces both employment and labor force participation. Fallon and Lucas (1991) show that strengthening job security regulations led to a strong decline in employment in India and Zimbabwe. More recent studies confirming the link between job security and lower employment include Nicolleti and others (2001) for OECD countries, Heckman and Pages (2000) for OECD and Latin American countries, Besley and Burgess (2002) for India, and Haltiwanger, Scarpetta, and Vodopivec (2003) for OECD and transition countries. Heckman and Pages (2000) attribute a reduction in employment of 5 percentage points to job security provisions in Latin America. OECD (1999b) finds insignificant effects on overall employment rates but notes that negative effects are concentrated among prime-age women, young people, and older workers. To the extent that severance pay increases youth unemployment, it has additional negative consequences for the persistence of their unemployment and their reduced future earnings capacity (on the long-term effects of youth unemployment, see Mroz and Savage 2000). Studies also show that severance pay increases part-time employment and self-employment. Consistent with theoretical predictions, the effects on unemployment of employment protection legislation (of which severance pay is one of the most important determinants) are largely inconclusive.

Mounting evidence also suggests that severance pay reduces inflows to and outflows from unemployment. By doing so, it contributes to longer unemployment spells (stagnant unemployment pool); flows through employment may not be affected as strongly (for a recent survey, see OECD 1999b; for evidence on transition countries, see Haltiwanger, Scarpetta, and Vodopivec 2003). Reduced labor market flows may hinder labor force adjustment and the reallocation of jobs, thereby slowing aggregate productivity growth (for a survey of the effects of job reallocation on aggregate productivity growth, see Davis and Haltiwanger 1999). But the question of whether job security stands in the way of productivity and growth has hardly been settled in industrial economies. Although recent studies show that efficiency in these countries depends critically on the ability to reallocate resources rapidly, Nickell and Layard (1999) argue that it would be wrong to assume a simple linear relationship between the pace of reallocation and economic growth.[12] To be able to evaluate the desirability of worker and job flows, one should therefore examine the scope and size of the contribution of worker and job flows to productivity and overall growth in transition and developing countries—an area that has hardly been addressed by researchers. In all like-lihood, however, individual country characteristics may well dictate differ-ent levels of labor reallocation (for example, the scope for labor reallocation is undoubtedly large in transition countries).

Severance pay does not create a moral hazard problem by lowering job-search effort, but it does affect incentives to enter unemployment and hence creates another moral hazard problem. De Ferranti and others (2000) report that large litigation costs arise from disputes over the cause of separation in Latin America.

Public Works

By providing job opportunities, albeit in a somewhat artificial environment, public works programs address equity and insurance considerations. But what are their efficiency consequences? In particular, how helpful are public works in increasing the probability that the unemployed obtain regular jobs, and how do they affect participants' reemployment wages? How large are the nonlabor costs of public works, and what is the wage gain for partici-pants over and above the forgone earnings (that is, above the gains from productive activities that participants have to give up so that they can par-ticipate in public works)? What is the "bang for the buck"—the share of gov-ernment expenditures that eventually reaches the poor?

Evaluations show that public works mildly reduce unemployment and increase employment. But they have strong substitution effects (which can reach 100 percent), and they reduce reemployment wages and the probabil-ity of employment in nonassisted jobs (see, for example, Calmfors 1994, Dar and Tzannatos 1999, and an update of the Dar and Tzannatos study in Betcherman, Olivas, and Dar 2003). Fretwell, Benus, and O'Leary (1999) find that the chances of public works participants in the Czech Republic, Hungary, and Poland finding a job are the same as or worse than those of nonparticipants and that their wages in jobs following public works partici-pation are likely to be no different from or lower than the wages of nonpar-ticipants. They argue that public works are mostly a way to provide income to the needy and are less suitable as a vehicle for increasing the employabil-ity of the unemployed.

The effects, however, may depend strongly on country-specific circum-stances and the design of the program. By shifting the focus from manual to skilled work, the Slovenian public works program succeeded in attracting more educated and younger workers than did programs in other transition countries (Vodopivec 1999). This may be why the program increased the chances of obtaining a regular job immediately upon leaving the program (due to stigmatization, the longer-term effects are negative). The study also finds that the positive effects on job-finding probability are concentrated among younger workers and that public works reduce the exit rate to inactivity.

Public works can also be expensive—and only a small share of govern-ment expenditures may reach the poor. Betcherman and others (2001) report annual costs per participant ranging from $786 in Madagascar to $5,445 in Senegal. Ravallion (1999a) lists four determinants of cost-effectiveness: labor intensity, targeting performance (the proportion of wages paid to the poor), the net wage gain (the difference between program pay and income forgone and other costs of participation), and indirect benefits to the poor (benefits derived from the assets created by public works). His simulations show that the cost to increase current earnings of the poor by $1 is $3.60 for low-income countries and $5.00 for middle-income countries. If indirect benefits are also accounted for, the cost of transferring $1 to the poor drops to $2.50 for both middle- and low-income countries, a result that still suggests significant leakage of resources. Ravallion cautions that these calculations do not account for the insurance function of the public works, which can be large. He also emphasizes that program performance depends on the design of the program.

Other Programs

Three other programs—social assistance, early retirement, and work-sharing—are used to address unemployment problems, primarily in industrial economies.

SOCIAL ASSISTANCE. High rates of withdrawal of a targeted transfer may create a poverty trap, as Atkinson argues (1995b). He quotes a study by Burtless (1990) showing that means-tested transfers have a statistically significant but small effect on the labor supply of low-income men and of women with children. Although assessments vary, incentives may be better structured under decentralized administration and financing of these programs, which facilitate flexibility in formulating and implementing appropriate solutions to local and individual problems. For example, the integration of social assistance with active labor market programs in the Nordic states has been attributed to the fact that local governments are responsible for financing these programs. To strengthen incentives, the national government may provide subsidies to enforce labor requirements and promote employment.

EARLY RETIREMENT. The prevalence of public early retirement programs has fallen drastically since the 1970s and 1980s, as these programs proved very costly and failed to free up jobs for younger workers as envisioned. Instead of encouraging exit to employment as a means to address unemployment, early retirement programs promote exit to inactivity. Gruber and Wise (1998) show that the structure of incentives and disincentives created by early retirement programs in Europe strongly encourages the early exit of older workers from the labor force. Studies of the effect of social security on early retirement in OECD countries confirm their findings.

The apparent success of early retirement programs has to be qualified in several ways, however. First, the withdrawal of older workers creates significant efficiency losses. Gruber and Wise (1998) show that the forgone productive capacity of older workers who withdrew from the labor force was sizable, ranging from 22 percent in Japan to 67 percent in Belgium for workers between 55 and 65. Second, the programs have failed to stimulate youth employment: Boldrin and others (1999) report that the early retirement of older workers has not reduced the unemployment rate among young workers in Europe. This is not surprising: if younger workers are complements—and not substitutes—for older workers, early retirement programs may even have a negative effect on the employment of young workers. Third, overall evaluations of early retirement programs have to account for complex general equilibrium effects. For example, the additional financial burden of supporting the pensions of early retirees may well contribute to an increase in social security contribution rates (higher taxes on earnings), thereby adding to labor costs. By reducing labor demand, early retirement programs may contribute to higher equilibrium unemployment.[13]

WORK SHARING. How valid is the popular belief that if each worker works fewer hours, more workers will be employed? An increase in employment is not the only possible outcome: if, for example, shorter hours puts upward pressure on wages, employers may substitute labor with other inputs. They may also be forced to reduce output.

An evaluation of hours reduction in Germany in the 1980s raises some doubts about the desirability of such a measure (Hunt 1996). In response to a one-hour reduction in hours worked, employment did increase but by very little (0.3–0.7 percent for hourly workers and 0.2–0.3 percent for salary workers), and the wage bill rose. Moreover, total hours worked fell sharply, which may have led to output losses.

Summary of Efficiency Effects

The main findings on the efficiency effects of income support programs are summarized in table 4.6. A consensus is emerging in some areas, but in others researchers are still far from agreement.

Different income support programs for the unemployed produce quite different efficiency effects. But there is a common thread through these results: while having efficiency increasing potential, none of the programs is without negative effects on efficiency. The challenge is to choose programs that minimize the negative effects while providing adequate income security to the unemployed—a challenge addressed in chapter 6.

UNEMPLOYMENT INSURANCE. The negative efficiency effects of unemployment insurance outweight the positive effects. Mounting evidence suggests that the generosity of unemployment insurance reduces the probability of exit from unemployment to employment, a result that is fairly robust across countries and labor market regimes. There is also significant agreement that unemployment insurance increases the equilibrium unemployment rate (the

Table 4.6. Summary of Efficiency Effects of Income Support Programs for the Unemployed

Program	Job-search effort and post-unemployment wages	Equilibrium labor market outcomes and persistence of unemployment	Enhancement of restructuring of enterprises and overall adjustment	Labor supply of other family members	Encouragement of taking regular versus informal jobs	Output and growth
Unemployment insurance	• Significant disincentives for leaving unemployment (moral hazard problem).[a] • Inconclusive evidence on improvement in job matching (as indicated by post-unemployment wages).[a]	• Increases equilibrium unemployment rate.[a] • Positive effect on labor force participation for some groups, but reductions in inactivity show up primarily as increases in unemployment.[a] • Benefits slow adjustment to shocks, make unemployment more persistent (in Europe, for example).[a]	• Increases attractiveness of restructuring. Strong evidence of increased temporary layoffs in United States (partial equilibrium results).[a] • Theory predicts that overall adjustment is not assisted because job creation is hindered.	• Reduces labor supply of spouses of unemployed workers.[a]	• Inconclusive evidence on entry into precarious jobs.[a] • Increases probability of entering self-employment in Brazil.[a]	• Reduces GDP losses during downturns by 10–15 percent by acting as automatic macroeconomic stabilizer.[a] • Theoretical predictions about effects on output are inconclusive. • Effects on growth are insignificant.[a]
Unemployment assistance	• Significant disincentives for leaving unemployment, particularly for low-wage earners.[a]	• Effects are similar to but milder than effects of unemployment insurance.	• Effects are similar to but milder than effects of unemployment insurance.	• Strong disincentive for other family members to take a job.[a]	• Effects are similar to effects of unemployment insurance.	• Effects are similar to but milder than effects of unemployment insurance.

Unemployment insurance savings accounts	• No moral hazard problem (theoretical prediction).	• Reduces unemployment relative to unemployment insurance (theoretical prediction).	• Conversion of severance pay into UISA increases both firing and hiring by firms (Colombia).[a]	• No evidence.	• No evidence.	• No evidence.
Severance pay	• No moral hazard problem with job-search effort, but incentives to enter unemployment increase. Large litigation costs from disputes over cause of separation.	• Strongly reduces employment, particularly of young workers.[a] • Increases self-employment.[a] • Effects on unemployment are inconclusive.[a]	• Negative effects on labor reallocation—economy's "sclerosis" increases: inflows into unemployment decline, but so does job creation.[a]	• No evidence.	• No evidence.	• Effects on growth have not been well documented.
Public works	If wages are kept sufficiently low, effect on job-search efforts is small.	Mildly reduces unemployment and increases employment.[a]	Negligible effects.	Negligible effects.	In transition countries, participants are stigmatized, more likely to take informal jobs or leave labor force after the completion of public works.[a]	Negligible effects.

Source: Derived from the text.

[a] Empirical evidence supports finding.

transmission channels are job-search intensity, wage bargaining, and possibly labor taxation). By interacting with adverse shocks, benefits also contribute to the persistence of unemployment. Moreover, while benefits make restructuring more attractive—and increase temporary layoffs—general equilibrium analyses show that overall adjustment is not assisted, because job creation is hindered. On the positive side, there is agreement that unemployment insurance is effective as an automatic macroeconomic stabilizer. But there are also important areas of disagreement. The evidence is inconclusive on the effects of benefits on post-unemployment wages and thus on the quality of job matches, on whether benefits enhance entry into regular jobs, and on whether they contribute to higher output and growth.

SEVERANCE PAY. There is remarkable agreement that severance pay lowers employment rates and reduces inflows to and outflows from unemployment. While the first effect is clearly negative, various interpretations exist on the efficiency effects of the second. Under some circumstances, the likely efficiency effects of reduced dynamics are negative (transition countries are a case in point). No evidence, however, exists about the effects of severance pay on job matches or on employment in regular jobs as opposed to informal ones.

OTHER INCOME SUPPORT PROGRAMS. Little evidence exists on the effects of unemployment assistance as a self-standing program. Almost no evidence exists on the effects of unemployment insurance savings accounts, because only a few such programs exist, most of them introduced only recently. Addressing this gap should figure prominently on the research agenda in the near future.

Suitability to Confront Different Shocks

When countries are affected by adverse shocks, do they adjust their income support programs for the unemployed, introduce new programs, or do both? How suitable are different programs for dealing with different types of shocks? Are income support programs for the unemployed countercyclical, that is, do they receive increased funding when an economy suffers from a recession and needs income support programs the most? What happens to marginal groups during a crisis? The following sections summarize how European transition countries and countries in East Asia and Latin America have reacted to economic shocks.

European Transition Economies

Reforms in transition countries in the early 1990s drastically reduced output and employment. Output decline was related largely to supply side shocks and structural imbalances that had accumulated for decades under the socialist regime (Holzmann, Gacs, and Georg 1995). The cumulative decline

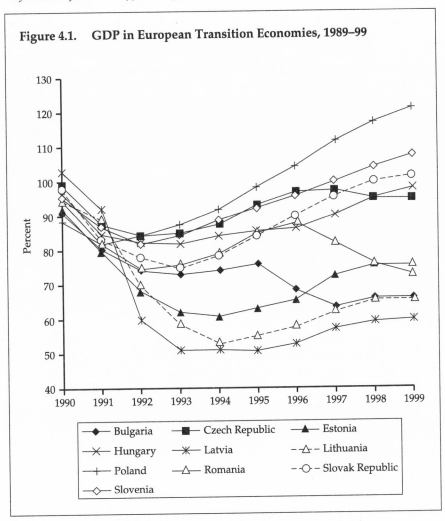

Figure 4.1. GDP in European Transition Economies, 1989–99

in GDP was about 25–35 percent in Central and Eastern European countries and about 40–50 percent in the Baltic republics (figure 4.1). Reductions in output invariably reduced employment and increased the number of unemployed and the number of inactive people. Due to the low probability of exit from unemployment, long-term unemployment—particularly prevalent among the unskilled—also became a serious problem, as did youth unemployment. The incidence of poverty among households with an unemployed member rose to twice that among households with no unemployed member (table 4.1).

The responses of countries to the emergence of large-scale unemployment varied. To reduce inflows into unemployment, some countries relied on employment protection (including severance pay) and job preservation subsidies. Hungary, Poland, the Slovak Republic, and Slovenia also devoted considerable resources to promoting early retirement (in 1992, for example, Poland spent 0.8 percent of GDP on early retirement).[14] To assist the unemployed, all countries introduced new labor market programs, both income support programs and active labor market programs.

In overhauling their cash benefit programs, European transition countries followed the blueprints of the European Union welfare states. Most important, they added two new programs, unemployment insurance/assistance and social assistance, to their existing programs of severance pay, family benefits, and pensions. In most countries, overall expenditures on unemployment benefits were less than 1 percent of GDP; in a few countries—Hungary, Poland, and Slovenia—they exceeded that level.

In addition, all transition countries maintained active labor market programs, including training, special measures for young people, employment subsidies, public works, and support for self-employment. With the exception of Hungary and Slovenia, the level of active support (0.15–0.30 percent of GDP in most countries) was much lower than in OECD countries. Hungary spent considerable resources on training and Slovenia on job preservation subsidies (a record 0.7 percent of GDP in 1992).

In evaluating income support programs for the unemployed in transition countries, Vodopivec, Wörgötter, and Raju (2003) note that due to fiscal pressures (and perhaps also to improve incentives), the initial generosity of unemployment insurance programs was scaled down: relative to the early 1990s, several countries reduced both replacement rates and the maximum duration of benefits. They also point out significant implementation problems of these programs. Scarpetta and Reutersward (1994) observe that the real value of unemployment benefits was reduced by imperfect indexation. Vodopivec, Wörgötter, and Raju note that while they were effective in promoting early exit from the workforce, early retirement programs proved fiscally expensive and did not increase the employment prospects of young workers. To address the nonperformance problem of severance pay, some transition countries (such as Slovenia) introduced public guarantee funds. Fretwell, Benus, and O'Leary (1998) argue that in many transition countries, public works proved mostly to be a way of providing income to the needy rather than a vehicle for increasing the employability of the unemployed.

Latin America and the Caribbean

Despite efforts to strengthen macroeconomic stability, many Latin American countries continue to be characterized by a high level of macroeconomic volatility (figure 4.2). The region has more and deeper recessions than most other areas of the world (standard deviations of key nonmonetary outcomes have been two to three times those of industrial countries), and reductions in output have a strong impact on poverty (Housmann and Gavin 1996). Mexico's contraction of output, for example, brought a sharp decline in per

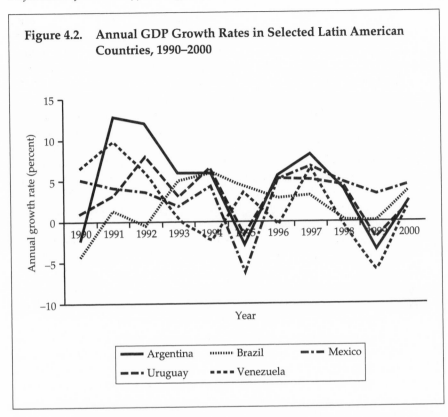

Figure 4.2. Annual GDP Growth Rates in Selected Latin American Countries, 1990–2000

capita GDP and consumption that increased poverty by 7 percentage points (Wodon 2000). In 1996 slightly more than a third of the region's population was poor, and about 16 percent were extremely poor.

Severance pay programs in Latin America and the Caribbean have been more generous than in any other region (table 3.6). But providing income security through severance pay and relying on the state to absorb labor surpluses—the dominant income support mechanisms in the past decades— has become increasingly untenable, particularly because these mechanisms serve the needs of only a small, privileged subset of the labor force. Increased job insecurity is one consequence: Rodrik (1999) reports that in the 1990s, the share of "unprotected" jobs (those without written contract or social benefits) increased in all seven Latin American countries under examination.

Other income maintenance programs in the region are specific and inno-vative. The region has not relied extensively on social insurance. Argentina introduced a limited program in 1991. Venezuela enacted legislation in 1989, but it has not yet implemented the program. In the 1990s Colombia and Peru transformed their severance pay programs into funded, individual account programs, which are uncommon outside Latin America. Chile has introduced an innovative income support program for the unemployed (see chapter 6). Other countries have introduced social funds and programs that provide cash to poor families to pay for basic health and schooling expenses as long as the children regularly visit health clinics and attend school (Chamberlin and Mason 2003; see chapter 6).

Latin American countries also used active labor market programs in the 1990s. These programs included public works (Argentina's Trabajar program), short-term training programs that targeted the unemployed (Mexico's Probecat program), wage subsidies for private sector employment, and credit for microenterprises (Marquez 1999). But Latin American countries spend much less than OECD countries on labor market programs. In the mid-1990s, for example, OECD countries spent an average of 0.38 percent of GDP on training, while Argentina, Brazil, Chile, Costa Rica, Jamaica, Mexico, and Peru averaged only 0.19 percent (Marquez 1999). OECD countries spent 0.34 percent of GDP on public works and subsidized employment compared with 0.22 percent in Latin America. Because Latin American countries spent very little on unemployment insurance programs, the difference in total expenditures on labor market programs is even greater: OECD countries spent on average 2.4 percent of GDP, while Latin America spent just 0.46 percent.

Many emergency programs were reintroduced or strengthened during crises (such as the Tequila crisis of 1995), and the virulence of the shock hastened the development and deployment of an assortment of programs, often at the expense of judicious planning and preparation. As a result, programs were poorly designed and incompatible with one another. In addition, notwithstanding the stated intent to assist workers in the most precarious positions, many emergency programs failed to reach them (Marquez 1999). De Ferranti and others (2000) report evidence for selected income support programs for the unemployed that shows that with the exception of the Probecat training program in Mexico and the Trabajar public works program in Argentina, program beneficiaries tend to come from the top three income quintiles.

There is also evidence that fiscal pressures associated with recessions reduced the capacity of governments to finance social spending. With a decline in output of 5.3 percent in 1995, targeted spending per poor person fell by 28 percent in Argentina, and the poverty rate increased by 5 percentage points (Wodon 2000). The only class of programs with a countercyclical pattern of spending were income security programs (old-age pensions, unemployment insurance, and family assistance) (de Ferranti and others 2000).

East Asia

The precipitous decline in economic growth during the recent East Asian financial crisis (figure 4.3) increased unemployment and reduced wages.

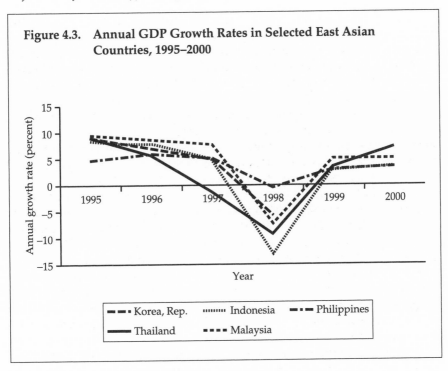

Figure 4.3. **Annual GDP Growth Rates in Selected East Asian Countries, 1995–2000**

Interestingly, while employment decreased in some countries, it increased in Indonesia and the Philippines (the so-called added worker effect). In the worst-affected countries of Indonesia, the Republic of Korea, and Thailand, the unemployment pool increased by about a million workers in each country. Between 1997 and 1998, the unemployment rate soared from 2.6 to 6.8 percent in the Republic of Korea and from 2.2 to 5.2 percent in Thailand, while Indonesia and the Philippines showed small increases. The effects of the crisis on marginal groups were severe (see chapter 5 for the effects in Indonesia).

Before the crisis, East Asia had little in the way of income support programs for the unemployed—the high economic growth environment during the 1980s and early 1990s acted as an effective emollient for many of the ills of the labor market. With the exception of the Republic of Korea, which instituted mandatory public unemployment insurance for firms employing more than 30 workers in 1995, and Thailand, where private pension programs (provident funds) were sometimes used to provide unemployment benefits, workers lacked access to unemployment insurance, and labor-intensive public works programs had been phased out in all countries by 1994. The only longstanding program available for workers was legislated severance pay, which covered only formal sector workers (Cox Edwards and Manning 2001).

The response to the crisis was similar across the worst-hit countries, with governments resorting to both employment-generation and income-maintenance programs (Betcherman and others 2001). Most countries adopted large-scale, labor-intensive public works programs as emergency measures. These programs involved 2.2 percent of the labor force in Indonesia, 2.6 percent in the Republic of Korea, and 5.2 percent in Thailand. Other programs were also introduced. Indonesia provided subsidized credit to small-scale firms and cooperatives. The Republic of Korea introduced job preservation and hiring subsidies to assist firms in dire circumstances. Indonesia, the Republic of Korea, and Thailand all created programs to promote self-employment.

Some changes were made in job security legislation to help displaced workers. In both the Republic of Korea and Malaysia, laws were amended to entitle workers who quit voluntarily to severance pay. But failure to remit severance pay was a problem. In Malaysia employers disbursed only 83 percent of the claims of laid-off workers in 1998 (Mansor and others 2001). Compliance was also low in Thailand, particularly among small employers (Mahmood and Aryah 2001). To address the problem, the Republic of Korea and Thailand introduced guarantee funds, which financed unmet claims from workers whose enterprises went bankrupt. Other legislative changes to extend income protection included widening public unemployment insurance coverage to smaller firms (those employing five workers or more). Since contributory requirements were left unchanged, the effect was minor and only about 10 percent of unemployed workers received unemployment benefits during the crisis (see box 6.13). The Philippines introduced the Emergency Loan Facility for Displaced Workers, which lets workers borrow based on their previous payments of social security contributions. The program resembles UISA programs in Latin American countries.

The limited evidence on the performance of income support programs for the unemployed during the crisis suggests that the programs had limited reach, leaving large numbers of displaced workers and their households to fend for themselves. Poor design and implementation impaired the effectiveness of public works programs, resulting in the leakage of benefits to the nonpoor and in low female participation rates (Horton and Mazumdar 2001).

Summary of the Responses

Although the nature of the crisis differed across the three groups of countries, the responses in terms of income support programs to the unemployed were similar. All introduced active labor market programs (public works, training programs targeting the unemployed, wage subsidies for private sector employment, and programs to assist self-employment). Transition economies also introduced new cash benefit programs, chief among them unemployment insurance and social assistance. This difference can be attributed to a more acute contraction in output as well as to the dearth of informal risk management mechanisms at the outset of the transition. The evidence shows that crises function as a strong promoter of institutional innovations—but also that there are advantages to having institutional support in place before a crisis hits.

What conclusions can be reached about the different income support programs with respect to their suitability in dealing with different types of shocks?

- *Unemployment insurance/assistance.* The experience of the transition countries shows that a massive increase in unemployment and the resulting increase in unemployment insurance expenditures can result in the scaling back of benefits. Unemployment insurance can effectively insure against individual shocks; it may not be as effective in insuring against large structural shocks (partly because of its vulnerability to political risk [see below]).
- *Severance pay.* Severance pay is effective in smoothing consumption regardless of the nature of the shock, but it may require a public guarantee fund or a prefunding arrangement to enhance availability (failure to remit severance pay was a problem in all three groups of countries).
- *Unemployment insurance savings accounts.* This program is more suitable for dealing with frequent but modest shocks than persistent and large shocks. (This insight follows from the theory of comprehensive insurance presented in chapter 2, which shows that self-insurance through savings is an appropriate way to smooth consumption given frequent and moderate shocks but that it is not appropriate for persistent and large shocks.)
- *Public works.* Large-scale, labor-intensive public works programs, providing both income support and provision of goods and services, are the most commonly used emergency measure. But funding per poor person declines during crises, showing vulnerability to covariant shocks.
- *Early retirement programs.* Early retirement programs are effective in dealing with sector risks, but they entail high efficiency and equity costs.

An assessment of the various income support programs is presented in table 4.7.

Resistance to Political Risk

By design or by default, income support programs typically involve income redistribution. To bring about this redistribution and to pay out benefits as stipulated by program rules, unpopular measures—such as increasing contribution rates—may be necessary. Some programs may be particularly prone to pressures to increase the generosity of benefits, expand coverage, or both. Once introduced, these programs develop their own constituencies,

Table 4.7.   **Ability of Income Support Programs for the Unemployed
to Confront Shocks**

Program	Ability
Unemployment insurance	Experience of transition countries suggests that unemployment insurance effectively insures against idiosyncratic, sectoral, and regional shocks but is less effective against large covariant shocks. Massive increase in unemployment can result in scaling back of benefits.
Unemployment assistance	Similar to unemployment insurance.
Unemployment insurance savings accounts	Suitable for frequent but modest shocks. Requires appropriate financial sector (instruments, regulations, supervision).
Severance pay	Suitable for all types of shocks. May require public guarantee fund or prefunding arrangement.
Public works	Suitable for idiosyncratic, catastrophic shocks; not well suited for dealing with covariant shocks. More effective if self-selection is strong; may provide little "bang for a buck."

Source: Derived from discussion in the text.

making reforms or their dismantlement difficult. These issues are elaborated below, where three aspects are distinguished: the ability of the program to maintain benefit levels during downturns, its susceptibility to pressures to increase benefit generosity, and its tolerance to reforms that attempt to reduce benefits.

Protection of Benefit Levels During Downturns

Financed largely on a pay-as-you-go basis, unemployment insurance programs create significant unfunded liabilities, which make payment of program benefits uncertain: it may not be possible to raise payroll contribution rates or obtain budgetary support necessary to provide benefits at levels as promised by the program, especially during economic downturns. In the transition countries in the 1990s, a substantial decline in payroll tax revenues together with a sharp increase in the number of unemployment benefit recipients resulted in the reduction of benefit levels of unemployment insurance programs: statutory replacement rates were reduced, and benefits were imperfectly adjusted to inflation (Vodopivec, Wörgötter, and Raju 2003).[15] In principle, programs that require prefunding of liabilities can reduce this kind of political risk, which is higher for publicly managed funds than for privately managed funds (Smetters 2000; see box 4.4).

Box 4.4. Should Assets Be Held by the Government or in Private Accounts?

Assets accumulated under insurance programs can be managed by the government (as they are in public insurance programs) or in private accounts (as they are for individual retirement accounts or unemployment insurance savings accounts). What is the likelihood that mismanagement or high administrative costs will eventually lead to the reduction of benefits under the two options? Smetters (2000) concludes that in the United States, political risks are higher under public management than under private management. He bases his conclusion on examination of the risks arising from the use of accumulated funds for other purposes; imprudent investment decisions and restrictions on investment; conflicts of interest; less redistribution than implied by the benefit formula; failure to set aside enough money; and administrative costs.

Smetter's conclusion can be extrapolated to developing countries that have the capacity to effectively regulate and supervise the financial institutions that will manage these funds. Publicly managed funds, particularly those in developing countries, have lower returns than privately managed funds (World Bank 1994). And public funds are often channeled to politically favored projects (Iglesias and Palacios 2000). In countries in which corruption is prevalent, the likelihood that publicly held accumulated funds will be used for other purposes is particularly high. The use of individual accounts also reduces the danger that the level of benefits is increased or new beneficiaries are added to the program.

True, several industrial countries have recently set up public management arrangements that may improve upon past poor performance. But as Palacios (2002) notes, the conditions necessary for such arrangements to succeed—good governance (accountability of the government, absence of corruption, good law enforcement); mature and liquid capital markets; developed asset management industry and related services; and good access to foreign exchange—are usually not found in developing countries.

Source: Palacios (2002); Smetters (2000); World Bank (1994).

Susceptibility to Pressures to Increase Benefit Generosity

As a largely pay-as-you-go program, unemployment insurance is highly nontransparent and therefore subject to a high degree of political interference (to increase or maintain benefits for selected groups, to expand program coverage). Many transition countries maintained generous benefits for older workers near retirement, while the generosity of benefits for others was reduced. Holmlund (1998) shows that higher union coverage should lead to higher replacement rates, confirming his hypothesis empirically for the OECD countries. (Note that this is consistent with the analysis of the incidence of unemployment benefit programs in chapter 3, which shows that the presence of trade unions facilitates the introduction of these programs.)

At the other extreme, the program most resistant to political interference is the UISA program, where the link between benefits and contributions is most direct. That program also allows self-policing (workers can monitor their own accounts).

Tolerance to Reforms that Reduce Benefit Generosity

Once instituted, income support programs for the unemployed are difficult to reform. Peru attempted to reduce the amount of severance pay in 1996 but ended up increasing its generosity after a popular backlash (MacIsaac and Rama 2000). France attempted to reduce pension benefits for its privileged public service employees at the end of 1996, but mass protests prevented it from doing so.

Several arguments have been furnished to explain why labor market reforms may be politically difficult. Analyzing redistribution through government programs using a median voter model, Meltzer and Richard (1983) argue that reforms that put the middle class at a disadvantage may be difficult to implement and that government programs are likely to favor the middle class, thus failing to reach the very poor (on the evidence, see Lal 1994). Lindbeck (1995) argues that the combination of specific benefits and general taxes creates pressures for increased social security spending that make it hard to curb this spending when needed. The perception that social security constitutes a social contract between the government and its citizenry makes it even more difficult to scale benefits back. In a similar vein, Hassler, Zilbotti, and Mora (1999) argue that social insurance institutions are naturally persistent: for example, highly specialized workers prefer more generous benefits in order to be able to pursue more selective search strategies; more generous benefits in turn reinforce higher specialization. Elmeskov, Martin, and Scarpetta (1998) apply the insider-outsider argument to contend that employed workers oppose labor market reforms that would reduce labor market rigidities, as they themselves are unaffected by these rigidities and fear that the reforms would reduce their bargaining power in wage negotiations. They also point to equity concerns as inhibiting reforms, given the widely held belief that there is a tradeoff between efficiency and equity. Buti, Franco, and Pench (1999) argue that reforms may be opposed if benefits are uncertain and remote and the costs are felt immediately. Under such circumstances, losers may outnumber winners, and there may be great uncertainty among groups that would actually gain. This view is supported by Forteza and Rama (2000), who show that organized political groups that stand to lose from economic reforms are successful in diluting these reforms. They find that countries with more organized groups and public employment are associated with weaker recoveries after adjustment programs.

Ravallion (1991) suggests that weak targeting may not necessarily be undesirable, as it could strengthen political support for income support programs. He finds that the "leakage" of benefits to nonpoor participants in the Maharashtra Employment Guarantee Scheme in India may have been instrumental in obtaining sustained budgetary support. The importance of leakages is also suggested by the fact that the ability of Argentina's public works program to reach the poor declined sharply with cuts to the program's aggregate budget (Ravallion 1999b).

Saint-Paul (1993) shows that reforms aimed at increasing the flexibility of the labor market are more likely if the labor market is flexible before the reforms are instituted—that is, if the employed are more vulnerable to unemployment. He points to the complementarity between the economic and political aspects of reform: the more flexible the labor market, the more the employed are exposed to unemployment and the greater the political will to fight it. Ravallion and Lokshin (1999) reach similar conclusions, pointing to the importance of future mobility (as opposed to downward mobility, as in Saint-Paul's model) in explaining government redistribution. They find that government redistribution in the Russian Federation is motivated not by considerations about current losses and gains but largely by expectations about future welfare: rich people who expect their welfare to decline favor redistribution, and poor people who expect their welfare to increase oppose it.

These insights prove useful for creating a strategy for reforms: while the welfare state was created in an incremental fashion, its scaling back may require bolder and more comprehensive measures. Elmeskov, Martin, and Scarpetta (1998) suggest that comprehensive rather than piecemeal labor market reforms may garner greater political support for two reasons: the costs are more widely and evenly distributed across different groups of workers (greater fairness), and broad reforms have a greater likelihood of producing gains that could be used to compensate losers. Moreover, Orszag and Snower (1998) point out the "political complementarities" associated with broad and concurrent reforms that facilitate their successful introduction—losers from one reform action can potentially be winners in another. Comprehensive reforms would also avoid "rule instability," whereby expectations of future changes destabilize the economy (Lindbeck 1995). Van Ours and Belot (2000) provide empirical support for these claims, showing that OECD countries that lowered unemployment implemented comprehensive sets of labor market reforms. They note the strong complementarities among institutions affecting unemployment.

Freeman (1992) argues that one way to convince losers that they will eventually gain from reforms is by creating clear examples of winners from reforms—a variant of Hirshman's "light at the end of the tunnel" effect. Freeman shows that even workers who initially lose from reforms may prefer greater inequality of earnings. Therefore, even from a political economy standpoint, policies that spur growth are more desirable than those that more abundantly compensate losers (as long as political support for reforms remains).

Several conclusions can be drawn from this literature. First, under stable conditions, public programs may favor the middle class and fail to reach the poor. Second, not only the current degree of income distribution but the proposed or perceived change in welfare may be an important determinant of support for income redistribution programs. Third, critical developments such as economic crises or changes in government have often paved the way for the introduction of major reforms (Elmeskov, Martin, and Scarpetta 1998). (Clearly, these are not sufficient conditions.) De Ferranti and others (2000) note that economic booms have not been conducive to labor market reforms and might even have reversed some policies that made growth possible in the first place (in Chile, for example). Finally, reforming income support programs may be more effective and feasible if the reform is part of a wider, comprehensive labor market reform initiative.

Table 4.8 summarizes the evaluation of the resistance of alternative programs to political risk. Its conclusions can be summarized as follows:

- *Unemployment insurance* offers low to medium protection of benefit levels during downturns (due to its largely unfunded liabilities and the public nature of fund management), exhibits high susceptibility to pressures to increase the generosity of benefits (because of its nontransparency), and has low to medium tolerance for reforms that would reduce the generosity of benefits (because social insurance may be perceived as a "social contract" and may exhibit "natural persistence").
- *Unemployment assistance* has similar properties as unemployment insurance, with less room for political maneuvering, since program rules are somewhat stricter due to means-testing.
- *Unemployment insurance savings accounts*, which are funded programs, offer high protection of benefit levels during downturns, exhibit low susceptibility to pressures to increase the generosity of benefits (due to a direct link between contributions and benefits), and have a low tolerance for reforms that would reduce the generosity of benefits (because each worker polices his or her own account).
- *Severance pay* offers medium protection of benefit levels during downturns (due to its largely unfunded liabilities), exhibits low to medium susceptibility to pressures to increase the generosity of benefits, and has low tolerance for reforms that would reduce the generosity of benefits (because "insiders" can effectively resist reforms that would primarily benefit "outsiders").
- *Public works* programs offer low protection of benefit availability during downturns, exhibit high susceptibility to pressures to increase the generosity of benefits (leakage to better-off participants makes the program more resistant to budget cuts), and have medium tolerance for reforms.

Table 4.8. Resistance to Political Risk of Income Support Programs for the Unemployed

Program	Protection of the level of benefits in downturns	Susceptibility to pressures to increase generosity	Tolerance to reforms that reduce benefits
Unemployment insurance	Low/medium. Unfunded liabilities make it difficult to raise contributions or obtain budgetary support; public management of funds susceptible to political investments and diversion of funds.	High. Pay-as-you-go program is nontransparent and thus easily manipulated.	Low/medium. Social insurance constitutes a "social contract" and exhibits "natural persistence."
Unemployment assistance	Low/medium.	Medium. Less room for maneuver than unemployment insurance.	Medium. Opponents to reform are less vocal than opponents of unemployment insurance.
Unemployment insurance savings accounts	High (funded program).	Low. Direct link between contributions and benefits.	Low (self-policing).
Severance pay	Medium. Not always available, particularly during downturns.	Low/medium. Largely outside the domain of the government, except if part of public retrenchment programs.	Low (insider-outsider argument).
Public works	Low (countercyclical funding pattern).	High. Leakage to the better-off makes program more resistant to budget cuts.	Medium. Target constituency may not be politically vocal.

Source: Derived from discussion in the text.

Concluding Remarks

Income support programs for the unemployed generate a great variety of effects, intended and unintended, anticipated and unanticipated. No program outperforms others in all aspects. One program may provide better insurance but create severe labor market disincentives—and a constituency that will block future reforms of the program. When introducing or improving income support programs, countries are therefore advised to carefully examine all aspects of performance. That said, countries may also want to set priorities regarding different aspects of performance—for example, which groups they would like to target—and then choose their programs accordingly.

Not all aspects of performance have been researched adequately. And in many areas where research has been conducted, the results are sometimes widely different or even conflicting. Given the complex interactions involved, theoretical studies of necessity abstract from important institutional features. Their validity thus has to be checked under country-specific circumstances by empirical studies. The dearth of empirical studies on transition and particularly developing countries makes transfer of programs from industrial countries to a transition or a developing country a particularly difficult and risky undertaking. When doing so, particular attention has to be paid to country-specific considerations—the task tackled in the next chapter.

Annex 4.1   Efficiency Effects of Income Support Programs

This annex complements the discussion of efficiency effects. For each type of income support program, it considers the following dimensions: job-search effort, post-unemployment wages, equilibrium labor market outcomes, enhancing restructuring of enterprises and overall adjustment, labor supply of other family members, encouragement of taking regular versus informal jobs, and output and growth. Where applicable, theoretical predictions about the effects are presented before the empirical evidence is reviewed.

Job-Search Effort

Unemployment Insurance and Unemployment Assistance

A stylized prediction from simple theoretical models is that an increase in the unemployment benefit increases the expected duration of unemployment. This follows from simple job-search models (in which the reservation wage is assumed to rise with the benefit level), as well as from simple labor supply models (because the presence of unemployment insurance modifies the budget constraint: because less income is forgone by staying unemployed, a utility-maximizing individual chooses a longer duration of unemployment). Search theory also implies that the reservation wage declines and the exit rate increases as beneficiaries near the expiration of benefits.[16] However, once more complexity is introduced in the models (by recognizing, for example, that unemployment benefits are paid only for a finite period and that by taking a job one requalifies for unemployment benefits), the increase in the benefit rate makes the transition to employment more attractive, not less (Atkinson and Micklewright 1991). Alternatively, one can argue that unemployment benefits increase the resources devoted to search and hence increase the probability of finding a job (in such a case, the job-offer effect prevails over the reservation wage effect). The theoretical predictions about the effects of longer duration and higher replacement rate on the probability of transition from unemployment to employment are thus ambiguous.

The empirical results are much clearer. In industrial economies most studies find a positive elasticity of the duration of unemployment with respect to the benefit replacement rate (table 4.4).[17] Layard, Nickell, and Jackman (1991) estimate a benefit elasticity of 0.2–0.9, depending on the time elapsed from the start of benefit receipt. Katz and Meyer (1990) estimate that a 10 percentage point increase in the benefit level is associated with about a 1.5-week increase in the duration of unemployment.

The duration of benefit entitlement significantly affects the duration of unemployment spells. Katz and Meyer (1990) estimate that the benefit duration elasticity of unemployment in the United States is 0.4–0.5. Moffitt (1985) finds that a 1-week increase in the benefit duration is associated with a 0.15 week increase in the duration of unemployment. Ham and Rea (1987) estimate the effect for Canada at 0.26–0.33 weeks.

Studies almost invariably find a sharp increase in the probability of exit to employment just before the benefit is exhausted. Meyer (1990) finds that the exit rate triples during the six weeks before benefits are exhausted. Carling and others (1996) show that in the three weeks before benefit exhaustion, exit rates to employment increase 170 percent in Sweden.

Similar to the evidence on industrial countries, empirical studies of transition countries overwhelmingly show that unemployment benefits reduce the probability of leaving unemployment to take a job. All but two studies (on Romania and the Slovak Republic) confirm these negative effects (see table 4.5 for a summary of the empirical findings). Ham, Svejnar, and Terrell (1998) estimate that a 1-week increase in the benefit duration is associated with a 0.30-week increase in the duration of unemployment in the Czech Republic and a 0.93-week increase in the Slovak Republics. Adverse incentive effects can be detected even in Estonia, the transition country with the least generous benefit program (Vodopivec, Wörgötter, and Raju 2003).

The effects of the replacement ratio are less pronounced. Ham, Svejnar, and Terrell (1998) find significant effects for the Czech Republic but not for the Slovak Republic; Vodopivec (1995) finds insignificant effects for Slovenia. Ham, Svejnar, and Terrell find the effects for the Czech Republic to be comparable to those in industrial economies. Micklewright and Nagy (1998) estimate that about 8 percent of unemployment benefit recipients in Hungary exit from unemployment to jobs at the point of benefit exhaustion. Vodopivec (1995) provides an estimate of about 6 percent for Slovenia, and Vodopivec, Wörgötter, and Raju (2003) provide an estimate of 32 percent for Estonia. Some of these studies confirm the disincentive effects of unemployment assistance, for which replacement rates are generally lower (Scarpetta and Reutersward 1994).

Unemployment insurance experiments conducted in the United States in the 1980s and 1990s provide strong evidence of the existence of moral hazard

(Meyer 1995). The experiments—prompted partly by unemployment insurance overpayments resulting from the failure of claimants to actively seek work—took two forms: cash bonuses for unemployment benefit recipients who found jobs quickly and kept them for some time and provision of varying levels of job-search assistance. In both cases, experiments used random assignment. The bonus experiments reveal that incentives matter: when offered a bonus for speedy reemployment, beneficiaries reduced unemployment benefit claims. In several cases, the reduction was statistically significant. Moreover, there was no evidence that speedier return to work reduced reemployment earnings. Job-search assistance experiments also underscore the presence of moral hazard: beneficiaries for whom oversight was reduced and job-search assistance was not provided showed a statistically significant increase in unemployment benefit claims.

There is little direct evidence on the intensity of job search of claimants of unemployment benefits in comparison to nonclaimants. In his analysis of job-search practices of British benefit claimants, Wadsworth (1991) finds that claimants search for jobs more extensively than nonclaimants. In the absence of better information, he takes the number of search methods as a measure of job-search effort.

Unemployment Insurance Saving Accounts

No empirical work has been done on the effects of unemployment insurance saving accounts on the probability of reemployment.

Severance Pay

Because it is not contingent on the duration of subsequent unemployment, the amount of severance pay does not alter the behavior of workers when searching for a job—that is, severance pay does not create a moral hazard problem pertaining to job-search incentives.

Post-Unemployment Wages

Unemployment insurance creates disincentives for exit from unemployment to employment. This effect could be seen in a less negative way if unemployment insurance produced a better match between workers and their new employers. If it did, the effect would show up as an increase in the post-unemployment wage.

Theoretical Predictions

Job-search theory yields ambiguous predictions with respect to the relationship between unemployment benefit levels and post-unemployment wages. On the one hand, an increase in the benefit level raises the reservation wage at the beginning of the covered unemployment spell. This improves the likelihood of a post-unemployment wage gain, as offered wages have to be higher to induce the recipient to exit compensated unemployment. On the other hand, a higher benefit level depresses job-search intensity and prolongs unemployment. The resultant downward adjustments in the reservation wage over the unemployment spell increase the likelihood of a post-unemployment wage loss. Wage offers are also negatively affected by the employers' perceptions of greater skill obsolescence and the loss of human capital from longer unemployment spells.

Empirical Evidence

There is no compelling evidence that unemployment benefits, by subsidizing job-search costs, improve job matches (Cox and Oaxaca 1990). Using U.S. data, Ehrenberg and Oaxaca (1976), Burgess and Kingston (1976), Holen (1977), and Barron and Mellow (1979) find a statistically significant and positive relationship between benefit levels and post-unemployment wages. Ehrenberg and Oaxaca (1976) estimate that a 10 percentage point increase in the benefit replacement rate increases post-unemployment wages by 7 percent for older men and 1.5 percent for older women. Using New Zealand data, Maani (1993) finds that a 10 percentage point increase in the benefit replacement rate is associated with a 4.5 percent increase in post-unemployment wages.[18] Other studies show a weak or negligible effect on post-unemployment wages. Blau and Robins (1986) and Kiefer and Neumann (1989) find a positive but statistically insignificant relationship between benefits and earnings. Addison and Blackburn (2000) find weak evidence of improved earnings, and Classen (1977) finds no effect. Meyer (1995) finds that re-employment bonuses shorten the duration of compensated unemployment without affecting post-unemployment wages.

Equilibrium Labor Market Outcomes

Theoretical Predictions

Most theoretical models predict that an increase in the level of unemployment benefits will increase the equilibrium unemployment rate.[19] In decentralized wage negotiations in union-bargaining models, a higher benefit level increases the negotiated wage at the firm level and hence overall unemployment. In Holmlund's (1998) model, for example, unemployment is very sensitive to the replacement rate: an increase in the replacement rate from 50 percent to 60 percent raises the equilibrium unemployment rate by almost 4 percentage points.

Equilibrium search models also predict an increase in equilibrium unemployment in response to an increase in the replacement rate. The increase is less intense than in a union-bargaining model—a rise in the replacement rate from 50 percent to 60 percent is associated with an increase in the equilibrium unemployment rate of 1 percentage point (the relationship is nonlinear) (Holmlund 1998). Calibration of models that include job creation and job destruction effects shows that halving the replacement rate reduces a typical unemployment spell from 3 months to less then 2.4 months, reducing the unemployment rate from 6 percent to 4.5 percent (Mortensen 1994).

Heer (2000), drawing on Fredriksson and Holmlund (2001), provides one of the rare explicit treatments of unemployment insurance and unemployment assistance as two components of a compensation program, with means-tested assistance available to individuals whose eligibility for unemployment insurance payments expires (as it does in several countries). His general equilibrium model predicts that both components of the program reduce equilibrium employment and that an increase in unemployment assistance payments has a strong disincentive effect on a worker's search effort. Optimal unemployment compensation declines over time.

General equilibrium models may reinforce partial equilibrium results, but they can also reverse them. The prediction that a higher benefit reduces the outflow from unemployment (given the level of labor market tightness) can be reinforced by general equilibrium models that endogenize wage setting and labor market tightness. But in some other general equilibrium models, the prediction that a higher benefit reduces the outflow from unemployment is reversed. If one assumes that in response to higher unemployment benefits the equilibrium wage distribution changes so that low-wage firms increase their wage offers, then the frequency of low-wage firms declines and the outflow from unemployment increases (Holmlund 1998). Moreover, the predictions of general equilibrium models are quite sensitive to changes in assumptions. The magnitude of the effects that an increase in the replacement rate has on unemployment in job-search models is very sensitive to the assumption about the value of leisure, for which no reliable estimates exist.

As for the effects on participation in the labor force, Friedman (1968) contends that the ability to claim unemployment benefits when unemployed makes it more attractive to enter the labor force (both to employment or unemployment)—the so-called "entitlement" effect. But this is a partial equilibrium result. By imposing additional costs associated with labor, unemployment insurance may also induce employers to reduce their demand for labor, which may increase equilibrium unemployment and, in turn, reduce labor force participation (through the discouraged worker effect, for example). Moreover, the effects of the availability of unemployment insurance may show up primarily as increases in wages, not as increases in employment; higher wages induce more people to enter the labor force, but they may also increase unemployment. Thus the effects on the labor force participation rate—and the employment rate—cannot be determined unambiguously.

The predicted effects of severance pay on unemployment are also ambiguous. Blanchard (1998) creates a model with explicit firing costs and shows that severance pay increases firing costs and therefore reduces the probability of an individual moving from employment to unemployment.

But by stifling job creation, severance pay also reduces the probability of entry to employment.

Pissarides (2001) argues that by delaying dismissals, advance notification and severance pay help prevent unemployment. But agreements on employment protection and wages must be left to the firms and workers, because government involvement can be counterproductive. Crucial for his argument is the ability of firms to lower wages in order to pay the additional costs associated with dismissal; if firms cannot reduce wages, employment protection legislation reduces the demand for labor and increases equilibrium unemployment. Addison, Barrett, and Siebert (1998) reach the same conclusion, showing that government mandating of worker protection (such as health insurance and dismissal costs) reduces output by reducing productive efficiency.

Empirical Evidence

By focusing on distinct features, different theoretical models reach different conclusions—conclusions that sometimes conflict with one another. Conflicting predictions reflect the fact that modeling of income support programs (particularly unemployment insurance and severance pay) has to account for various and complex institutional elements that are impossible to capture in a single model if analytical tractability is to be retained. Empirical research is needed to determine which effects—and theoretical models—dominate. Several studies have tried to explain differences in labor market outcomes by pointing to differences in institutions and other control variables (such as the stage of the business cycle and differences in earnings).[20]

EFFECTS ON UNEMPLOYMENT. One of the best known studies in this area—Layard, Nickell, and Jackman (1991)—finds that in the mid-1980s the replacement rate of unemployment benefit programs in OECD countries significantly affected the average unemployment rate, with a 10 percentage point increase in the benefit rate producing an estimated 1.3 percentage point increase in the unemployment rate. This study also confirms the positive effect of the potential duration of unemployment benefits on the unemployment rate. Nickell and Layard (1999) obtain similar results for the 1983–94 period. Two other recent studies, also for OECD counties, are broadly in line with these results. OECD (1999b) finds significant effects of the replacement rate (but insignificant effects of the potential entitlement duration); Daveri and Tabellini (2000) find mostly significant effects of the potential entitlement duration (they do not report results for replacement rates).

Consistent with theoretical predictions, the effects of employment protection legislation on unemployment are largely inconclusive (for a survey of the effects, see OECD 1999b). According to Mortensen (1994), however, a calibration of a general equilibrium model applied to the U.S. economy shows that the introduction of severance pay increases unemployment, because the reduction in job creation imposed by firing costs more than off-sets the intended effects of firing costs to reduce unemployment by discouraging layoffs. Several studies find positive effects of severance pay on long-term unemployment.

EFFECTS ON EMPLOYMENT. The effects of unemployment benefits on employment rates are often statistically insignificant (see, for example, Nickell and Layard 1999). In contrast, there is strong evidence that strict employment protection—particularly severance pay—reduces employment. Lazear (1990) shows that increasing severance pay by one month reduces employment per capita by about 0.4 percent and reduces the labor force participation rate by 0.3 percent. OECD (1999b) finds that negative effects are concentrated among prime-age women, young people, and older workers. Haffner and others (2001) find a negative association between the extensiveness of employment protection legislation and employment rates in OECD countries. Heckman and Pages (2000) also confirm the link between job security and lower employment and attribute a 5 percentage point reduction in employment in Latin America to job security provisions. Indirect support of the negative effects of severance pay on employment is also provided by a study of severance pay in Peru by MacIsaac and Rama (2000). They find that firms bear the higher firing costs due to severance pay, since the earnings of covered workers differ insignificantly from the earnings of noncovered workers. The fact that severance pay lowers employment rates in Latin America can also be interpreted as indirect evidence that severance pay pushes workers into the informal sector.

Lazear (1990) shows that severance pay contributes to turning full-time jobs into part-time jobs. OECD (1999b) finds a strong link between stricter employment protection legislation and higher rates of self-employment, a result confirmed by other studies.

Enhancing Restructuring of Enterprises and Overall Adjustment

Theory does not support the argument that, to facilitate the restructuring process by overcoming political resistance, the optimal level of insurance protection against unemployment is higher during the transition process. Blanchard (1997) shows that more generous benefits do indeed add to the attractiveness of restructuring but that they also hinder (private) job creation. He concludes that "the case for increasing unemployment benefits on efficiency grounds is limited" (p. 114). Measured by the dynamics of job creation and job destruction, the intensity of labor reallocation in transition countries is not associated with the generosity of unemployment benefits. Haltiwanger and Vodopivec (2002) find much higher gross worker and job flows in Estonia than in Slovenia, despite the fact that Estonia has one of the most frugal and Slovenia one of the most generous programs of unemployment benefits among transition countries.

Of course, restructuring programs that provide workers with a sufficiently generous compensation (at the extreme, full insurance, or income support at a 100 percent replacement rate) are successful in the sense that they facilitate the downsizing of a particular enterprise to a desirable level. But in their evaluation of 41 public sector retrenchment projects, Haltiwanger and Singh (1999) provide a mixed picture of the success of these projects when gauged by a broader measure. Financial returns were high—most of the surveyed projects recovered their direct costs in as little as two years. But 40 percent of programs for which data existed rehired some of the same workers they had shed during the retrenchment, a sign that economic returns may be less clear. Active labor market measures, which may be part of retrenchment programs, may also have dubious economic effects (Dar and Tzannatos 1999).

Haltiwanger and Singh (1999) find that individually tailored severance payments based on skills and age, in combination with a mix of strategies for employment reduction, are less often associated with rehiring. Although they find that such an approach can be financially expensive, they argue that it has "a potentially large payoff in productivity gains and in lower adjustment costs" (p. 52). The specific conditions prevailing in a particular country must be carefully evaluated before applying any of the general principles. Given that many of the relevant data to evaluate the effects of these programs are not available (particularly on the costs side), the economic effects of such programs are difficult to pinpoint.

Labor Supply of Other Family Members

Unemployment Insurance

Theoretical considerations suggest that higher replacement rates will suppress the labor supply of other family members through the income effect. Empirical evidence confirms such predictions. Cullen and Gruber (cited in Gruber 1999) find that the labor supply of wives of unemployed workers is very responsive to unemployment benefits received by their husbands: a $1 increase in the unemployment benefits of a husband reduces the earnings of his wife by 36 cents.

Unemployment Assistance

Theoretical predictions differ from those associated with unemployment insurance, reflecting differences in program rules. Because unemployment assistance requires means-testing, it could be expected to create disincentives for other family members to take a job. Empirical evidence supports such predictions. Garcia (1989) shows that if such disincentives were removed, the overall participation rate of the wives of the unemployed would increase by 8 percentage points. Similar evidence is found in transition countries. Terrell, Lubyova, and Strapec (1996) report that in the Slovak

Republic the presence of an unemployed spouse lowers the probability of exit to employment of unemployment assistance recipients by 72 percent for females and 82 percent for males. Boeri (1997) reports similar effects for Poland.

Decision to Enter Regular versus Informal Job

The existence of unemployment insurance may encourage people to enter regular employment rather than work in the informal sector. It should have this effect if the expected unemployment benefits exceed the cost of paying the contributions (if the government or the employer covers part of the cost).

The evidence on this issue is scant and inconclusive. On the one hand, two studies of France find that the availability of unemployment benefits significantly reduced entry into precarious jobs (Atkinson and Micklewright 1991). Boheim and Taylor (2000) find that while the occurrence of unemployment severely reduced the duration of subsequent job tenure, the duration of unemployment had no deleterious impact—in fact, longer durations of unemployment were rewarded by longer job tenures, presumably because a longer period of job search improves the probability of a better worker-job match.[21] On the other hand, Addison and Portugal (1998) find no evidence that unemployment benefits facilitate entry into stable jobs in Portugal. And Cunningham (2000) shows that an increase in the generosity of unemployment insurance in Brazil led to increased participation in the self-employment sector. This result suggests that in Brazil, the lack of liquidity represents a barrier to entry into self-employment. It supports the view that markets in Brazil are well integrated and participation in the informal sector is not an inferior choice.

Output and Growth

The dynamic general equilibrium model of Acemoglu and Shimer (1999) shows that unemployment insurance helps an economy produce higher output than an economy without unemployment insurance, since unemployment insurance contributes to the creation of high-quality, high-wage jobs with greater unemployment risk. Calibrations of their model show that moderate increases in the replacement rate or the duration of entitlement lead to a rise in the share of good jobs as well as to increases in both welfare and output (the resulting increase in unemployment is due primarily to better-insured workers looking for higher wage jobs) (Acemoglu and Shimer 2000). Acemoglu and Shimer show that states in the United States with higher replacement ratios experience higher unemployment but also a relative increase in the number of high-wage occupations and industries and higher productivity growth. Other research also shows that unemployment insurance may improve the allocation of resources (see, for example, Diamond 1981).

Central to the efficiency-increasing effect argument of Acemoglu and Shimer is their claim that unemployment insurance helps create high-quality, high-wage jobs. But there is also evidence that points to the contrary. Anderson and Meyer (1993) find that the industries consistently receiving subsidies from the unemployment insurance program in the United States are construction, manufacturing, and mining—industries that do not generate high-quality, high-wage jobs. Their finding is consistent with the prediction that the program subsidizes unstable employment, as workers are more willing to take more unstable jobs (such as seasonal jobs) if they can count on unemployment benefits.

The efficiency-enhancing literature has to be contrasted with the literature on optimal unemployment insurance, which focuses on the moral hazard associated with search effort and models the tradeoff between efficiency and equity. Wang and Williamson (1996) conclude that the introduction of optimal unemployment insurance in the United States would reduce the steady state unemployment rate by 3.4 percentage points and increase output by 3.64 percentage points.[22] Similarly, using a job creation/job destruction model, Mortensen (1994) finds that halving the replacement rate of unemployment insurance would increase job creation and thus aggregate output.

Attanasio and Rios-Rull (2000) provide a different perspective that also suggests that the introduction of unemployment insurance may reduce welfare. They observe that a government-mandated program may crowd out private insurance programs by breaking down the social fabric that maintains private transfers. They show that when both aggregate and idiosyncratic risks are shared among members of extended families and idiosyncratic risk is less than fully insured because of enforceability problems, the provision of mandated insurance programs is almost surely inefficient, because it crowds out private insurance against idiosyncratic shocks. Their findings suggest that before introducing unemployment support programs, policymakers should consider the substitution effects such a program may have on private arrangements.

Notes

1. The informal sector is increasingly viewed as an "unregulated entrepreneurial sector," which generates many unemployed (see Arango and Maloney 2000).

2. This summary measure takes into account the support provided not only by unemployment benefits but also by other welfare programs and active programs, including social assistance and family, housing, employment-conditional, and single-parent benefits. It is calculated for a period of more than 60 months for four different household types (single, married couple, couple with two children, and a single parent with two children) and two alternative earnings possibilities (an average production worker and one earning two-thirds of the average).

3. These are upper bounds of poverty-reduction effects, as calculations do not account for behavioral responses (in the absence of unemployment benefits, the

unemployed would probably have responded differently to the wage loss, in particular, by resorting to coping mechanisms to compensate for the loss).

4. Coady, Grosch, and Hoddinott (2002) compare the individual assessment, based on means-testing or proxy means-testing (that is, construction of a targeting index from income and wealth attributes); categorical targeting (such as child allowances); self-selection methods (such as public works and food subsidies); and community assessment.

5. Coady, Grosch, and Hoddinott (2002) find that community involvement in some countries helps improve targeting. In contrast, Galasso and Ravallion (forthcoming) find evidence that the less equal the distribution of assets in a village, the better positioned are the nonpoor to capture the benefits of the program.

6. If the inflow of workers into unemployment is assumed to be invariant to the increase in unemployment benefits, then the increase in the duration of unemployment increases the equilibrium unemployment, which is determined by the average duration of unemployment and the inflow into unemployment.

7. Cross-country studies have been criticized as suffering from the problem of reversed causality.

8. Negative effects may apply only in the short run—long-run effects may be less pronounced, as some studies find that employment is insensitive to the level of total taxes in the long run (see, for example, Gruber 1997b).

9. But Forteza and Rama (2001) show that greater mandated benefits (represented by the wedge on wages created by social security contributions) do not stand in the way of recovery after economic reforms are undertaken.

10. Indeed, the evidence shows a strong positive effect of imperfect experience rating—where employers bear only part of the cost of unemployment benefits drawn by their laid-off workers—on temporary layoffs. The fact that employers bear only part of the cost creates incentives for increasing temporary layoffs during economic downturns. Card and Levine (1994) attribute 50 percent of temporary layoff spells to imperfect experience rating, Topel (1983) as much as 30 percent, and Anderson and Meyer (1994) more than 20 percent.

11. The literature on the effects of worker management, cooperation, and participatory approaches in management finds mildly positive effects of these features on productivity of firms but cannot pinpoint the features or interactions that contribute to success. Levine and Tyson (1990) single out measures to enhance actual participation as instrumental for higher productivity, but it is unclear to what extent employment protection boosts such measures.

12. Abraham and Houseman (1994) find that despite slower employment adjustment, stricter employment protection legislation in Europe leads to adjustments in hours that are similar to adjustments in the United States.

13. The results of Daveri and Tabellini (2000) confirm the view that increased labor costs contribute to unemployment and slow economic growth.

14. Unless otherwise noted, data on labor market programs in this subsection are from Vodopivec, Wörgötter, and Raju (2003).

15. This has been the case with pension benefits even in OECD countries, where benefits have been cut according to a preset schedule since the 1980s (Schwarz and Demirguc-Kunt 1999).

16. Mortensen's seminal paper (1977) implies three types of effects. First, for the qualified unemployed worker, the exit rate increases as the benefit expiration date nears. Second, a rise in benefits reduces the exit rate for an insured worker who has recently become unemployed and increases the exit rate for the insured worker who

is close to benefit expiration. This follows from the fact that a higher benefit level increases both the value of continued search and the value of accepting an offer. The immediate value of higher benefits is small for workers close to benefit exhaustion, because their situation is similar to that of workers who do not qualify for the benefit. Third, a rise in benefits increases the exit rate for an unemployed worker who does not qualify for benefits (the entitlement effect).

17. For a survey of studies that do not find significant effects of benefits on unemployment duration, see Pedersen and Westergård-Nielsen (1993).

18. The results of some of the studies that do find a positive effect of benefits on wages are considered questionable because of shortcomings in the data and the approaches used (Welch 1977). One significant problem in studies of earnings-related unemployment benefit programs is the difficulty of disentangling the effect of the benefit on post-unemployment wages from previous wages.

19. In contrast to the discussion of the search-effort effects, this discussion focuses on general equilibrium results.

20. OECD (1999b) uses variables characterizing wage bargaining, income support for the unemployed, taxation of labor, and spending on active labor market programs.

21. This finding may be confounding the effects of job search with the effects of other variables that are not controlled for in the analysis, such as the receipt of unemployment insurance, which may capture the difference in unobserved differences between recipients and nonrecipients.

22. The large positive effects on employment and output are driven largely by a sharp decline in unemployment inflow that results from switching to an optimal unemployment insurance program. The empirical foundation for this sharp reduction is not very strong.

5

Design and Implementation Criteria: Exploring Country-Specific Conditions

Much is known about the performance of income support programs for the unemployed under the conditions that usually prevail in industrial countries. But these conditions may not exist in transition or developing countries. Policymakers in those settings need to carefully take account of country-specific features as they introduce new institutions or try to improve existing ones, because those features will determine how a program will work in a particular country.

This chapter reviews some of the most important country-specific features that policymakers need to consider when introducing or improving income support programs in developing and transition countries. Some of these features relate to the interactions of income support programs with other social risk management mechanisms. Others relate to the desirability of different programs or to specific conditions that are likely to strongly affect the performance of various programs. The following features are examined:

- interactions with labor market institutions and shocks
- administrative capacity for program implementation
- characteristics of unemployment
- size of the informal sector
- prevalence and pattern of interhousehold transfers
- nonsocial insurance and self-protection
- the nature of shocks
- cultural and political factors

Interactions with Labor Market Institutions and Shocks

Interactions between an income support program and other labor market institutions and shocks affect the impact the program has on labor market outcomes. The impact of unemployment insurance benefits on the equilibrium level of unemployment depends on the interaction of benefits with wage-setting mechanisms; the impact of an adverse shock on the persistence of unemployment depends on the interaction of the shock with institutions, above all on the interaction with unemployment insurance and employment protection legislation (including severance pay).

Impact on Equilibrium Unemployment: The Interaction of Income Support Programs with Wage-Setting Institutions

Theoretical studies suggest that the presence of unemployment insurance is likely to strengthen the bargaining power of trade unions and thus increase the equilibrium unemployment rate. Under decentralized wage setting in which bargaining takes place at the firm level, union-bargaining models predict that an increase in the level of unemployment benefits will positively affect equilibrium unemployment, as workers' reservation wage increases (Holmlund 1998). Depending on the level of coordination and centralization of collective bargaining, the effect on unemployment can be significant. Centralized and highly coordinated programs as well as fully decentralized programs have been shown to restrain insiders' pressure for wage increases; uncoordinated and fragmented bargaining is likely to lead to stronger wage pressure (Calmfors and Drifill 1988; Elmeskov, Martin, and Scarpetta 1998).

Other interactions may also influence the effects of unemployment insurance. Mortensen and Pissarides (1999) suggest that an increase in the benefit replacement rate has a stronger impact on the equilibrium unemployment rate when payroll taxes are higher. Orszag and Snower (1998) argue that there are complementary effects between unemployment benefits and payroll taxes.[1]

Impact on Persistence of Unemployment: The Interaction of Income Support Programs with Shocks

The presence of unemployment insurance programs and employment protection exacerbates the effects of adverse shocks (Blanchard and Wolfers 2000). (Their argument is summarized under the explanations of the rise of European unemployment in chapter 4.)

Implications for Program Choice and Design

Other things equal, the level of coordination and the degree of centralization of collective bargaining matter: the introduction of unemployment insurance is less likely to raise the equilibrium unemployment rate in an economy with a centralized and coordinated wage-bargaining system or in a fully decentralized system. Unemployment benefits also interact with payroll taxation. Moreover, through their interaction with adverse covariant shocks, more generous unemployment insurance or assistance and more protective employment legislation contribute to the persistence of unemployment.

Administrative Capacity for Program Implementation

An important consideration in choosing an income support program is the administrative capacity necessary to implement it. Underscoring the importance of good monitoring and enforcement, recent studies suggest that effective monitoring and the use of sanctions strongly reduce the average duration of unemployment benefit payments and increase the transition rate to employment (see chapter 6). This section focuses on the capacity to evaluate initial and continuing program eligibility as well as to pay out benefits. It examines the capacity to pay out benefits and to generate and process information on the payment of contributions by or on behalf of workers as well as information on workers' employment/unemployment status, job-search efforts, income from other sources and assets, and family circumstances (number of family members, their incomes, and their assets).

With recent advancements in information and communication technology, keeping track of payments of insurance premiums and disbursements of funds has become increasingly affordable, even in low-income countries. Such technology is instrumental in maintaining records on premium payments. Even low-income countries have pension systems, which typically require a long history of contributions for individual workers. The same kind of information system is necessary to administer unemployment insurance, unemployment assistance, and unemployment insurance savings accounts.

Information technology is of only limited help when it comes to checking additional eligibility requirements under unemployment insurance or unemployment assistance programs. The need for additional screening of applicants arises from the fact that these programs are prone to moral hazard problems: the status of unemployment, coupled with sufficiently low family earnings, triggers the payment of unemployment assistance benefits, creating disincentives to take a job or work longer hours. In addition to checking whether recipients are working, the program also has to monitor whether they are available and willing to take a job and actively searching for one.

Monitoring of eligibility conditions under unemployment insurance and unemployment assistance is challenging even for industrial countries and transition countries. First, it is not clear how best to monitor "availability for work," the requirement often used to curtail informal employment. Different countries use different approaches, all of which have shortcomings. Recent amendments to the unemployment benefit law in Slovenia require that benefit recipients make themselves available for contacts by employment offices for three hours a day, but preliminary results show little effect on disqualification. Moreover, such a requirement may backfire, because it forces employment counselors to assume two opposing roles, job facilitator and police officer. Second, monitoring the requirement to actively seek employment is not easy, and because it entails many different aspects, it cannot easily be incorporated in legislation. What can reasonably be expected from the unemployed may well depend on individual circumstances (skills, qualifications, experience, length of the unemployment spell), as well as on vacancies in the

---

Box 5.1.   Disqualifying Benefit Recipients in Transition Countries

Micklewright and Nagy (1994) report that disqualification from unemployment insurance benefits receipt rarely occurs in Hungary. Among the March 1992 cohort of benefit recipients, just 4 percent of spells ended with disqualification of benefits. The risk of disqualification was much higher for the young, the less educated, blue-collar workers, and those living in Budapest. While such differences could conceivably occur with the same degree of enforcement of the rules, in all likelihood enforcement varies widely within as well as across countries.

The risk of benefit disqualification in Slovenia is much lower than in Hungary: in 1998 only 1 percent of spells ended with disqualification; in 1999 the figure was just 0.65 percent, despite changes in legislation aimed at improving the monitoring of benefit eligibility. Casual evidence suggests that in Estonia during the 1990s, when unemployment benefits were extremely modest, employment offices sometimes sided with the unemployed and did not take actions that would have resulted in disqualification—precisely because the benefit was so low.

Source: Vodopivec, Wörgötter, and Raju (2003).

---

local labor market. Third, it is difficult to determine what constitutes a "suitable job" and the amount of work that may be undertaken without losing benefit eligibility. It is thus not surprising that disqualification from unemployment benefits rarely occurs and that this practice differs across as well as within countries (see box 5.1 for evidence on transition countries and OECD 2000a for evidence on OECD countries).

Monitoring labor market status—particularly availability for work and earnings obtained from informal employment—is even more difficult in developing countries. The existence of a large informal sector, together with the ease of entry into—and exit from—informal sector activities, makes verifying the status of unemployment as well as earnings more difficult. Monitoring eligibility is somewhat easier in countries with interlinked administrative bases of individuals (box 5.2). Such interlinked programs rarely exist in developing countries, where information technology at local and public employment service offices is limited. Even in the absence of information problems, rules are not always strictly enforced. Recognizing its inability to monitor labor market status effectively, Argentina recently introduced an unemployment insurance program that dispenses altogether with checking the continuing eligibility of unemployment insurance recipients. Instead, it cross-checks whether benefit recipients are also on the social security payment rolls (box 5.3).

Monitoring eligibility requirements under unemployment insurance and unemployment assistance is more challenging in developing countries—and

---

Box 5.2.   Using Advanced Technology to Fight Fraud and Reduce Costs in Poland and Germany

Advanced information and communication technology and the existence of interconnected administrative data bases can help prevent fraud and reduce administrative costs. A pilot management information project in the Poznan region of Poland reduces benefit leakage by checking whether unemployment benefit recipients have already taken a job. To do so, employment offices contact the social security administration and tax office, using advanced communication technology. Estimates suggest that reducing leakage will allow the project to recoup its costs in about two years.

In Germany the staff of employment offices make field visits to check whether workers are legally employed. Equipped with computers and mobile phones, employment office staff can log on to institutional databases from the field to check if a worker contributes to the unemployment insurance and pension funds and is receiving unemployment compensation.

Source: Leipold (2000).

---

their capacity to do so is much more limited than that of industrial countries. None of the offices of the Filipino public employment service has the capacity to check a claimant's labor force status and job-search efforts or to conduct means-testing. Even in the more developed regions of the Philippines, most offices have only one employee, and the offices are active only in periods of high seasonal unemployment. These offices may also be influenced by local chief executives and therefore (mis)used for political purposes.

Additional administrative costs can be expected under means-testing programs, such as unemployment assistance, eligibility criteria for which include determining the income and assets of applicants and their families. Minimizing leakages of program benefits to the nonpoor may require significant resources, especially in developing countries. The University of the Philippines screens applicants for tuition fee subsidies and allowances, using information requirements similar to those required under unemployment assistance. The screening costs about $10 per applicant—equivalent to total per capita social sector spending in the Philippines (Esguerra, Ogawa, and Vodopivec 2001). Coady, Grosch, and Hoddinott (2002) report that the median cost of 100 means-tested programs they evaluated in developing countries was 28 percent of total benefit expenditures—one and a half times the 19 percent for non–means-tested programs. Atkinson (1995b) reports that the administrative costs of an income- and asset-tested program in the United Kingdom in the early 1990s were 5.3 percent of total benefit expenditures—almost two and a half times the 2.2 percent for the universal child benefit program.

Box 5.3.   Identifying Ineligible Benefits Recipients in Argentina

Argentina introduced its unemployment insurance program in 1992, follow-ing a macroeconomic crisis that raised the fear of large-scale unemployment. The total number of recipients is relatively small—on average, only about 100,000–125,000 out of 2 million officially unemployed workers receive bene-fits. Administration of the program (the processing of claims and payment of benefits) was handed over to the social security system (ANSES—Adminis-tración Nacional de la Seguridad Nacional), which operates a national net-work of offices and reports to the Ministry of Labor and Social Security. Workers go to one of 150 local ANSES offices to register and receive their checks; no job placement or other reemployment services are provided.

While the administration of benefits has seemingly proceeded smoothly (workers are informed of their eligibility and receive payments on a timely basis), the program only recently acquired the capacity to identify recipients who have found new jobs in the formal sector—and it still applies few mea-sures to prevent the leakage of benefits to those who have found jobs in the informal sector. Through a newly introduced program of common personal identification numbers, the government has been able to cross-check whether unemployment insurance recipients are also on social security payment rolls. (Personal identification numbers were introduced in 1994, but it took several years to develop this cross-checking capability.) The cross-checking capability allows significant numbers of benefit recipients actually working in the formal sector to be purged from the benefit receipt lists. Nevertheless, far more recip-ients are likely to be working in the informal sector, with no measures taken to detect them and terminate their benefits.

Source: Mazza (1999).

Less administrative capacity is needed to implement public works pro-grams, and such capacity is usually stronger in developing countries, where many local governments are familiar with the procedures involved in pro-viding public works.

Implications for Program Choice and Design

The administrative capacity needed to implement income support pro-grams varies greatly across programs. Some programs—severance pay, public works, some versions of unemployment insurance savings accounts (UISAs)—have relatively modest informational and organiza-tional demands, and developing countries usually have adequate capacity to administer these programs. Other programs, such as unemployment insurance, unemployment assistance, and UISA-cum-solidarity-funding, require extensive and sophisticated information that often cannot be read-ily provided by developing countries, particularly low-income countries.

Eligibility monitoring is more demanding and costly in developing countries, because of a larger informal sector, which provides more abundant informal employment opportunities, and weaker administrative databases, which prevent cost-effective methods of cross-checking benefit receipt. At the same time, capacity is much weaker.

The lack of administrative capacity to effectively monitor continuing eligibility and impose sanctions suggests that the moral hazard problem that arises from asymmetric information will be particularly prominent in developing countries. Under such conditions, insurance principles suggest that social insurance should impose deductibles, copayments, or both. Within the traditional unemployment insurance program, that means imposing a waiting period, limiting the duration of benefits, and having a declining level of benefits during individual unemployment spell (see the discussion on the design features of unemployment insurance in chapter 6). Alternatively, unemployment insurance can be combined with savings accounts, as it is in the new Chilean program (see chapter 6).

Characteristics of Unemployment

The characteristics of unemployment—the frequency and duration of unemployment, the characteristics of unemployed workers—affect the choice of program. Because the provision of income security may come only at a cost in terms of efficiency or access to (formal) employment, policymakers need to know which groups are most likely to benefit from which programs.

If unemployment spells are frequent and short, self-insurance measures may be more appropriate (Gill and Ilahi 2000). Less frequent and longer unemployment spells speak in favor of public insurance programs.

Other characteristics of unemployment in developing countries also need to be considered. A peculiarity of low-income countries is that poor people may be less than proportionally represented among the unemployed (Cox Edwards and Manning 2001). In Brazil and Peru the poor experience disproportionately less unemployment than the rich. The pattern is reversed in Mexico and Uruguay, but unemployment is still heavily represented among the richer quintiles (de Ferranti and others 2000). In the Philippines, where 25 percent of the population lives in poverty, only 12.1 percent of households whose heads were unemployed were poor in 1997 (Balisacan 2001). And although households whose heads were unemployed represented 12.7 percent of the total population, they made up just 6.1 percent of the total number of poor people. In Sri Lanka unemployment has been closely related to status in the household and the availability of income support from relatives, both critical factors for allowing extended periods of job search (World Bank 1999). Members of poorer households apparently cannot afford to stay unemployed for a prolonged period of time. They therefore cushion the loss of earnings by opting for low-productivity jobs (mostly in the informal sector) while they continue to search for better-paying jobs.

In some low-income countries, the most deprived groups are underemployed rather than unemployed. In the Philippines these are mostly unskilled workers—self-employed subsistence farmers and fishers, seasonal workers, and workers in the informal sector (Esguerra, Ogawa, and Vodopivec 2001). In contrast to unemployment, underemployment in the Philippines is higher in rural areas.

Implications for Program Choice and Design

The characteristics of unemployment have important implications for both equity and efficiency aspects of income support programs. First, equity considerations suggest that the underemployed—not only the unemployed—should be regarded as an important potential client group for income support programs. Second, the efficiency effects of an insurance-type income support program are difficult to predict. The fact that poor workers prefer underemployment to unemployment suggests that moral hazard problems may figure prominently once insurance-type public income support programs are offered. Some workers who in the absence of unemployment benefits choose temporary jobs because they cannot afford to stay out of work (the underemployed) would prefer unemployment if offered unemployment benefits—insurance would reduce the need to take self-protection measures. Such efficiency losses could be high, because activities forgone due to public income support may not be much less productive than those carried out in formal production units, due to the low capital intensity of labor in the formal sector. But if unemployment benefits contribute to more effective job search—that is, if the recipients find better-paying jobs or find jobs more rapidly—efficiency is enhanced.[2] In the absence of empirical evidence in developing countries, it is not possible to determine which of these effects dominates. Third, if unemployment spells are less frequent and longer, self-insurance measures may become inadequate and public insurance programs needed.

Size of the Informal Sector

The informal sector is a pervasive and persistent economic feature in most of the developing world, particularly in low-income countries, where it is a significant source of employment, production, and income generation.[3] In developing countries it is estimated to account for about 20–80 percent of nonagricultural employment.[4] In developing countries in Asia and Africa it accounts for an estimated 25–40 percent of annual output. The importance of the informal sector as a source of employment and income is brought into sharp relief when juxtaposed against the sluggish formal private sector and the shrinking public sector that characterizes many developing countries.[5] The informal sector absorbs much of the slack in the labor force, particularly in urban centers, and it often acts as a "shock absorber" during economic crises, providing employment for workers displaced from formal sector jobs—as it did during the recent economic crisis in Southeast and East Asia.

Informal sector employment is characterized by a high degree of insecurity. In Argentina informal sector workers are twice as likely as formal sector workers to become unemployed (Arango and Maloney 2000). The adverse income and consumption consequences of unemployment are also more severe than in the formal sector, as income support measures for the unemployed are typically lacking in the informal sector. Of particular concern is the lack of statutory social security coverage of informal sector workers in the developing world. Coverage is lowest in Sub-Saharan Africa and South Asia, where just 5–10 percent of the labor force has social security protection (Van Ginneken 1999). Other regions have higher coverage rates but exhibit high intraregional variation, with rates ranging from 10 to 80 percent in Latin America, 10 to 100 percent in Southeast and East Asia, and 50 to 80 percent in Central and Eastern Europe. Coverage is generally on the decline in Sub-Saharan Africa and South Asia, level in Latin America, and on the rise in Southeast and East Asia.

Excluded from programs in which eligibility is conditional on social security contributions, workers in the informal sector are much more vulnerable to the adverse effects of unemployment than formal sector workers. Even small disruptions to their income flows can cause a severe, sometimes permanent deterioration in their economic circumstances. Informal sector workers and their households have been largely left to their own devices, although they may have access to public works.

Implications for Program Choice and Design

The existence of a large informal sector has important implications for both the design and the mix of income support programs. A large informal sector underscores the importance of providing programs that reach workers in the informal sector, particularly as many of these workers are less able to self-protect than formal sector workers. Reinforcing the importance of wide access to income support programs is the fact that the informal sector can be viewed as an "unregulated entrepreneurial sector," which itself generates much unemployment (Arango and Maloney 2000). Given the abundant and diverse employment opportunities in the informal sector, the need for monitoring the continuing eligibility of unemployment benefit recipients (particularly availability for work) is likely to be great.

Prevalence and Pattern of Interhousehold Transfers

In many countries, private transfers make a significant contribution to consumption smoothing. These transfers represent a mechanism of social risk management that should not be overlooked. Cox and Jimenez (1995) show that in 1988, transfers in the Philippines generally flowed from rich to poor households, accounting for 12 percent of overall household income. Urban households in the lowest quintile benefited most, increasing their income by 80 percent as a result of the transfers. Absent these private transfers, income poverty rates would have been one-third higher. The scope and intensity of interhousehold transfers were uneven across regions.

What is the nature of these transfers? How should the existence of private transfers affect the design of public income support programs? Using detailed data on gifts, loans, and asset sales, Fafchamps and Lund (1997) find that transfers among rural Filipino households are triggered by shocks (such as the loss of work or crop failure). According to them, the system is best described as a system of quasicredit, in which mutual insurance is provided by tightly knit networks of friends and relatives through flexible informal loans, combined with pure transfers. Mutual insurance does not appear to take place at the village level: households receive help primarily through networks of friends and relatives. This finding suggests that even the proximity and familiarity provided by living close together may not suffice to provide reliable modes of monitoring and ensure willingness to reciprocate transfers in the future. Loans are taken for consumption purposes. Most borrowers and lenders have exchanged loans before, and many have switched roles in the transaction. Indeed, having provided transfers to other households entitles the provider to call on the support of the borrower once he or she requires support. Few loans require collateral or have a set repayment schedule, and loan contracts are rarely interlinked with other contracts. The majority of informal loans—80 percent—carry no interest charge.

Fafchamps and Lund (1997) reject models of risk-sharing that portray informal lending as an efficient mix of perfectly enforceable credit and insurance contracts: full insurance cannot be rejected for funerals and for the unemployment of household heads or their spouses, but it can be rejected for all other categories of risk, such as those associated with acute or mild sickness. They also find that poor households, whose capacity to reciprocate is limited by their poor human capital endowments, may not receive as much support as they need.

Several studies that examine how private transfers are affected by the presence of social insurance programs find significant crowding out effects. Based on empirical estimates of a private transfers function, Cox and Jimenez (1995) simulate the effects of the introduction of unemployment insurance in the Philippines, assuming a 50 percent replacement rate. Their simulations show that the reduction of private transfers would erode 91 percent of the income received from the public program, yielding very little net gain. Schoeni (2002) finds a much smaller reduction of private transfers for the United States, estimating that 24–40 percent of private transfers are displaced by unemployment benefits. Modest crowding out effects of the public pension scheme have also been established for Peru, where Cox and Jimenez (1992) estimate that without pension benefits private transfers from young to old would be nearly 20 percent higher. It is also worth recalling that Attanasio and Rios-Rull (2000) show that the introduction of unemployment benefits may even be welfare-reducing, because the existence of public insurance program may destroy the social fabric necessary to support private insurance arrangements and thus crowd out private transfers.

Consistent with this argument—and pointing to the cultural differences across countries as determinants of the size of private transfers—Bentolila and Ichino (2000) show that despite low unemployment benefits, the unemployed reduce their consumption less in the Mediterranean countries than in Germany, the United States, or the United Kingdom. In the absence of other compelling explanations, they attribute the difference to higher private transfers in the Mediterranean region.

Implications for Program Choice and Design

Private transfers have diverse and far-reaching implications for program choice and design. First, although they may be sizable, private transfers are vulnerable to covariant risks and offer only limited insurance against income shocks, particularly to the poor. This suggests that there is scope for public income support programs, including those focusing on the unemployed. Second, the size and nature of private transfers, and the likely substitution effects of public insurance programs, have to be considered before such programs are introduced. Simple analyses that do not account for private transfer responses to the expansion or introduction of public income support programs overstate the effectiveness of these programs. Empirical evidence suggests that these responses could consist of sharp cutbacks in private transfers, particularly for programs in which the main beneficiaries are likely to be the nonpoor, whose transfers are more responsive to income shocks. If the introduction of a public program of insurance breaks down the habit of self-help, the overall effect may be welfare-reducing. If, of course, the providers of private transfers are themselves poor, crowding out of private transfers by the public program would be desirable, assuming that financing of the public program is reasonably progressive. Third, regional unevenness in the size of transfers suggests that some regions are more in need of supplementary public programs, such as public works, than others (indeed, the relative size of interhousehold transfers may be taken as one of the indicators of targeting of such programs).

Nonsocial Insurance and Self-Protection

While nonsocial insurance and self-protection mechanisms may provide adequate protection against income shocks for high-income workers, many other workers in developing countries, particularly those employed in the informal sector, remain vulnerable to even small income shocks. Surveys show that during the recent East Asian crisis, the poor in the Philippines had to resort much more frequently than the rich to changing their eating patterns, taking their children out of school, working longer hours, and migrating to urban areas or other countries (table 5.1). Similar were the crisis-induced responses in Indonesia, where households, particularly poor households, reduced the share of consumption on education (box 5.4). The ability of the poor to maintain their consumption in the face of crisis-induced income

Table 5.1.   **Responses to the 1998 East Asian Financial Crisis by Households in the Philippines (percent)**

Income decile	Changing eating pattern	Taking children out of school	Migrating to city or other countries	Receiving assistance from friends or relatives	Receiving assistance from government	Increasing working hours
1 (poorest)	56.7	12.4	7.8	16.5	10.7	37.5
2	52.3	9.3	5.4	17.1	8.8	36.8
3	50.7	7.3	5.4	16.3	8.4	33.6
4	51.0	8.7	5.2	17.0	6.8	33.1
5	47.8	7.1	4.5	17.2	5.9	29.4
6	48.3	5.6	3.8	16.4	5.7	27.0
7	47.0	5.0	3.7	15.0	4.5	26.1
8	44.1	3.5	3.4	12.5	2.9	22.3
9	41.4	3.2	3.1	13.8	3.9	23.1
10 (richest)	33.3	1.2	3.5	12.0	2.6	18.2
Total	47.5	6.4	4.6	15.4	6.1	28.9

Source: Esguerra, Ogawa, and Vodopivec (2001).

shocks is more limited than the ability of the nonpoor (World Bank 2000).[6] Moreover, different types of shocks frequently result in the exhaustion of savings set aside for consumption smoothing and—if they are covariant—in a reduction in the ability of households to provide support to one another.

Even in industrial countries the savings and wealth of the unemployed offer inadequate self-insurance. Gruber (1999) finds that the median worker in the United States who becomes unemployed has sufficient financial assets to replace 75 percent of his or her realized income loss. He finds that the wealth of older and white workers relative to income losses from unemployment is larger and that wealth holdings are much less adequate for minorities and for those with long unemployment spells. But evidence also shows that unemployment benefits crowd out precautionary savings. Engen and Gruber (cited in Gruber 1999) find that a 10 percent increase in the generosity of benefits reduces savings by 2.8 percent. Bird and Hagstrom (1999) find a somewhat smaller elasticity (-0.18) for both unemployment insurance and means-tested benefits.

Workers in the formal sector—at least those higher in the income distribution—have access to consumer credit, and larger companies frequently have private retirement, education, and accident and life insurance plans for their workers. But access to credit and fringe benefits is highly uneven. In the Philippines only 30 percent of the highest-paid workers have access to consumer credit, and they tend to be concentrated in metropolitan

---

Box 5.4.   The 1998 East Asian Crisis: Who Was Affected and How?

After almost three decades of sustained economic growth, Indonesia was severely hit by the East Asian crisis: output in 1998 contracted 13.7 percent, commodity prices sharply increased, and consumption decreased.

Wages took the brunt of the adjustment, with median wages falling 20–30 percent between 1997 and 1998, with even larger declines for men and urban workers. While men's employment remained unchanged, women's employment rose, primarily because more women worked as unpaid family workers. Fewer men, but not women, held secondary jobs in addition to their primary job, and average working hours for both men and women increased. Younger workers had better access to jobs than older workers, and men in rural areas had better access than men in urban areas. Younger, better-educated, and urban residents were also more likely to have moved between 1997 and 1998.

As a result of reduced consumption, poverty in the Philippines rose, with larger households and those headed by younger heads particularly likely to fall into poverty. Households spent relatively more on food and less on education and health care. The share of the household budget spent on education decreased from 3.43 percent in 1997 to 2.93 percent in 1998, with poor households reducing their expenditures on education the most. Fewer children attended school in 1998, and both decreases in enrollment and increases in drop-outs were largest for children from the poorest households (nonattendance among poor children increased from 5 percent to 10 percent).

About 2 percent of the workforce participated in emergency public works, with more than proportional representation of men and rural residents. In rural areas better-off households were significantly less likely to receive assistance from friends and family and only marginally less likely to receive assistance from the government and NGOs. In contrast, in urban areas households received assistance from friends and family regardless of how wealthy they were, but wealthy families were less likely to receive assistance from the government or NGOs.

Source: Beegle, Frankenberg, and Thomas (1999).

Manila and its vicinity; outside of these regions, only about 10–15 percent of workers have access to consumer credit (Esguerra, Ogawa, and Vodopivec 2001). For poor workers in urban areas, pawnshops are a means of generating cash—at very high interest rates.

Among poor workers in rural areas, insurance is less institutionalized. Because rural financial markets are segmented and highly incomplete, in many countries only a minority of small farmers can obtain agricultural loans from banks or other lending institutions, and crop insurance is very limited. Covariance of risk and moral hazard problems make the establishment of credit and insurance programs particularly difficult, as the poor experience of programs in rural areas suggests (Hazell, Pomaseda, and

Valdez 1986). Often farmers resort to costly informal substitutes for precautionary savings, such as distress sales of productive assets and accumulation of excess grain supplies and farm animals (Rosenzweig and Wolpin 1993). According to Rosenzweig and Binswanger (1993), "farmers in riskier environments select portfolios of assets that are less sensitive to rainfall variation and thus less profitable" (p. 58).

Households are much less likely to use costly risk-reducing measures (such as precautionary holding of assets) if they have access to consumption credit or can enter the labor market. Kochar (1995) reports that households in central India use wage income to smooth crop shocks; informal borrowing and private transfer are less important. Specific informal insurance mechanisms have been developed in some countries. In the Philippines small farmers use share-tenancy, which allows tenants to borrow from their landlords using their share in farm produce as collateral. This arrangement reduces the magnitude of the income loss to the farming household if there is crop failure.

In dealing with income shocks, the household, not the individual, is the locus of distress. The response to the shock affects all household members. During the recent East Asian crisis, predominantly male industries (agriculture, manufacturing, construction) in the Philippines were more adversely affected, and male unemployment increased more than female. As a result, secondary income-earners, particularly young people, entered the labor markets, resulting in significant declines in high school enrollment rates. Similar responses took place in Indonesia.

Implications for Program Choice and Design

The ability of low-income workers and farmers to buy insurance in the market, to self-insure, and to self-protect is limited. While the presence of social insurance is likely to reduce their incentives to self-protect (by taking informal jobs, for example) and to self-insure (by saving for precautionary reasons), it also reduces their vulnerability to income shocks. Interestingly, in Brazil unemployment benefits foster self-protection by promoting self-employment (Cunningham 2000). Other ways to improve self-insurance and self-protection include programs that address imperfections in financial and insurance markets (such as replications of Bangladesh's Grameen Bank savings programs) and various types of publicly supported livelihood programs. Such programs not only encourage group savings institutions, they also help participants "graduate" from programs in which they are primarily beneficiaries of grants to programs that allow them to tap the formal financial program. Strengthening the financial sector also promotes self-insurance, by allowing individuals and households to hold more diversified saving portfolios, thereby increasing the attractiveness of precautionary savings. In addition, to discourage counterproductive coping mechanisms, such as taking children out of school and reducing childcare, income support programs can target vulnerable family members of the unemployed (by providing school subsidies, for example).

The Nature of Shocks

The choice of income support program also depends on the nature and frequency of the shock typically faced by a country. Unemployment can be caused by various types of shocks, including macroeconomic volatility, structural and technological shocks, and geography and climate. Sometimes the resulting unemployment is *idiosyncratic*—that is, the probability that an individual becomes unemployed is unrelated to the probability that others will be unemployed. Sometimes it is *covariant*—that is, an individual's probability of becoming unemployed is related to the probability that other people will become unemployed. Covariant risk can affect workers of an enterprise or industry in need of structural adjustment (*meso-risk*), or it can affect an entire economy (*macro-risk*). Moreover, risk can be catastrophic (large and rare) or noncatastrophic (modest and frequent).

Macroeconomic Volatility

Many countries are subject to large swings in economic activity, with recessions resulting in significant reductions in employment and increases in unemployment. Macroeconomic volatility could be produced by trade liberalization and ensuing increase in international competition, and globalization. Capital account liberalization and misalignment of the exchange rate could also increase macroeconomic instability. The recent Asian financial crisis highlighted the problem in a part of the world that once seemed immune to recessions.

Structural and Technological Shocks

Countries can experience radical changes in input and factor prices (OPEC shocks in the 1970s), systemic and political changes (the fall of the socialist system in Soviet Union and Eastern Europe), or technological shocks (the reduction in total factor productivity growth in Western Europe in the past 30 years) that put workers at risk of unemployment. Policymakers need to consider the magnitude, duration, and frequency of such shocks when designing income support programs, as well as the interaction of such programs with the shocks themselves.

Geography and Climate

In some developing countries, geography and climate cause significant employment and income insecurity. The drought caused by the El Niño phenomenon resulted in a strong decline in agricultural production in Southeast Asia. For countries in the monsoon belt, typhoons represent a significant source of job and income insecurity.

Shocks from Civil Strife, Wars, and Social Upheavals

Ethnic, racial, religious, and linguistic differences sometimes result in social fragmentation that can escalate to violent confrontations and wars. These are covariant shocks, affecting regions and nations. The consequences involve destruction of and reduced investment in physical and human capital, disruption of markets, diversion of human resources and public expenditures away from productive activities, and migration of highly skilled workers (World Bank 2001b).

Implications for Program Choice and Design

Not all programs are equally well-suited for all types of unemployment risks. The selection of programs should take into account the prevalence and severity of shocks typically confronted. Individuals tend to self-insure against relatively frequent and modest shocks, but they are often unable to take effective protective measures when shocks are large and rare, particularly if the shocks are covariant. Public programs, which pool resources across larger groups, are needed to deal with these shocks. A menu of programs is generally needed in order to address different types of shocks and the different abilities of individuals to self-insure and self-protect. During recessions, for example, many unemployed workers exhaust their unemployment insurance benefits, and fewer first-time job-seekers find jobs without a period of initial unemployment. Public works and public training programs may be needed. In dealing with meso-risks, special redundancy programs may be needed to promote enterprise restructuring. Unemployment caused by natural disasters is best dealt with through flexible, rapidly deployable programs, such as public works. To deal with the consequences of civil strife and wars, special programs—such as programs to help reintegrate former combatants economically and socially—may be needed.

Cultural and Political Factors

As a result of different social and cultural norms, societies differ in their propensity to resort to informal mechanisms (such as reciprocal gift-giving) to deal with economic hardships. In transition countries, for example, decades of state paternalism have reduced private transfers. As a consequence, the introduction of formal, public income support programs for the unemployed may not have crowded out private transfers on a large scale or displaced existing social networks that would have supported private transfers. In other societies the receipt of state transfers—or participation in public works—may be stigmatizing and redistributive programs opposed. Countries also differ in their susceptibility to corruption.

Income support programs must be attuned to the prevailing social norms and culture and take advantage of existing institutions. Programs that are

Table 5.2. Design and Implementation Criteria of Income Support Programs for the Unemployed

Item	Unemployment insurance	Unemployment assistance	Severance pay	Unemployment insurance savings accounts	Public works
Interactions with labor market institutions and shocks	• Benefits are less likely to raise equilibrium unemployment rate in economy with centralized and coordinated wage bargaining or economy with fully decentralized system. • Due to interaction with shocks, more generous unemployment insurance contributes to stronger or longer lasting impacts on unemployment. • Benefit replacement rate has a stronger impact on equilibrium unemployment rate when payroll taxes are higher.	Similar to unemployment insurance.	Due to interaction with shocks, more protective employment legislation contributes to the persistence of unemployment.		

(continued)

147

Table 5.2. (continued)

Item	Unemployment insurance	Unemployment assistance	Severance pay	Unemployment insurance savings accounts	Public works
Administrative capacity for program implementation	• Extensive and sophisticated informational requirements are needed to monitor continuing eligibility. • Cross-linking of administrative databases helps identify ineligible benefit recipients.	Similar to unemployment insurance. Additional capacity needed for means-testing.	• Informational demands for administering the benefit are modest. • May impose a burden on the legal system to resolve disputes about the cause of separation.	Informational demands similar to those for pension systems.	Informational and organizational requirements less demanding than those for other programs.
Characteristics of unemployment	• More appropriate if unemployment spells are less frequent and longer. • If underemployment is significant, moral hazard problems may be pronounced.	Similar to unemployment insurance.		More appropriate if unemployment spells are more frequent and shorter	• More suitable if unemployment has strong seasonal component. • Potential to serve the underemployed.

Size of the informal sector	Abundant informal sector employment opportunities increase costs of monitoring continuing eligibility of benefit recipients.	Similar to unemployment insurance, but monitoring also includes activities of household members.		Potential to serve informal sector workers.	Potential to serve informal sector workers—many unemployed come from informal sector and are ineligible for contribution-based public programs.
Interhousehold transfers	Crowding out likely (reduction of private transfers may be welfare-reducing).	Crowding out somewhat less likely than under unemployment insurance, because transfers to poor offer more limited insurance.	Crowding out likely.	Crowding out likely.	Regional unevenness of size of transfers suggests that some regions are more in need of supplementary public programs, such as public works, than others.

(continued)

Table 5.2. (*continued*)

Item	Unemployment insurance	Unemployment assistance	Severance pay	Unemployment insurance savings accounts	Public works
Nonmarket insurance and self-protection	• Benefits are likely to reduce incentives to self-protect (by taking informal job, for example) and to self-insure (to save for precautionary reasons, for example). • Unemployment insurance fosters self-employment in Brazil (Cunningham 2000).	Similar to unemployment insurance.	Some evidence that severance pay fosters self-employment.		Particularly valuable to the poor in rural areas, who are especially vulnerable and not eligible for public programs requiring contributions.
Existence of shocks	Suitable if country is prone to sectoral or regional shocks rather than large, aggregate shocks.	Similar to unemployment insurance.		Suitable if shocks are modest and frequent.	Suitable in countries with frequent natural disasters.
Cultural and political factors	Less appropriate in country prone to corruption and political risk.	• Some societies may stigmatize beneficiaries. • Less appropriate in country prone to corruption and political risk.	Less vulnerable to political risk than most other programs.	• Less vulnerable to political risk than most other programs. • Existing programs and institutions can be upgraded.	Tradition of collective support in rural communities benefits the program.

Source: World Bank staff.

more prone to political risk must be avoided in countries with more corrupt governments. Targeting income support to the poor through public works can benefit from presenting the program as rooted in a tradition of rural communities' collective support.

Concluding Remarks

Country-specific features must be considered when introducing or improving public income support programs. If they are not, countries may adopt solutions that work well in other countries without examining the prerequisites needed and the conditions conducive to their successful functioning— and without anticipating the likely consequences when such prerequisites and conditions are missing.

One size does not fit all, for several reasons. First, labor markets and institutions in developing and transition countries may be very different from those in industrial countries, where most income support programs have been tested. Second, the desirability of alternative income support programs depends crucially on the interactions of these programs with other social risk management mechanisms, which may be very different in developing and transition countries. Third, developing countries and transition economies may lack the capacity to administer income support programs effectively.

Table 5.2 summarizes the key country-specific features that determine the appropriateness of different income support programs for the unemployed. In the next chapter, these considerations are used to provide guidelines for choosing appropriate programs.

Notes

1. Interestingly, Elmeskov, Martin, and Scarpetta (1998) do not find empirical support for the hypothesis that the combination of restrictive employment protection legislation and generous benefits leads to particularly high unemployment.

2. According to Klassen and Woolard (2001), the absence of unemployment benefits in South Africa affects household formation and residential choices in ways that are detrimental to job finding. The program forces the unemployed to base their location decisions on the availability of economic support, which is generally available in rural areas, often from parents, rather than on the availability of job openings. Klassen and Woolard conclude that the absence of unemployment benefits may not only lower welfare of the unemployed and their dependents, it may also fail to reduce—or actually increase—the duration of unemployment.

3. The informal sector is defined in various ways. For statistical purposes, informal economic activities are generally defined on the basis of their legal organization (unincorporated enterprises). Household and labor force surveys often define the informal sector based on the size of the enterprise, with firms with fewer than six workers, for example, considered informal. For a discussion of definitions, see ILO (2000).

4. The estimates in table 3.6 are in a similar range. Note that they refer to the share of informal employment in capital cities.

5. It has been argued that job creation in the formal sector is inhibited partly by the high costs of social security contributions, which makes the informal sector more attractive.

6. The findings of de Ferranti and others (2000) deviate somewhat from these results. They find that the poor are affected more than the rich when the shocks are large but less when the shocks are small. They also report that in Latin America school enrollment is insensitive to aggregate economic fluctuation.

6

Improving Income Support Programs for the Unemployed in Developing Countries

This chapter provides guidelines for developing and transition countries for choosing and designing income support programs for the unemployed. The guidelines are based on two sets of criteria: performance criteria and design and implementation criteria. Drawing on findings from previous chapters, the guidelines identify the strengths, weaknesses, and country-specific circumstances that are conducive to good performance of alternative income support programs. The chapter also examines some important design features of unemployment insurance and presents options for improving income support for informal sector workers. It concludes by presenting some general principles for improving income support for the unemployed.

Choosing the Right Program

Under what circumstances is it desirable to introduce unemployment insurance or some other income support program for unemployed workers? What factors do policymakers need to consider in choosing a program?

When Does Unemployment Insurance Work Well?

The evaluation of the unemployment insurance system in chapter 4 suggests that the program has three key strengths:

- Thanks to the pooling of resources across a wide base, it provides good protection by enabling a high degree of consumption smoothing for all categories of covered workers.
- It performs well under idiosyncratic, sectoral, and regional shocks.
- By automatically injecting additional resources—and reducing taxes—during recessions, it acts as an automatic stabilizer, moderating the magnitude of the downturn.[1]

The program also has important weaknesses:

- It creates reemployment disincentives and wage pressures, which increase the equilibrium unemployment rate of the economy.
- By interacting with adverse shocks, it contributes to the persistence of unemployment.
- Because the program is nontransparent, it may create large unfunded liabilities and be susceptible to political risk.
- It protects only formal sector workers.

A host of country-specific considerations related to both institutional and labor market features determine how well unemployment insurance works in a particular setting (see chapter 5). These conditions include the following:

- Strong administrative capacity to monitor initial and particularly continuing eligibility. The stricter the monitoring of the behavior of the recipients, the weaker the disincentives unemployment insurance creates.
- Modest size of the informal sector. The larger the informal sector, the more abundant the opportunities for undeclared paid work and the higher the costs of monitoring.
- An environment that is not conducive to political risk.
- A decentralized or encompassing wage-bargaining structure. Unemployment insurance in conjunction with fragmented and uncoordinated collective bargaining is likely to generate strong pressures on wages. A decentralized and encompassing wage-bargaining structure moderates wages.
- Low total tax wedge. The higher the total tax wedge, the greater the impact of benefits on the equilibrium unemployment rate.
- Low share of underemployed workers. The existence of benefits may attract the underemployed into insured unemployment, reducing their incentives for self-protection.
- Low incidence of private transfers. If the introduction of public insurance breaks down the custom of self-help among local communities, replacing private transfers by social insurance may be welfare-reducing.

Absent these conditions, unemployment insurance does not perform well, increasing inefficiencies, reducing welfare gains, or both. For example, reemployment incentives depend crucially on a country's monitoring capacity. This capacity determines how strictly the conditions of initial and, perhaps even more important, continuing eligibility are imposed. As the experience with Argentinean unemployment insurance suggests (see box 5.3), the capacity to screen initial eligibility has not been a problem—the program draws on the capacity of other social protection programs—but the country still has to monitor continuing eligibility. Effective monitoring and the use of sanctions can make a difference—by strongly reducing the average duration of unemployment benefit payments and increasing transition rates to employment. Deficient monitoring thus not only creates leakages, adding to overall costs (and possibly indirectly affecting unemployment), it also undermines the legitimacy of the program, as the program de facto ignores its own rules.

How do such problems affect the decision to introduce unemployment insurance? Prompted by increased exposure to foreign markets and fearing future international crises, some developing countries (the Philippines and Thailand, among them) are contemplating introducing unemployment insurance. Yoo (2001) argues against introducing unemployment insurance in the short term in the Philippines (box 6.1). Gill and Ilahi (2000) note that many Latin American countries lack the capacity to run an efficient unemployment insurance program. They argue that although introducing unemployment insurance should be a long-term goal of these countries, doing so in the medium term is either infeasible or too costly. They propose that Latin American governments augment other instruments, such as self-insurance, to overcome the lack of market insurance in the medium term.

Sometimes historical or political conditions speak in favor of introducing unemployment insurance. If providing unemployment insurance is the only politically acceptable way to reform badly performing institutions, doing so may be worthwhile even though other considerations suggest that introduction is premature—provided, of course, that the program is attuned to local circumstances. Sri Lanka is facing just such a dilemma: political consensus was reached that reform of its nontransparent, discretionary, and extremely

---

Box 6.1.   Should the Philippines Introduce Unemployment Insurance?

Introducing unemployment insurance may not always be appropriate, as Yoo (2001) argues in the case of the Philippines. He recommends against introducing the program immediately, because of the lack of consensus by social partners (trade unions, employer associations, and government) that unemployment insurance is a top policy priority; concerns on the part of employers and workers about its affordability; and concerns about the financial stability of a program, given the low level of industrialization and per capita income. Yoo proposes introducing unemployment insurance in the medium term—comprehensive insurance that would also provide some active measures, as it does in the Republic of Korea. He recommends that in the short term the Philippines develop social assistance programs for the poor, create the conditions for sound and continuous growth, begin a national dialogue among social partners to determine the best unemployment program for the future, and build capacity in employment and training systems and in record-keeping and fee collection within the social security administration.

Source: Yoo (2001).

costly severance pay program could be implemented only if unemployment insurance were introduced. Under these circumstances, introducing unemployment insurance may make sense if the reform indeed leads to substantially more flexible employment protection legislation, including severance pay, and the design of the unemployment program is adapted to Sri Lanka's realities (particularly the lack of administrative capacity and the abundant opportunities to work in the informal sector). To minimize adverse effects and to ensure affordability and a smooth start, the program would have to be introduced on a small scale (only in enterprises with more than 15 workers, for example) and provide modest benefits. The needed support infrastructure would have to be put in place before the program starts, and the design of the program would have to take advantage of new, innovative solutions that help reduce labor market disincentives. On the other hand, introducing an unemployment insurance program is not justified if it is costly, financed by the government, not tailored to Sri Lanka, and leaves the existing severance pay essentially intact. Such a program would add another protection program to the already privileged group of formal sector workers and could worsen labor market performance, thus failing to produce desirable equity and efficiency gains.

What are the likely welfare and efficiency implications of introducing unemployment insurance (box 6.2)? Many workers would benefit, but in

---

Box 6.2.   Benefits and Costs of Introducing Unemployment Insurance

Unemployment insurance increases welfare by smoothing consumption patterns. Bird (1995) estimates that individuals in Germany and the United States are willing to pay 5–9 percent of their disposable income for insurance that would smooth their incomes.

These positive, direct effects on welfare have to be qualified in several ways. First, because the program is limited to the formal sector, the beneficiaries are limited to a subset of workers who, by and large, belong to better-off segments of the population. Indeed, the likely effect of unemployment insurance on the reduction of income inequality is small. Second, unemployment insurance may not reduce poverty, as the likely beneficiaries—particularly in low-income countries—are concentrated in the nonpoor segments of the population. Third, public programs displace some private transfers, thus reducing the net effect of benefits on individuals' welfare.

The welfare benefits of introducing unemployment insurance have to be weighed against the likely efficiency costs, including disincentives for leaving unemployment, higher equilibrium unemployment, and more persistent unemployment. These efficiency effects also have negative distributive consequences. Any increase in unemployment due to the introduction of unemployment insurance would most likely affect the worse-off workers in the society—marginal workers in the formal sector (young workers, workers on fixed-term contracts) and informal sector workers, hindering their access to formal sector jobs.

low-income countries the likely beneficiaries tend to be concentrated among already better-off segments of the population. Introducing unemployment insurance would likely cause efficiency losses and negative distributive consequences.

How suitable is unemployment insurance, then, for developing countries? Weak administrative capacity (even in upper middle-income countries, like Argentina) means that the program may not perform well from an efficiency viewpoint, particularly if weak administration is coupled with unfavorable labor market conditions (such as a high tax wedge and a wage mechanism that is not conducive to containing pressures). A large informal sector is likely to produce negative efficiency and distribution effects. High political risk—common in developing countries—means that unemployment insurance is likely to be susceptible to political economy pressures. In developing countries—particularly low-income countries in which large shares of workers are underemployed or work in the informal sector and there is no general program of social assistance—it is hard to justify the expenditure of public funds on unemployment insurance program, the benefits of which go to those who work in the formal sector. Unemployment benefits in these countries should be financed by employers, by workers, or both; they should not be subsidized by the government. The case for introducing unemployment insurance in developing countries is thus less compelling than it is in industrial countries.

Transition economies, which have stronger administrative capacity than most developing countries, a smaller informal sector, and lower private transfers, were right to introduce unemployment insurance. But some of these countries could benefit from tailoring their programs to their circumstances. Introducing a flat-rate benefit—which would have improved incentives, made benefits more progressive, reduced fiscal costs, and simplified administration—may have been more appropriate in some of these countries, particularly the low-income ones.

Unemployment Assistance: How Attractive Is Means-Tested Targeting?

Unlike unemployment insurance, which grants benefit to all workers with sufficient employment histories and paid contributions, unemployment assistance screens potential benefit recipients with a means test. Does this targeting of benefits improve incentives and produce savings?

Eliminating potential claimants by means-testing would seem bound to produce savings. But the experience of Australia and New Zealand—two of the few countries with self-standing unemployment assistance programs—does not provide evidence that it does. Measured by the average cost of unemployment benefits per percentage point of unemployment, the costs in both countries exceed the comparable costs of unemployment insurance programs in 12 OECD countries (see Vroman 2002) (box 6.3). Australia's unemployment assistance program failed to produce savings, but it undoubtedly reaches all those whose income is below some stipulated income

---

Box 6.3.   The High Cost of Australia's Unemployment Assistance Program

Because unemployment assistance is a means-tested program, one would expect its expenditures to be lower than expenditures under unemployment insurance. But Australia's unemployment assistance program has proved more expensive. Measured as the percentage of unemployment benefits in total wages divided by the unemployment rate, the average cost of unemployment insurance in 12 OECD countries was 0.25 in 1992 (ranging from 0.032 in Greece to 0.697 in Sweden); the average cost of Australia's unemployment assistance program in the 1990s was about 0.28.

Why are the costs under the Australian program so high? First, the basic income guarantee (25 percent of the average wage) is high, producing replacement rates of 60–90 percent. Because income guarantee is so high, the majority of the unemployed qualify for benefits, despite the income test. In fact, since 1995 the number of recipients has exceeded the number of unemployed. Second, employed workers are eligible for unemployment assistance, and about 20 percent of claimants are employed. Third, Australia's high marginal tax rates create labor supply incentive problems.

Administrative costs under unemployment assistance are higher than under unemployment insurance (these costs were not included in the calculation of costs above). Additional costs are associated with the costs of monitoring income, for both initial and continuing eligibility. These costs typically exceed the costs of initial eligibility determination under unemployment insurance, which are incurred once per claim. The costs of monitoring availability for work and job search are similar in the two programs.

Source: Vroman (2002).

---

guarantee and smoothes consumption. The program is also very progressive: roughly 60 percent of cash benefits are paid to those in the bottom three deciles of the income distribution.[2]

Estonia and Hong Kong (China) show that unemployment assistance can indeed be provided at low cost. The generosity of unemployment assistance programs in these countries (in terms of costs per percentage point of unemployment) is significantly lower than the average generosity of benefit programs in OECD countries (Vroman 2002).

Several factors need to be considered before adopting an income- or means-testing program (Atkinson 1995b). First, administrative costs associated with identifying and monitoring the eligibility of individuals or households can be high (see chapter 5). Second, eligible recipients do not always take advantage of programs that involve income- or means-testing. According to Atkinson, in OECD countries at least a third of potential claimants never receive benefits (because of information problems, administrative complexities, and stigmatization of recipients). Third, programs that condition benefits on low current income create incentive problems.

In summary, the major advantages of unemployment assistance are the potential to provide benefits to informal sector workers and to workers with little work experience and the ability to target beneficiaries more effectively (table 6.1). However, relative to unemployment insurance, unemployment assistance does not necessarily generate savings, it provides less protection for high-income workers, it imposes higher administrative costs, it reduces the labor supply of family members, and it may stigmatize recipients. In addition, it suffers from some of the same weaknesses as unemployment insurance, by creating reemployment disincentives, increasing the equilibrium unemployment rate, and contributing to the persistence of unemployment.

What are the implications for the use of unemployment assistance in developing and transition countries? First, in most developing countries, the fact that eligibility does not require prior contributions renders these programs nonviable. With large segments of the labor force underemployed or unemployed, providing an income support program that fails to exclude people who have not made contributions would be fiscally unsustainable. Unemployment assistance programs in developing countries would therefore have to condition benefit eligibility on the prior payment of contributions. Second, the administrative constraints typically faced by low-income countries mean that few, if any, would be able to carry out the required level of monitoring. Third, because of abundant employment opportunities in the informal sector, the problem of employment disincentives for other members of the household would be more severe than in industrial countries. Ineffective monitoring would produce large leakages; effective monitoring would impose large administrative costs and force workers to forgo significant earnings. Unemployment assistance thus seems appropriate only in countries with relatively developed administrative capacity and small informal sectors and in which tight budgetary constraints are in place, perhaps as a transition program to unemployment insurance. Transition economies could be candidates.

Unemployment Insurance Savings Accounts: How Much Insurance Can They Provide?

Several new approaches have been developed in an effort to avoid the adverse incentives created by traditional income support programs. The most radical is unemployment insurance savings accounts (UISAs). These accounts have several key strengths:

- By internalizing the costs of unemployment benefits, UISAs eliminate the moral hazard inherent in traditional unemployment insurance and encourage individuals to make efficient choices about their labor market activity.[3] This may be the most important advantage of the program.
- Because UISAs are payable in cases of voluntary separations, they encourage labor reallocation and cut down on the litigation costs incurred under severance pay.

Table 6.1. Summary of Factors Affecting Choice of Income Support Systems for the Unemployed

Support system	Strengths	Weaknesses	Key country-specific features conducive to introduction and successful performance
Unemployment insurance	• Provides good protection (wide pooling) • Performs well under idiosyncratic, sectoral, and regional shocks • Acts as automatic stabilizer, moderating severity of contractions	• Creates reemployment disincentives • Increases equilibrium unemployment rate • Contributes to persistence of unemployment • Susceptible to political risk • Does not cover informal sector workers	• Strong administrative capacity to establish initial and monitor continuing eligibility • Modest informal sector (lower costs of monitoring) • Low political risk • Decentralized or encompassing wage bargaining structure—wage-moderation effects • Low total tax wedge • Small share of underemployed workers • Low incidence of private transfers (unemployment insurance may be welfare-reducing if it breaks down social fabric that maintains private transfers)
Unemployment assistance	• Similar to strengths of unemployment insurance • Allows workers with little prior work experience and informal sector workers to participate • More progressive than unemployment insurance	• Failure to exclude people without prior work experience (and hence without payments of program contributions) may undermine program's fiscal sustainability • Offers less protection for high-income workers than unemployment insurance • Imposes higher administrative costs than unemployment insurance • Reduces labor supply of family members • May stigmatize participants	• Similar to unemployment insurance • Additional capacity needed for means-testing

| Unemployment insurance savings accounts (UISAs) | • Improves work incentives
• Provides good protection if combined with public insurance
• Potential to attract informal sector workers
• Encourages labor reallocation and reduces litigation costs
• Low political risk
• Largely unexplored and insufficiently tested | • Pure UISA version allows for only intertemporal risk pooling of individual (no cross-section pooling)
• Allowing individuals to borrow from UISA creates incentives to withdraw from formal sector and find a job in informal one, thereby avoiding repayment of debt, and reduces gains in terms of reemployment incentives.
• Requires well-functioning financial sector
• Higher administrative costs than under unemployment insurance | • For pure UISA version, modest, nonpersistent shocks. If different shocks are present, combination of UISA and public insurance particularly desirable
• Self-policing (of reemployment incentives) imposed by UISA is a greater advantage in countries with weak monitoring capacity
• Existing mandatory forced-savings type of schemes for employed workers in developing countries facilitate introduction of UISAs
• Introduction of personal accounts reduces nonpayments of social security contributions by employers
• Reasonably developed financial sector
• Nonperformance mitigated by presence of guarantee fund
• Possible reforms include streamlining severance pay systems, converting them to funded systems and linking them to unemployment benefit or pension reforms |
| Severance pay | • Minimizes disincentives for subsequent job search
• Requires simple administration
• Offers risk-pooling at level of firm | • Provides weak income protection because of nonperformance, inefficient protection (benefits are paid regardless of unemployment duration), reduced job access by marginal groups, lack of coverage of informal sector workers
• Creates inefficiencies by reducing employment rates, reducing labor market dynamics, and creating significant litigation costs | |

(continued)

Table 6.1. *(continued)*

Support system	Strengths	Weaknesses	Key country-specific features conducive to introduction and successful performance
Public works	• Effective in reaching the poor • Good targeting properties • Substantial capacity to redistribute income from rich to poor • Potential to attract informal sector workers • Allows flexible and fast response • Administratively less demanding than other schemes	• High nonwage costs reduce the effectiveness of public works in reaching the poor • May stigmatize participants • Difficult to raise funding during crises • Program's redistributive character makes it difficult to gain political support, so some leakage to nonpoor may be necessary • Possible problems with maintenance of infrastructure built through public works	• Attracts informal sector workers and those with low forgone earnings • Useful when undeveloped insurance and financial markets prevent market insurance, self-insurance, and self-protection • Appropriate for dealing with geographic and climatic shocks, as well as mono-crop areas vulnerable to cyclical and structural shocks • Requires less complex administration and can be quickly set up in areas affected by various shocks • Can benefit from traditions and values that emphasize cooperation and collective support

Source: Derived from chapters 4 and 5.

- Relative to unemployment insurance, UISAs reduce political risk.
- If backed by government subsidies, UISAs have the potential to attract informal sector workers.

A UISA program also has several shortcomings:

- By its very design, the program—in its pure form—does not pool risk among individuals. It may therefore offer less protection than programs that do so explicitly (such as unemployment insurance) or implicitly (such as programs financed from general tax revenues). Young workers may not be able to accumulate enough savings at the time of separation to be able to self-finance their unemployment. This lack of risk-pooling is the program's most serious shortcoming.
- The UISA-cum-borrowing version (in which individuals can borrow from their UISAs) may suffer from a moral hazard problem by creating incentives for workers to withdraw from the formal sector and find jobs in the informal sector in order to avoiding repaying the debt.
- The program may impose large administrative costs, and its administration requires a relatively well-functioning financial sector.

Under certain circumstances, the absence of pooling across individuals may not be critical. When shocks are modest and frequent, self-insurance through savings may provide adequate consumption-smoothing (Ehrlic and Becker 1972). To better address large and persistent shocks, some UISA proposals combine individual accounts with public insurance (Feldstein and Altman 1998; Guasch 1999). Under the proposal of Feldstein and Altman, unemployed workers can draw benefits monthly, as under traditional unemployment insurance; the government lends money to accounts in which the balance falls below zero. The consumption-smoothing properties of such a program would be no worse than under traditional unemployment insurance, because individuals with negative balances would still receive benefits, as rules of withdrawal would be the same as under unemployment insurance. But the UISA program would reduce labor market disincentives for workers who end their working careers with positive UISA balances. This version of the program reduces the gains in terms of reemployment incentives but increases its insurance function.

A similar approach—combining self-insurance and social insurance—is applied in the new unemployment insurance program Chile introduced at the end of 2002. Employers and workers pay contributions into individual savings accounts, and employers and the government pay contributions into a solidarity fund. The unemployed first draw benefits from their individual accounts; if they qualify, upon depletion of these funds they withdraw from the solidarity fund (box 6.4). (Guasch proposed introducing solidarity funding in 1999.)

What is the rationale for public intervention under the UISA program? The pure UISA program is just a form of self-insurance: it supports consumption during spells of unemployment by drawing on the savings an individual

---

Box 6.4.   Combining Self-Insurance and Social Insurance: Chile's New Unemployment Benefit Program

In 2002 Chile introduced an innovative new unemployment insurance program that combines social insurance with self-insurance. Unemployment contributions are split between individual accounts and a common solidarity account, which is partly financed by the government. Both workers and employers pay contributions. By doing so, employers reduce their severance payments obligations. The new unemployment insurance program is thus partly replacing severance pay. The program is effectively a funded program, with funds of individual accounts managed by a freestanding administrator selected through competitive tender.

To stimulate reemployment, the program requires that benefit recipients first draw from their own accounts; upon depletion, they can draw from the solidarity fund. Withdrawals from individual accounts are triggered by separation from the employer, regardless of the reason. Withdrawals from the common fund are triggered once individual accounts are depleted, if the claimant satisfies the usual conditions of continuing eligibility under unemployment insurance (not working, being available, searching for job) but are limited to two withdrawals every five years. Benefits are linked to past earnings, with a declining schedule.

Source: Acevedo and Eskenazi (2003).

---

generated while working. The UISA in this case is nothing but a forced-savings mechanism. While the program is likely to create few inefficiencies, it offers income protection only under very restrictive conditions (short expected durations of unemployment), and it fails to protect some groups of workers (such as workers at the beginning of their working careers, whose savings accounts accumulations are likely to be low).[4] The pure UISA program thus cannot be advocated on the basis of correcting market failures. It can, perhaps, be advocated to correct "government failures." For example, a case could be made for such a program if it were the only politically palatable way to reform a badly performing public income support program or if the government could not commit itself not to bail out unprofitable firms in order to avoid politically unacceptable increases of unemployment (such bail-outs have occurred often in Latin America). The pure UISA program may be preferable to traditional unemployment insurance if traditional unemployment insurance creates severe inefficiencies, particularly if the risk of unemployment is frequent and moderate.

The rationale for public intervention under the UISA-cum-borrowing is twofold. First, the program helps smooth consumption by providing access to credit. It thus corrects for capital market imperfections that prevent borrowing against future earnings—a problem faced in particular by developing countries. Second, this version—and the UISA-cum-solidarity-fund version—combines self-insurance with social insurance (because the debt of workers who end their working lives with negative balances has to be financed through solidarity). The rationale for public intervention is thus widened to all considerations that underlie the public provision of unemployment insurance.

The UISA-cum-borrowing version thus potentially offers several advantages. First, it addresses capital market imperfections. Second, it enables widespread risk-pooling and offers other advantages of publicly provided unemployment insurance (for example, public agencies can monitor benefit eligibility better than private agents). Third, it addresses the moral hazard problem inherent in unemployment insurance by introducing self-policing. The UISA-cum-borrowing version therefore compares well with other programs. Relative to traditional unemployment insurance, this program can improve incentives. If individual accounts foster self-insurance, moral hazard will be lower than in traditional unemployment insurance. Relative to the pure UISA system or prefunded severance pay system, it improves income protection, because it allows widespread risk-pooling. And it improves access to credit, because it allows the option of borrowing from the UISA accounts. Simulations by Hopenhayn and Hatchondo (2002) show that when the parameters are selected appropriately, the UISA-cum-borrowing indeed comes very close to the welfare properties of the optimal unemployment insurance program.

The efficiency properties of the UISA-cum-borrowing program can be improved by combining several risks under one program. Orszag and others (1999) and Yun (2001) propose an integrated unemployment insurance program that combines unemployment insurance not only with the pension program but also with other programs, such as health, disability, and life insurance. Such a program would integrate intertemporal pooling of various risks of the individual with cross-sectional pooling. By doing so, it could be expected both to provide better insurance and to significantly reduce disincentives relative to traditional unemployment insurance (box 6.5).

Some design and implementation considerations speak in favor of introducing a UISA program in middle- and upper-middle-income developing and transition countries:

- Weak monitoring capacity in these countries exacerbates the moral hazard problem inherent in traditional unemployment insurance and encourages other misuses of the program. Hence the self-policing nature of the UISA program represents a greater advantage.
- Converting the various income support programs already in place in developing countries into UISA–type programs could greatly facilitate its introduction. The Philippines has several mandatory forced-savings schemes that could, together with severance pay, be merged and transformed into a UISA program (Esguerra, Ogawa, and Vocopivec 2001).

Box 6.5.   Advantages of the Integrated Unemployment Insurance Program

Recent proposals to improve the welfare and efficiency effects of income support programs for the unemployed include the Integrated Unemployment Insurance Program. Under this program, unemployment insurance is provided by integrating unemployment insurance with the pension program. Benefits are financed through a combination of withdrawals from individual savings accounts—in which workers accumulate their contributions for unemployment and for old-age pensions—and, under certain circumstances, from a public unemployment insurance fund (which operates on a pay-as-you-go basis). By combining intertemporal pooling of risk of an individual with pooling under the traditional unemployment insurance program, this program combines self-insurance through savings and public insurance. In addition, by pooling the self-insurance components and thus combining several risks under one program, the integrated program reduces the amount of savings needed to provide a given level of insurance under separate programs. (Indeed, there are also proposals to include other social insurance programs, such as disability and health care, under the same roof. Under certain conditions, these proposals can be welfare-improving [Orszag and others 1999].)

The integrated program is expected to provide better insurance (and thus consumption smoothing) and to significantly reduce disincentives relative to traditional unemployment insurance. To improve the distributive properties of the program, the government could subsidize low-wage workers. Because of the direct link between contributions and benefits, the program has the potential to attract informal sector workers. While details of the program still need to be determined, theoretical modeling suggests that the more risk averse the individual and the lower the job-search elasticity (that is, the less sensitive is the reemployment probability to job search), the higher the level of optimal borrowing from the public part of the program (Yun 2001).

Source: Orszag and others (1999); Yun (2001).

- Employers in developing countries sometimes fail to pay program contributions under traditional unemployment insurance. Introducing personal accounts allows workers to monitor such payments themselves, making UISAs less susceptible to political risk.
- The administrative demands of UISAs are not great. Old-age insurance programs introduced in many Latin American countries require similar information systems.[5]

UISAs may create adverse incentive problems of their own, however, which may be difficult to deal with. First, the program may produce excessive turnover, by encouraging workers to choose to become unemployed in order to "get their money back"—a problem that has plagued the Brazilian Fundo de Garantia do Tempo de Servico program because of the low return yielded by the program funds. Setting administrative limits on when workers can access funds may help, but doing so would limit labor mobility. Second, a UISA-cum-borrowing program may create incentives to "dive and run," that is, borrow and then withdraw from the formal sector and find a job in the informal sector, thereby avoiding repayment of the debt upon reemployment in the formal sector. Conceivably, one could use pension contributions as "collateral" in an integrated UISA–pensions program. But integration assumes that workers have very long time horizons, which may not be the case. (Indeed, if workers had long horizons, they would save for themselves and there would be no need for a forced-savings mechanisms such as the pure UISA program.)

In sum, the UISA program with solidarity funding—and its variant, an integrated unemployment insurance program—may be promising options, particularly in East Asia and Latin America, where the existence of severance pay programs may ease the transition to an UISA program. There is a need, however, for further investigation—and piloting—of the program. Too little is known about the working of the UISA program to know for which groups of workers and under what conditions the program works best and yields positive results. Design parameters of the program (contribution rates and rules for withdrawal, for example) also need to be examined.

Severance Pay Programs: Can They Be Reformed to Improve Protection and Reduce Distortions?

Severance pay is often considered one of the least appropriate means of providing income protection: it not only provides inadequate and incomplete protection, it also distorts the behavior of firms and workers and imposes other efficiency costs. Yet except in low-income countries, severance pay is the most prevalent income support program in developing countries. The question of how best to reform existing severance pay programs is therefore an important one.

Severance pay has three key strengths:

- Because the amount of severance pay is not contingent on the duration of subsequent unemployment, the program minimizes disincentives for subsequent job search.
- The program is easy to administer.
- It offers risk-pooling at the level of the firm.

Severance pay also suffers from several weaknesses both on income protection and efficiency front.

Income protection

- It suffers from nonperformance (many workers do not receive the severance pay to which they are entitled), with the problem related to limited risk-pooling and the nonfunded nature of severance pay.

- The same amount of severance pay is paid regardless of the duration of the unemployment spell.
- Coverage is limited to formal sector workers only.

Efficiency

- It reduces labor market flows and employment rates.
- It pushes workers into informal sector and limits job accessibility for disadvantaged groups.
- It creates significant litigation costs.

In light of these shortcomings, it is not surprising that several countries (including industrial ones) have started to reform their severance pay programs. Reforms include streamlining severance pay programs as well as converting them to funded programs and linking them to unemployment benefit or pension reforms.

STREAMLINING CURRENT SEVERANCE PAY PROGRAMS. Severance pay programs may elicit undesirable responses from firms and workers, impose large monetary and other costs, and be poorly synchronized with other income protection programs. To streamline their severance pay programs, some countries could simplify program rules. Latin American countries might reconsider forcing employers to make additional payments for "dismissals without cause" (which almost invariably include economic dismissals). Doing so would not only reduce the costs of the program, it would also reduce the costs of litigation. To reduce uncertainty about firms' ability to lay off workers, the lack of transparency and the discretionary nature of severance pay programs in some countries should be removed (box 6.6). Moreover, countries with both social insurance and severance pay programs could save on costs without reducing insurance by better coordinating payments under the two programs. Unemployment insurance eligibility rules could be adjusted so that insurance benefits would start only after severance benefits "expire," that is, after n months if the individual received n months' wages as severance payment (such a program is in place in some industrial countries, such as Canada). To address the nonperformance of the program, some countries could consider introducing public guarantee funds, thereby creating pooling at the above-firm level.

PREFUNDING SEVERANCE PAY PROGRAMS. A more radical reform is converting severance pay into a funded program. Such a reform converts conditional obligations to laid-off workers under traditional severance pay into unconditional obligations to all workers paid regularly to their individual accounts. The reform addresses the nonperformance problem and seeks to reduce some of the inefficiencies severance pay creates (by removing obstacles to labor market flows and reducing litigation costs). Converting severance pay into a funded program creates a kind of savings accounts. Austria introduced prefunding in 2003, converting its severance

---

Box 6.6. Costs of Sri Lanka's Severance Pay Program

Sri Lanka's severance pay program is one of the most expensive in the world. It provides extremely high compensation to laid-off workers and imposes correspondingly high costs on employers. In addition, its discretionary nature and lack of transparency impose additional costs by creating uncertainty about the ability to lay off workers (the government has the authority to reject employer's demands) and requiring lengthy procedures.

The Termination of Employment of Workman Act (TEWA) of 1971 requires employers with more than 15 workers to inform the Commissioner of Labor about their intended layoffs and to obtain the commissioner's authorization (for each individual case, not only for mass layoffs). The act requires that the request be examined and a response provided in three months, but it does not determine the compensation to be provided for the laid-off workers. In addition, a separate severance payment, called a *gratuity*, paid by employers with more than 15 workers, is paid to all of their workers upon termination of their employment, provided that they have more than five years' services with the employer. Gratuity payment amounts to one month's salary for every two years of service.

The level of compensation under TEWA has been as high as 6 months' wages per year of service; the average was 1.6 months' wages per year of service in 2000 and 3.1 months' wages in 2001 (ILO 2003). Pay-outs to laid-off workers have been large, with the maximum amounting to 36–50 monthly wages (ILO 2003). The time needed to process requests has been unpredictable, taking six months on average, sometimes much more. What is more, the procedure has usually involved hearings, in which employers describe their financial performance and business plans to government bureaucrats to justify the layoffs.

Source: Discussions with Sri Lankan officials by the World Bank mission team, May 2003.

---

pay to a fully funded, contributory program that pays unemployment and retirement benefits (box 6.7). The program allows withdrawals only after a three-year vesting period, which may hinder worker mobility.

Colombia introduced prefunding in 1990. Kugler (1999, 2002) finds that the reform reduced labor market distortions by increasing employment and labor mobility. She concludes that severance payments under the new program continued to play a consumption-smoothing role. Because prefunding improved the likelihood of receiving such payments, the insurance function of severance pay also improved (box 6.8). The prefunding reform does not require sophisticated information systems (requirements are the same as under pension programs), but it calls for management of accumulated assets and thus imposes additional administrative costs.

Conversion to a funded scheme reduces the nonperformance problem of severance pay, but it only transforms severance pay into a forced-savings scheme in which workers insure themselves. A further step to improve the

---

Box 6.7.   Severance Pay Reform in Austria

In January 2003 Austria converted its severance pay to a fully funded, contributory program akin to unemployment insurance savings accounts. The reform extended entitlement to workers with short tenures and removed obstacles to worker mobility, granting full portability and allowing the accumulation of benefits from the beginning of an employment spell. Employers make contributions of 1.5 percent of each worker's pay. The funds are held in a central account and invested in the capital market. Laid-off workers with job tenure of three years or more can withdraw accumulations in their accounts or keep them and claim them upon retirement (workers who separate voluntary and those with tenures of less than three years cannot immediate withdrawals).

Source: Felderer and others (2003).

Box 6.8.   Reforming Severance Pay in Colombia

In 1990 Colombia introduced a program of fully funded severance pay savings accounts. The program required employers to deposit a percentage of wages into guaranteed individual accounts available to workers in the event of job separation. Limited access to funds while employed was also foreseen.

The reform reduced labor market distortions, reducing wages and increasing employment measured by weekly hours. Wages fell as employers shifted 80 percent of severance payment costs to workers in the form of lower wages; total compensation of workers (wages plus deposits to their savings accounts) increased, however. In addition, because the reform removed the discretionary nature of severance payments, both firing and hiring increased under the new program.

By transforming uncertain conditional payments into unconditional payments monitored by a third party (the government), the reform also enhanced the insurance function of severance pay. Before the reform, nonperformance of severance pay was a serious problem (firms about to go bankrupt could simply not pay or negotiate a package substantially below what they owed in severance payments). The prefunding requirement increased the likelihood that the legal entitlement to severance pay is actually carried out. Among those who received severance payments, consumption smoothing was equally effective before and after the reform (an increase of 1,000 pesos in severance payments increased the consumption of nonemployed heads of households by 240 pesos). Substantial crowding-out effects are also reported: severance pay strongly reduced in-kind and monetary transfers from relatives, as well as government-mandated transfers, received by severance payments beneficiaries.

Source: Kugler (1999, 2002).

insurance function of the program would be to add a social insurance component in order to increase the pooling of the employment risk to the national level.

In summary, severance pay programs are important because they are already in place in many developing and transition countries. To improve their protection and efficiency, countries could streamline these programs by simplifying program rules and adjusting their generosity to bring them in line with international experience. More radical reforms may introduce prefunding to reduce nonperformance of severance pay, ameliorate labor market rigidities, or both, as well as introduce a social insurance component supplementing individual savings to enhance the insurance properties of the program.

Public Works: What Makes These Programs Suitable for Developing Countries?

Public works programs have several strengths:

- They are effective in reaching the poor, do a good job of targeting beneficiaries, and have substantial capacity to redistribute income from the rich to the poor.
- They can reach informal sector workers.
- They allow flexible and rapid responses to shocks.
- They are administratively less demanding than other public income support programs for the unemployed.

The programs also suffer from several weaknesses.

- High nonwage costs reduce the effectiveness of public works in reaching the poor.
- The countercyclical pattern of funding means that it is difficult to raise funding during crises, when support is needed most.
- Because of the highly redistributive character of public works, it may be difficult to gain political support, so some leakage to the nonpoor may be necessary.
- Maintaining the infrastructure built by public works may be difficult.
- Participants may be stigmatized.

Many conditions prevailing in developing countries make public works especially suitable for these countries:

- The informal sector is large. Informal sector workers do not have access to public income support programs that require social security contributions and thus remain vulnerable to even small income shocks.
- Due to a strong seasonal farm workload, particularly in mono-crop areas, public works can be cheaply deployed in nonfarm activities in nonpeak periods. The program thus provides an opportunity to productively engage temporary surplus labor while minimizing forgone earnings and maximizing poverty-reduction effects.

- The existence of large mono-crop areas leaves large segments of the population vulnerable to cyclical and structural shocks. Similar exposure is caused by geographic and climatic shocks. In the absence of market insurance, public works can provide effective insurance in such cases (box 6.9).
- Compared with other programs, public works programs do not require complex administration, and they can be quickly set up in areas hit by shocks.
- Obtaining public support for public works program can benefit from linking the programs to traditions and values that emphasize cooperation and collective support, particularly in rural areas.
- Public works in transition countries do not increase employability and may stigmatize participants. These programs therefore seem less desirable in these countries.

Box 6.9. Helping Coconut Farmers Weather El Niño Droughts

A disastrous drought in 1998 brought severe hardship to Filipino coconut farmers—suppliers of 60 percent of the world's coconut oil production—and revealed their extreme vulnerability to risk. The risks facing the sector are both cyclical (caused by drought) and structural (caused by emerging substitutes to coconut oil). But despite the risks, intercropping is rarely practiced, and more than half of coconut farms are mono-crop plantations.

Coconut farmers have little access to market insurance, and their ability to self-insure and self-protect is limited. There are few opportunities for generating nonfarm income that do not covary with activity on coconut farms. As a consequence, interfamily transfers and other community-based modes of informal insurance and collective savings provide inadequate insurance. Moreover, farmers face severe barriers to diversifying production, including the limited size of the local market for nonfood products, the high transactions costs of selling non-coconut products to urban markets (because of losses due to spoilage and the difficult access to urban centers), and the lack of capital for starting new ventures.

Labor-intensive public works can reduce exposure to the risks coconut growers face without rendering unnecessary the possible use of other policy instruments (such as commodity price stabilization programs). Public works would not only smooth income streams of very poor workers during the lean seasons, it would also put in place the infrastructure needed to improve linkages to product and labor markets in urban areas, going a long way toward reducing barriers to income and risk diversification (such as intercropping). Households and community organizations with more diversified income sources would enhance their ability to tap bank credit for their investment needs. The fact that adverse shocks to the coconut sector do not necessarily coincide with those in the rest of the economy may also increase the funding possibilities of such a program.

Source: Esguerra, Ogawa, and Vodopivec (2001).

In designing public works programs, policymakers should be guided by several general principles. First, forgone earnings should be minimized by attracting workers with low alternative earnings opportunities (Ravallion 1999a). Second, displacement effects should be avoided by carefully selecting the types of public works projects. Third, while the program should in principle be open to anyone, wages should be set low enough to trigger a self-selection mechanism that will attract only those in need. (Low wages also encourage participants to search for regular jobs.) Fourth, to maximize the "bang for the buck," programs should avoid projects that require heavy nonlabor costs, particularly during crises (Maloney 2001). Public works programs should be more labor intensive than required by pure maximization of present value of the assets created. According to Ravallion, to enhance the impact on poverty, program design should stress cost-recovery form the nonpoor, labor intensity, and provision of indirect benefits to the poor. Box 6.10 presents the key design elements of a successful public works program.

Ravallion also argues that a well-designed public guarantee program should become a permanent program, to enable it to address both covariant risks during crises and idiosyncratic risks during noncrisis times. Making the program permanent would also reduce political pressures to increase wages.

Complementarity of Programs and Policies

Most countries rely on several programs simultaneously, for several reasons:

- Different programs have different objectives. While the primary goal of income support programs is generally compensation for lost

---

Box 6.10.   Key Design Elements of a Successful Workfare Program: Argentina's Trabajar Program

Argentina's Trabajar program allocates funds across provinces based on the distribution of the unemployed poor. Municipalities and nongovernment organizations submit proposals to use the funds. These proposals are approved at the regional level, based on a system of points tied to poverty in the area and the merits of the proposed project. The government pays for the costs of unskilled labor, the sponsoring units pay for equipment, materials, and skilled labor. The wage for unskilled labor is set at two-thirds of the average wage for the poorest decile in the capital city. In principle, no restrictions are placed on the eligibility of beneficiaries to participate in the program, but in practice rationing occurs. The financing of the Trabajar program as a matching grant scheme not only induces local governments to commit to the project, it also induces local governments to use more labor. The use of labor-intensive approaches is enhanced by giving incentives to local governments rather than through instructions to contractors and engineers.

Source: de Ferranti and others (2000).

wages, some programs may also emphasize other objectives, including developing human resources (training, severance pay); countering the psychological effects of unemployment (training, public
works); and providing goods and services (public works). Combining various programs can allow countries to more effectively serve
the needs of different population groups, at different stages. In some
stages, for example, such as transition to a market-based economy,
the goal of reallocating labor may deserve special attention. Complementary programs should be flexible and adaptable to changing circumstances in order to provide help when needed.

- Workers in the informal sector are ineligible for certain programs,
  such as unemployment insurance or severance pay. It is important
  that the government also provide programs that are open to everyone
  (public works, training programs).

- Different programs have different eligibility rules. Some programs
  limit participation. Others are open to anyone, and individuals decide
  whether or not to participate. Self-selection can be a very powerful
  targeting mechanism (Ravallion 1999a).

- All programs are not equally well suited to address all types of
  shocks. Some programs, such as unemployment insurance, are suitable to confront various types of shocks, including some covariant
  shocks occurring at the national level (such as macroeconomic instability). Other programs are less suitable for certain type of shocks.
  Severance pay, for example, may offer insufficient protection against
  large idiosyncratic shocks—and perhaps for covariant shocks—if
  these shocks exacerbate the nonperformance problem of severance
  pay (firms may be less likely to meet their obligations to workers
  during recessions). Public works programs, which provide both
  income and goods and services, are particularly well suited for dealing with natural disasters.

Among complementary programs, active labor market programs (training,
employment subsidies, job-search assistance, promotion of self-employment,
youth programs) are particularly important. Depending on the country's
fiscal position, objectives, and conditions, these programs may be used to
increase the employment opportunities of the unemployed.

While discussion of these programs is beyond the scope of this book,
two points bear mention. First, active programs should be carefully coordinated with income support programs for the unemployed. If, for example,
participation in an active program qualifies individuals for benefits upon
completion, it may create perverse incentives for enrollment and weaken
incentives for reemployment. Second, active labor market programs may be
used to screen participants in income support programs. One way to test
recipients' willingness to work is by requiring proof of job search, such as
proof of regular job offers. But especially when unemployment is high, this
kind of test may not adequately reveal job-search activity and may impose

unwarranted costs on both claimants and employers. Placement in active labor market programs provides a suitable alternative. Those who are not genuinely looking for a job may prefer to lose the benefit than participate in a program. Indeed, recent empirical work shows that the "threat" of being exposed to a labor market program reduces the average duration of benefit payments (Benus and others 1997).

Complementarity issues also arise from the fact that the locus of distress is often the household, rather than the individual. To discourage counter-productive coping mechanisms, such as taking children out of school and reducing health care, income support programs could target vulnerable family members of the unemployed providing school and health subsidies (such programs are known as conditional cash transfers). Successful examples include Mexico's PROGRESA and Brazil's PETI, which give grants to poor families provided that their children attend school and visit health centers regularly. Evaluations show that these programs can raise school enrollment and attendance rates and improve child health and nutrition (Rawlings and Rubio 2003). They thus undoubtedly reduce poverty in the long run.

Important complementarities also exist between income support programs and government policies, particularly labor market and financial policies. A well-functioning labor market can substantially increase opportunities for self-protection (by reducing the risk of unemployment) and self-insurance (by contributing to short unemployment spells). Moreover, as Gill and Ilahi (2000) note, to ensure balanced, market-augmented social risk management, the government should foster the development of insurance and financial markets, which can greatly improve self-protection and self-insurance mechanisms.

Summary Evaluation

Alternative income support programs for the unemployed have both strengths and weaknesses (see also the summary in table 6.1):

- *Unemployment insurance,* which involves wide risk-pooling, enables a high degree of consumption smoothing for all categories of workers and performs well under various types of risks. It also acts as an automatic stabilizer. It creates reemployment disincentives and wage pressures, however, and thus increases the equilibrium unemployment rate. In addition, it contributes to the persistence of unemployment and is prone to political risk. Because successful performance relies on strong administrative capacity to monitor program eligibility, conducive labor market conditions, a modest-size informal sector, and an environment of low political risk—conditions typically lacking in developing and transition countries—the case for introducing unemployment insurance in these countries is less compelling than it is in industrial countries. The existence of unemployment insurance may also reduce incentives for self-protection and break down the habit of self-help among local communities, which may be welfare-reducing. Introducing unemployment insurance is thus viewed as a longer-term goal for many of these countries.

- *Unemployment assistance* enables more effective targeting, but it may not yield savings in comparison with unemployment insurance. In fact, it may prove fiscally unsustainable, due to the increased pool of potential applicants created by the program's failure to base eligibility on contribution payments deriving from prior work history. In addition, compared with unemployment insurance, unemployment assistance offers a lower level of protection for high-income workers, imposes higher administrative costs, and may suffer from similar employment disincentives. Its applicability is thus limited, perhaps to countries with relatively developed administrative capacity and a small informal sector—a rare breed among developing and transition countries.

- *Unemployment insurance savings accounts* (UISAs), particularly the version that combines the accounts with social insurance, may be an interesting option for developing and transition countries. By internalizing the costs of unemployment benefits, the program reduces the moral hazard inherent in traditional unemployment insurance and thus improves reemployment incentives—given the weak monitoring capacity of developing countries, an important advantage. The UISA-cum-social-funding variant—which combines self-insurance and social insurance and thus allows for broad-based risk-pooling—may improve work incentives while in principle offering the same income protection as traditional unemployment insurance. It also has the potential to attract informal sector workers. By allowing individuals to borrow from their UISA accounts, some versions of the program introduce problems of their own, creating incentives to withdraw from a formal sector in order to avoid repaying the debt. Because the program has been largely untested, further investigation of its effects and design parameters, including piloting of the program, is needed.

- *Severance pay* is important because it is available in many developing and transition countries, but it offers few advantages. To improve its protection and efficiency effects, countries may consider streamlining these programs and reducing their costs if they are too generous. A more radical reform may introduce prefunding, to improve nonperformance and reduce labor market rigidities.

- *Public works* programs are effective in reaching the poor, have good targeting properties and a substantial capacity to redistribute income from the rich to the poor, are able to attract informal sector workers and provide flexible and fast response to shocks, and are administratively less demanding than other public income support programs. Despite their weaknesses—high nonwage costs, the likely countercyclical

pattern of funding, and in some countries stigmatization of participants—they are suitable for developing countries, particularly as
complementary programs.

Designing Unemployment Insurance

What principles should guide policymakers as they design unemployment
insurance? The guidelines provided here suggest ways of dealing with the
moral hazard problem. They try to strike the right balance between the
insurance function of a program and the disincentives the program creates.

The analysis shows the usefulness of imposing "deductibles," sanctions
for noncompliance with program rules, and strict job-search monitoring.
Evidence on the level of benefits is less clear-cut, although there is support
for declining benefits over time. Allowing for different entitlement durations helps equalize the probability of finding a job within the entitlement
period and is thus justified from a fairness point of view.

The starting point in designing an unemployment insurance program is
recognition that some of the key conditions conducive for good performance
of formal insurance programs are generally missing in the case of unemployment insurance. In general, insurance works well in the presence of
large, rare, idiosyncratic shocks and in the absence of moral hazard and
adverse selection problems. Many of these key conditions are often missing
in the case of unemployment insurance. Unemployment insurance is often
provided under less than ideal conditions: large variations in the probability
of risk; extremely asymmetric information, with limited and costly opportunities for the insurer to obtain relevant information about individuals, which
creates strong moral hazard and adverse selection problems; and high
covariant risk.

Given these problems, how can unemployment insurance be designed?
First, to address the adverse selection problem, unemployment insurance
programs usually require mandatory membership. Second, because frequent shocks are better insured through self-insurance, and to reduce the
moral hazard, public insurance should not crowd out self-insurance com-
pletely. Such self-insurance could take the form of a waiting period before
benefit eligibility starts, of limited duration of unemployment benefits, or of
withdrawals from individual accounts, as in Chile (box 6.4). Third, to reduce
the moral hazard problem, unemployment insurance programs should
monitor job search activities and impose benefit sanctions. Fourth, in countries with weak administrative capacity, disincentive effects can be minimized by providing a flat-rate benefit at a low level. Some countries that
have used such a design—notably the United Kingdom, where unemployment and social assistance benefits have recently become essentially the
same—have succeeded in maintaining low unemployment.

Underscoring the importance of quality monitoring and enforcement,
recent studies suggest that effective monitoring and the use of sanctions can
strongly reduce the average duration of unemployment benefit payments

and increase the transition rate to employment. In a recent review of the literature, OECD (2000a) reports the results of studies of various OECD countries that show that compulsory intensive interviews reduced the volume of benefit claims, that the imposition of stricter job search requirements led to a reduction in the average duration of unemployment benefit payments, and that the imposition of sanctions on unemployed workers significantly raised the subsequent transition rate to employment (box 6.11). In a theoretical search equilibrium model, Boone and others (2001) show that monitoring and sanctions are welfare-improving and suggest that the optimal level of sanctions is well above those typically observed in Europe.

Should Unemployment Benefits Decrease over Time?

In a world free of reemployment disincentives created by unemployment benefits, welfare maximization dictates constant (flat) benefits, in order to smooth consumption. Once moral hazard is introduced, the optimal unemployment insurance literature suggests that benefits should be "front loaded," that is, that the replacement rate should be a declining function of the time spent in unemployment (Shavell and Weiss 1979); Hopenhayn and

---

Box 6.11.   Monitoring and Sanctions Can Speed Reemployment

Evidence suggests that by deterring undesirable and promoting desirable behavior, stricter monitoring and benefit sanctions can substantially increase the job-finding rate of benefit recipients. In the 1994 Maryland Unemployment Insurance Work Search Demonstration, stricter job-search requirements and reporting reduced the average duration of unemployment by about two weeks (17 percent) relative to no reporting requirement (Benus and others 1997). An experiment that increased the number of employer contacts required from two to four per week reduced the average duration of benefit payments by 0.7 weeks. Informing claimants that reported contacts would be verified with the employer reduced average duration by 0.9 weeks; dropping the requirement for reporting of contacts (claimants were still told that they must search for work) increased average duration by 0.4 weeks. Similar evidence was found in the United Kingdom following the introduction of new unemployment benefit legislation in 1996 (Martin and Grubb 2001).

Fredriksson and Holmlund (2003) report strong effects of benefit sanctions on the transition from unemployment. Two studies conducted in the Netherlands show that the transition rate from unemployment to employment more than doubled after sanctions were imposed cutting benefits by 5–35 percent conditional on failure to meet certain search requirements. Strong evidence was also found for Switzerland, where both warning and enforcement significantly increased the outflow rate from unemployment.

Source: Benus and others (1997), Martin and Grubb (2001), Fredriksson and Holmlund (2003).

Nicolini 1997). This makes intuitive sense: in order to provide optimal incentives for reemployment, the program should penalize failure to find a job by reducing the unemployment benefit. A strongly decreasing time structure of unemployment benefits can be avoided by imposing a permanent employment tax upon reemployment (Hopenhayn and Nicolini 1997). The reemployment tax imposes a penalty for opportunistic behavior while at the same time allowing for a higher income replacement rate later in the spell, thus providing better consumption-smoothing.

Other considerations in addition to moral hazard also suggest that unemployment benefits should decline over time. Cremer, Marchand, and Pestieau (1996) show that such a policy can follow from an adverse selection problem arising from the inability of the benefit administration office to distinguish between workers who wait for a job that fits their preferences or productivity and workers employed in informal jobs who refuse to accept any job offers. Wright (1986) shows that in an economy in which less than half of all workers are unemployed, the median voter will choose a declining benefit schedule. Moreover, by increasing the transition rate from unemployment, declining benefits reduce the incidence of long-term unemployed and thus contribute to a smoother aggregate response to shocks (Blanchard and Wolfers 2000).

Cahuc and Lehmann (2000) show that the case for declining benefits is reduced when endogenous wage determination through collective bargaining is introduced in moral hazard models. Such general equilibrium modeling shows that given the tax rate of wages used to finance unemployment benefits, moving from a flat to a declining profile of benefits, while indeed increasing the intensity of job search of the unemployed, could have two undesirable effects. First, the reduction in the equilibrium unemployment rate is much more modest than in the case of exogenous wage formation—and declining benefits could even increase the equilibrium unemployment (in the case of a mildly declining profile instead of a flat profile). Second, the welfare of the long-term unemployed suffers and the society moves away from the Rawlsian justice criterion.

Two other criticisms of declining benefits have also been voiced. Meyer (1995) notes that providing declining benefits overlooks the increased incentives of the unemployed to enter unemployment (this criticism assumes that when changing the time structure of benefits, the initial replacement rate is raised). Gruber (1999) finds that the capacity of the long-term unemployed to self-insure is particularly low, providing an argument against lowering unemployment benefits over time. (Gruber's findings also speak in favor of a waiting period.)

Should the Maximum Length of the Entitlement Period Be Equal for All?

Allowing for different entitlement durations may help equalize the probability of finding a job within the entitlement period. Micklewright and Nagy (1994) show that the expected length of unemployment varies tremendously across different groups of unemployed: for a 21- to 25-year-old man who finished college, worked as a nonmanual worker, lives in the capital, and enters unemployment directly from previous employment, the expected length of unemployment is nine months; for a 45- to 50-year-old man with only a primary education, who worked as a manual worker, and lives outside the capital, the expected length of unemployment is more than three times higher.

Several countries (including Austria, Germany, and Slovenia) determine the potential entitlement duration on the basis of claimants' work experience. This seems to be a suitable variable to take as a basis for differentiation. Work experience is not only correlated with the probability of exit from unemployment, it also fosters the program's insurance principles, as experience determines the contribution period. Micklewright and Nagy (1994) also show that age—and therefore experience—is one of the main determinants of exit probability: according to their estimates, a 10 percent increase in age leads to an 8 percent drop in the probability of exit from unemployment to employment.

Improving Income Protection of the Informal Sector

Informal sector workers are often unable to adequately self-protect and self-insure against income shocks, and their chances of participating in public income support programs are often very low. Why is statutory social security coverage in developing countries low? Why are informal sector workers excluded? Low coverage is attributable largely to the inappropriateness of existing statutory programs for the informal sector. Qualifying conditions and contribution requirements of statutory programs are often inconsistent with the nature of informal enterprises (single-person or small workforces), employment (nonwage and often irregular), and earnings (low and often irregular), effectively precluding participation by informal sector workers. Furthermore, the benefits from participation in these programs are often incompatible with the social protection needs of informal sector workers (van Ginneken 1999).

Several other factors also hinder extension of social protection coverage to informal sector workers. In many countries the long-standing state bias against informal sector activity has resulted in the neglect of the social protection needs of informal sector workers. But even if those needs were recognized, extending coverage would pose many practical challenges given the diversity, complexity, and obscurity of informal sector activities. These attributes make it difficult to ascertain the nature of risks and the demand for social protection in the informal sector—that is, they create a serious problem of asymmetric information—hampering efforts to develop suitable risk management measures. Given that the informal labor market is largely unmonitored, information on the extent, frequency, and duration of unemployment is for the most part unavailable. Because informal sector workers operate largely outside the purview of regulatory authorities, monitoring and enforcing social security requirements can also prove challenging. Dealing with these problems is costly and requires administrative capacity that many developing countries may not have.

Lack of awareness about various public and private social security provisions has also kept social security coverage low. In addition, in many countries the red tape associated with participating in public programs often discourages employers and workers from doing so. Workers in the informal sector may also fear participating in social security programs lest participation expose them to the heavy hand of the state for not complying with other regulations (van Ginneken 1999).

In most countries the only forms of publicly provided income support available to informal sector workers and their households are public works and social assistance programs, both of which are noncontributory and target individuals in economic need. Absent these programs, informal sector workers and their households have been largely left to their own devices. For the vast majority, who are subsistence earners, saving to insure against risk is impossible. For the poorest of the poor, therefore, even the slightest disruption to income flows can cause a severe, sometimes permanent, deterioration in their economic circumstances.

Without external assistance the informal sector has shown great ingenuity, developing informal, community-based measures to prevent, mitigate, and cope with various risks on a limited scale.[6] One such mechanism has been the pooling of resources by the community to assist members in economic need. Traditional arrangements have been supplemented or supplanted by private, often larger-scale arrangements—cooperatives, mutual benefit societies, rotating credit societies—many of them with outside assistance from nongovernmental organizations. (Some well-known examples include the Grameen Bank in Bangladesh, the Bank Rakyat in Indonesia, and BancoSol in Bolivia [Siegel, Alwang, and Canagarajah 2001].) Nongovernmental organizations have also introduced other programs to help workers improve their livelihoods and strengthen their risk management strategies. The most widespread has been the provision of microcredit to establish, continue, or expand employment- and income-generating activities. Technical assistance and training for microenterprise development and self-employment as well as the adoption of new, innovative technologies and techniques have been less common.[7]

These community-based arrangements have strengthened the capacity of the poor to address risks. Various insurance instruments have been introduced to pool risks faced by low-income households and reduce their exposure to risk-induced losses. Health insurance to cover the cost of limited health care has been the most prevalent. But more and more microinsurance products and services are being designed and implemented to cover contingencies such as death, disability, and maternity, as well as loss of productive assets, housing, or property due to natural catastrophes or other causes (box 6.12). In addition, measures are being taken to reduce risk by improving working and workplace conditions, preventing disease, and raising

---

Box 6.12.   The SEWA Integrated Social Security Program in India

The Self Employed Women's Association (SEWA), based in Ahmedabad, India, is a trade union organization made up primarily of poor, self-employed women. The association provides credit, technical assistance, and training for income-generating activities. In the 1990s it also introduced an integrated social security program, in response to the need expressed by members for protection against the adverse impacts on household incomes caused by sickness, death, and destruction to property and assets caused by natural catastrophes. Consultations and member participation were integral in designing and implementing the program.

The insurance-based, voluntary scheme is administered principally by the SEWA Bank, with involvement by national insurance institutions. Premiums are financed in equal shares by beneficiary contributions (facilitated through flexible payment arrangements), grants, and subsidies from insurance agencies. In the late 1990s the program insured about 32,000 members (14 percent of total membership).

The integrated social security scheme covers sickness, natural or accidental death and disability, maternity, and loss of or damage to housing and productive assets. The health insurance component has been particularly favorably received: members are willing to pay, because the service places strong emphasis on quality and is sensitive to their health needs. But program effectiveness and attractiveness have been undermined by the exclusion of household members other than the insured SEWA member and of certain diseases and treatments. And the insurance benefit amount has proved inadequate in half of all cases. In addition, most clients are from the urban center of Ahmedabad, and efforts to expand the clientele base to include members in rural areas have been hampered by the overcentralization of administrative procedures. Administrative difficulties related to claims-processing have also been reported. SEWA is trying to strengthen the administrative capacity, long-term financial sustainability, and quality and effectiveness of the integrated scheme by decentralizing operations, expanding coverage and benefits, and restructuring premiums.

Source: Jain (1997) and Lund and Srinivas (2000).

---

awareness. These community-based interventions have succeeded where formal provisions have failed, mainly because they have been designed with a recognition of the circumstances and social protection needs of beneficiaries. These interventions have been ad hoc and narrowly targeted, however, and critical questions regarding program sustainability, cost-effectiveness, feasibility, and replicability remain unanswered.

Policymakers need to examine how existing statutory social security provisions can be extended to cover informal sector workers—and how new institutions that better serve the needs of informal workers can be introduced. Extending coverage of existing programs is possible only if programs are adapted to the circumstances and needs of informal sector workers. Qualifying conditions for social insurance schemes, for example, need to be relaxed to allow for the unique characteristics of firms, occupations, and employment in the informal sector. And innovative solutions involving new arrangements and mechanisms need to be sought. Arango and Maloney (2000) argue that income support programs need to be delinked from jobs in order to reach informal sector workers. By making a clear link between contributions and benefits, unemployment insurance savings accounts could function in this role, but successful penetration might require temporary government subsidies (by matching the contributions made by the poor).[8] Other proposals include involving nongovernmental organizations in collecting contributions, delivering benefits, and monitoring beneficiaries (Sethuraman 1997). These organizations often organize workers into associations, making it easier for the state to provide coverage. Nongovernmental organizations have successfully mobilized informal sector workers in many developing countries (box 6.12).

Concluding Remarks

When choosing among income support programs for the unemployed, policymakers need to evaluate alternative programs, taking into account the effects and features of different programs and examining how the programs fit the specific circumstances facing their countries. Before choosing a program, they need to identify who their target beneficiaries are and assess the importance of specific aspects of program performance. Doing so will allow them to weigh different aspects of performance of the programs against each other in order to rank options.

Three general principles can guide policymakers as they choose a program:

- Adopt a holistic view. Income support programs must be seen in the wider context of other formal and informal mechanisms of social risk management. Particular attention should be devoted to developing financial and labor markets, which help individuals self-protect and self-insure.
- Strike the right balance. Policymakers should strike a balance between publicly provided programs and self-insurance and self-protection mechanisms, as well as a balance between cash benefit and in-kind benefit public programs. In-kind benefit programs that provide basic education and health services can significantly improve the long-term chances for self-protection.
- Be prepared for crises. The 1998 financial crisis in East Asia and recurrent crises in Latin America demonstrate the advantages of having income support programs in place before a crisis hits. The recent introduction of unemployment insurance in the Republic of Korea cushioned the impact of the crisis for many unemployed workers there—although only a small minority of workers was covered (box 6.13). Of course, only some income support programs (such as public works) can be created and put on hold.

Box 6.13. Cushioning the Blow of the East Asian Crisis in the Republic of Korea

The oil shocks of the 1970s stimulated discussions about the need for an unemployment insurance program in the Republic of Korea, but concerns about work disincentives and weak administration capacity prevailed. Two decades of rapid growth changed perceptions. In 1995, after more than two years of intense discussions and hearings, Korea introduced a compulsory unemployment insurance. Together with training and job information service, the program forms the country's employment insurance system.

When unemployment insurance was introduced, it was limited to workers in firms with at least 30 workers and covered about 21 percent of employed workers. Although coverage was expanded during the financial crisis to workers in smaller firms, coverage increased only modestly. In mid-1998, at the height of the financial crisis, insurance was extended to firms with five or more workers, but just 24 percent of employed workers were covered. In December 1999 coverage was extended to all firms and 57 percent of all wage workers (see table).

During the crisis of 1998, Korea was able to provide unemployment benefits to the unemployed. Still, at the height of the crisis only 7.6 percent of unemployed workers received unemployment benefits. By February 2003 this figure had doubled.

Further expansion of coverage is limited by the large informal sector, estimated to amount to more than a third of total employment, and a large segment of temporary and daily workers. Workers in both groups, who constitute about 80 percent of the unemployed, are ineligible for unemployment insurance.

Month/year	Benefit recipients as percent of unemployed	Unemployment rate	Percent of employed covered by unemployment insurance
December 1995	0	1.8	20.8
June 1998	7.6	7.1	22.3
December 1999	9.6	4.9	29.3
March 2003	14.3	3.6	32.9

Source: National Statistical Office of Korea (various years) and Ministry of Labor of Korea (various years).

Notes

1. Key strengths, weaknesses, and country-specific features conducive to the successful performance of each program discussed in this chapter are summarized in table 6.1.

2. Comparative data for 13 OECD countries in 1995 show that the overall share of transfers going to the bottom three deciles ranged from 20.8 percent in Italy to 53.5

in France and 58.0 percent in Australia. The top three deciles in Australia received 7.4 percent of transfers, the lowest percentage among the 13 countries (Vroman 2002).

3. Another way of looking at the improved incentives is noting that the UISA system is based on lifetime income, not current income, which is much more volatile. The system thus eliminates the "piggy-bank" function of unemployment insurance (redistribution across the life cycle). This redistribution represents the majority of spending in welfare states (Barr 2001 reports that two-thirds to three-quarters of welfare-state spending is life-cycle redistribution). Eliminating this function reduces taxes and disincentives (Folster and others 2002).

4. One could advocate such a system by claiming that workers are irrational—that they have too high a discount rate or underestimate the risk of becoming unemployed— so that left to themselves they make inadequate provision in private savings for the risk of becoming unemployed. But this is a weak argument, which ignores the distortions arising from overriding individual preferences about savings.

5. Smetters (2000) assesses the risk of high administrative costs of private pension accounts in the United States as low to medium; a similar assessment holds for unemployment insurance savings accounts and other countries as well. To keep the costs of private accounts low, Smetters proposes that investment funds be approved and regulated by the government and subject to standard auditing controls (to reduce fraud). He also proposes placing limits on investment charges and on free movements of money between funds. If these changes were made, most of the administrative costs would come from collecting contributions from individual workers.

6. These arrangements are extremely fragile, however, and are particularly vulnerable when a large-scale adverse event, such as an epidemic or natural catastrophe, occurs.

7. Usually provided through nongovernmental organizations, training has mostly been ad hoc and provided on the job (through apprenticeships, for example). Microfinance institutions provide some technical assistance and training to their clients.

8. By subsidizing the cost of participation of low-income households, the Republic of Korea significantly expanded health insurance coverage to this group.

References

Abraham, K., and S. Houseman. 1993. *Job Security in America: Lessons from Germany*. Washington, DC: Brookings Institution.

———. 1994. "Labor Adjustment under Different Institutional Structures: A Case Study of Germany and the United States." Kalamazoo, MI: Upjohn Institute Staff Working Paper 94–26.

Acemoglu, D., and R. Shimer. 1999. "Efficient Unemployment Insurance." *Journal of Political Economy* 107 (5): 893–928.

———. 2000. "Productivity Gains from Unemployment Insurance." *European Economic Review* 44 (7): 1195–1224.

Acevedo, G., and P. Eskenazi. 2003. "The Chilean Unemployment Insurance: A New Model of Income Support for the Unemployed?" Association of Pension Funds, Santiago.

Adamchik, V. 1999. "The Effect of Unemployment Benefits on the Probability of Re-employment in Poland." *Oxford Bulletin of Economics and Statistics* 61 (1): 95–108.

Adato, M., and L. Haddad. 2001. "Targeting Poverty through Community-Based Public Works Programs: A Cross-Disciplinary Assessment of Recent Experience in South Africa." FCND DP 121. International Food Policy Research Institute, Washington, DC.

Addison, J.T., C.R. Barrett, and W.S. Siebert. 1998. "Mandated Benefits, Welfare, and Heterogeneous Firms." Discussion Paper No. 98–46, Zentrum for Europaische Wirtschaftsforschung, Mannheim, Germany.

Addison, J.T., and M.L. Blackburn. 2000. "The Effects of Unemployment Insurance on Postunemployment Earnings." *Labour Economics* 7 (1): 21–53.

Addison, J.T., and P. Portugal. 1998. "Unemployment Benefits and Joblessness: A Discrete Duration Model with Multiple Destinations."

Discussion Paper No. 99–03, Zentrum for Europaishe Wirtschafts-forschung, Mannheim, Germany.

Addison, J.T., and P. Teixeira. 2001. "The Economics of Employment Protection." IZA Discussion Paper No. 381, Bonn, Germany.

Aghion, P., and O. Blanchard. 1994. "On the Speed of Transition in Central Europe." *NBER Macroeconomics Annual* 9: 283–320. Cambridge, MA: National Bureau of Economic Research.

Amadeo, E.J., I.S. Gill, and M.C. Neri. 2002. "Assessing the Impact of Regulations on Informal Workers in Brazil. In *Crafting Labor Policy: Techniques and Lessons from Latin America*, eds. J.S. Gill, C.E. Montenegro, and D. Domeland. Washington, D.C.: World Bank.

Anderson, P.M., and B.D. Meyer. 1993. "Unemployment Insurance in the United States: Layoff Incentives and Cross Subsidies." *Journal of Labor Economics* 11 (1): 70–95.

————. 1994. "The Effects of Unemployment Insurance Taxes and Benefits on Layoffs Using Firm and Individual Data." NBER Working Paper No. 4960, National Bureau of Economic Research, Cambridge, MA.

Arango, C., and W.F. Maloney. 2000. "Unemployment Dynamics in Latin America: Estimates of Continuous Time Markov Models for Mexico and Argentina." World Bank, Latin America and Caribbean Region Poverty Reduction and Economic Management, Washington, DC.

Asaad, R. 1999. "Matching Severance Payments with Worker Losses in the Egyptian Public Sector." *World Bank Economic Review* 13 (1): 117–154.

Atkinson, A.B. 1995a. *Incomes and the Welfare State. Essays on Britain and Europe.* Cambridge: Cambridge University Press.

————. 1995b. "On Targeting Social Security: Theory and Western Experience with Family Benefits." In *Public Spending and the Poor: Theory and Evidence*, eds. D. van de Walle and K. Nead, 25–68. Baltimore: John Hopkins University Press.

Atkinson, A.B., and J. Micklewright. 1991. "Unemployment Compensation and Labor Market Transitions: A Critical Review." *Journal of Economic Literature* 29 (4): 1679–1727.

Attanasio, O., and J.V. Rios-Rull. 2000. "Consumption Smoothing in Island Economies: Can Public Insurance Reduce Welfare?" *European Economic Review* 44 (7): 1225–1258.

Balisacan, A.M. 2001. "Poverty in the Philippines: An Update and Reexamination." *Philippine Review of Economics* 38 (1): 16–51.

Barr, N. 1990. *The Economics of the Welfare State.* London: Weidenfeld and Nicolson.

————. 2001. *The Welfare State as Piggy Bank: Information, Uncertainty and the Role of the State.* Oxford: Oxford University Press.

Barron, J., and W. Mellow. 1979. "Search Effort in the Labor Market." *Journal of Human Resources* 4 (3): 389–404.

Beegle, K., E. Frankenberg, and D. Thomas. 1999. "Measuring Change in Indonesia." Labor and Population Program, Working Paper Series 99–07. RAND, Santa Monica, CA.

Bentolila, S., and A. Ichino. 2000. "Unemployment and Consumption: Are Job Losses Less Painful near the Mediterranean?" Discussion Paper No. 2539, Centre for Economic Policy Research, London.

Benus, J., J. Joesch, T. Johnson, and D. Klepinger. 1997. "Evaluation of the Maryland Unemployment Insurance Work Search Demonstration: Final Report." Report 98-2. Batelle Memorial Institute, in association with Abt Associates Inc.

Besley, T., and R. Burgess. 2004. "Can Labor Regulation Hinder Economic Performance? Evidence from India." *Quarterly Journal of Economics* 119 (1): 91–134.

Besley, T., and S. Coate. 1995. "The Design of Income Maintenance Programs." *Review of Economic Studies* 62 (211): 187–221.

Betcherman, G., A. Dar, A. Luinstra, and M. Ogawa. 2001. "Active Labor Market Policies: Policy Issues for East Asia." In *East Asian Labor Market and the Economic Crisis: Impacts, Responses, and Lessons*, eds. G. Betcherman and R. Islam, 295–344. Washington, DC: World Bank.

Betcherman, G., and R. Islam. 2001. *East Asian Labor Market and the Economic Crisis: Impacts, Responses, and Lessons.* Washington, DC: World Bank.

Betcherman, G., K. Olivas, and A. Dar. 2003. "Impacts of Active Labor Market Programs: New Evidence from Evaluations with Particular Attention to Developing and Transition Countries." World Bank, Human Development Network, Washingon, DC.

Bird, E.J. 1995. "An Exploratory Comparisons of Income Risk in Germany and in the United States." *Review of Income and Wealth* 41 (4): 405–426.

Bird, E.J., and P.A. Hagstrom. 1999. "The Wealth Effects of Income Insurance." *Review of Income and Wealth* 45 (3): 339–352.

Blanchard, O. 1997. *The Economics of Post-Communist Transition.* Oxford: Oxford University Press.

————. 1999. "European Unemployment: The Role of Shocks and Institutions." Bafi Lecture, Rome. http://econ-www.mit.edu/faculty/download_pdf.php?id=804.

————. 2000. "The Economics of Unemployment. Shocks, Institutions, and Interactions." Lionel Robbins Lectures, London School of Economics. http://econ-www.mit.edu/faculty/download_pdf.php?id=800.

Blanchard, O., and P. Portugal. 1998. "What Hides Behind an Unemployment Rate: Comparing Portuguese and U.S. Unemployment." NBER Working Paper 6636, National Bureau of Economic Research, Cambridge, MA.

Blanchard, O., and J. Wolfers. 2000. "The Role of Shocks and Institutions in the Rise of European Unemployment: The Aggregate Evidence." *Economic Journal* 110 (462): C1–C33.

Blau, D.M., and P.K. Robins. 1986. "Job Search, Wage Offers, and Unemployment Insurance." *Journal of Public Economics* 29 (2): 143–197.

Blaustein, S.J. 1993. *Unemployment Insurance in the United States*. Kalamazoo, MI: Upjohn Institute.

Blöndal, S., and S. Scarpetta. 1997. "Early Retirement in OECD Countries: The Role of Social Security Systems." *OECD Economic Studies* 29 (2): 7–54.

Boeri, T. 1997. "Labor Market Reforms in Transition Economies." *Oxford Review of Economic Policy* 13 (2): 126–135.

Boeri, T., and S. Edwards. 1998. "Long-Term Unemployment and Short-Term Unemployment Benefits." *Empirical Economics* 23 (1–2): 31–54.

Boeri, T., and V. Steiner. 1996. "'Wait Unemployment' in Economies in Transition: The Case of Poland." *Konjukturpolitik* 3 (2): 287–311.

Boheim, R., and M.P. Taylor. 2000. "The Search for Success: Do the Unemployed Find Stable Employment?" University of Essex, United Kingdom.

Boldrin, M., J. Dolado, J.F. Jimeno, and F. Peracchi. 1999. "The Future of Pensions in Europe." *Economic Policy* 29 (14): 289–320.

Boone, P., P. Fredriksson, B. Holmlund, and J. van Ours. 2001. "Optimal Unemployment Insurance with Monitoring and Sanctions." Discussion Paper No. 3082, Centre for Economic Policy Research, London.

Botero, J., S. Djankov, R. La Porta, F. Lopez-de-Silanes, and A. Shleifer. 2002. "The Regulation of Labor." NBER Working Paper No. 9756, National Bureau of Economic Research, Cambridge, MA.

Burdett, K., and R. Wright. 1989. "Optimal Firm Size, Taxes, and Unemployment." *Journal of Public Economics* 39 (3): 275–287.

Burgess, P.L., and J.L. Kingston. 1976. "The Impact of Unemployment Insurance Benefits on Reemployment Success." *Industrial and Labor Relations Review* 30 (1): 25–31.

Burtless, G.S. 1990. "Unemployment Insurance and Labor Supply: A Survey." In *Unemployment Insurance*, eds. W.L. Hansen and J.F. Byers, 69–107. Madison: University of Wisconsin Press.

Buti, M., D. Franco, and L.R. Pench. 1999. "Reconciling the Welfare State with Sound Public Finances and High Employment." In *The Welfare State in Europe: Challenges and Reforms*, eds. M. Buti, D. Franco, and L. R. Pench, 3–54. Cheltenham, United Kingdom: Elgar.

Caballero, R.J., and M.L. Hammour. 2000. "Institutions, Restructuring and Macroeconomic Performance." NBER Working Paper 7720, National Bureau of Economic Research, Cambridge, MA.

Cahuc, P., and E. Lehmann. 2000. "Should Unemployment Benefits Decrease with the Unemployment Spell?" *Journal of Public Economics* 77 (1): 135–153.

Calmfors, L. 1994. "Active Labour Market Policy and Unemployment: A Framework for the Analysis of Crucial Design Features." OECD Economic Studies No. 22. Paris.

Calmfors, L., and J. Drifill. 1988. "Bargaining Structure, Corporatism, and Macroeconomic Performance." *Economic Policy* 6 (3): 14–61.

Calmfors, L., and B. Holmlund. 2000. "Unemployment and Economic Growth: A Partial Survey." *Swedish Economic Policy Review* 7 (1): 109–153.

Card, D., and P. Levine. 1994. "Unemployment Insurance Taxes and the Cyclical and Seasonal Properties of Unemployment." *Journal of Public Economics* 53 (1): 1–29.

Carling, K., P. Edins, A. Harkman, and B. Holmlund. 1996. "Unemployment Duration, Unemployment Benefits, and Labor Market Programs in Sweden." *Journal of Public Economics* 59 (3): 313–334.

Cazes, S., and S. Scarpetta. 1998. "Labour Market Transitions and Unemployment Duration: Evidence from Bulgarian and Polish Microdata." *Economics of Transition* 6 (1): 13–144.

Chamberlin, C., and A.D. Mason. 2003. "Overview: Social Protection in Latin America and the Caribbean." *Spectrum* (Fall), World Bank, Washington, DC. Available at wbln0018.worldbank.org/HDNet/HDdocs.nsf/vtlw/a0ccca5343b6dc3b85256d9d0069de99?OpenDocument.

Chimerine, T., T.S. Black, and L. Coffey. 1999. "Unemployment Insurance as an Economic Stabilizer: Evidence of Effectiveness over Three Decades." *Unemployment Insurance Occasional Paper* 99-8. U.S. Department of Labor, Washington, DC.

Clark, K.B., and L.H. Summers. 1982. "Unemployment Insurance and Labor Market Transitions." In *Workers, Jobs, and Inflation*, ed. M.N. Bailey, 279–323. Washington, DC: Brookings Institution.

Classen, K.P. 1977. "The Effect of Unemployment Insurance on the Duration of Unemployment and Subsequent Earnings." *Industrial and Labor Relations Review* 30 (4): 438–444.

Coady, D., M. Grosch, and J. Hoddinott. 2002. "The Targeting of Transfers in Developing Countries: Review of Experiences and Lessons." Social Safety Net Primer Series, World Bank, Washington, DC.

Cortazar, R. 1996. "Sharing Risk in Volatile Labour Markets." *Securing Stability and Growth in Latin America, Policy Issues and Prospects for Shock–Prone Economics,* eds. R. Housmann, and H. Reisen, 215–231. Paris: OECD.

Cox, D., and E. Jimenez. 1992. "Social Security and Private Transfers in Developing Countries: The Case of Peru." *World Bank Economic Review* 6 (1): 155–169.

———. 1995. "Targeting and the Effectiveness of Public Income Redistribution in the Philippines." In *Public Spending and the Poor: Theory and Evidence,* eds. D. van de Walle and K. Nead, 321–346. Baltimore: Johns Hopkins University Press.

Cox, J.C., and R.L. Oaxaca. 1990. "Unemployment Insurance and Job Search." *Research in Labor Economics* 11 (2): 223–240.

Cox Edwards, A.C., and C. Manning. 2001. "The Economics of Employment Protection and Unemployment Insurance Schemes: Policy Options for Indonesia, Malaysia, the Philippines, and Thailand." In *East Asian Labor Market and the Economic Crisis: Impacts, Responses, and Lessons,* eds. G. Betcherman and R. Islam, 345–378. Washington, DC: World Bank.

Cremer, H., M. Marchand, and P. Pestieau. 1996. "The Optimal Level of Unemployment Insurance Benefits in a Model of Employment Mismatch." *Labour Economics* 2 (4): 407–420.

Cunningham, W.V. 2000. "Unemployment Insurance in Brazil: Unemployment Duration, Wages, and Sectoral Choice." World Bank, Latin America and Caribbean Region Social Protection Sector, Washington, DC.

Dar, A., and Z. Tzannatos. 1999. "Active Labor Market Programs: A Review of the Evidence from Evaluations." Social Protection Discussion Paper No. 9901, World Bank, Washington, DC.

Datt, G., and M. Ravallion. 1994. "Transfer Benefits from Public Work Employment: Evidence from Rural India." *Economic Journal* 194 (427): 1346–1369.

Daveri, F., and G. Tabellini. 2000. "Unemployment, Growth and Taxation in Industrial Countries." *Economic Policy* 15 (30): 49–104.

Davis, S., and J. Haltiwanger. 1999. "Gross Job Flows." In *Handbook of Labor Economics*, eds. Orley Ashenfelter and David Card, 2711–2805. Amsterdam: North Holland.

Decker, P.T. 1997. "Work Incentives and Disincentives." In *Unemployment Insurance in the United States, Analysis of Policy Issues*, eds. C.J. O'Leary and S.A. Wandner, 285–320. Kalamazoo, MI: Upjohn Institute for Employment Research.

De Ferranti, D., G.E. Perry, I. S. Gill, and L. Serven. 2000. *Securing Our Future in a Global Economy*. World Bank Latin and Caribbean Studies, Washington, DC.

Diamond, P. 1981. "Mobility Costs, Frictional Unemployment, and Efficiency." *Journal of Political Economy* 89 (4): 798–812.

Dungan, P., and S. Murphy. 1995. "The UI System as an Automatic Stabilizer in Canada." Human Resources Development Canada, Hull, Quebec.

Dunson, B.H., S.C. Maurice, and G.P. Dwyer, Jr. 1991. "The Cyclical Effects of the Unemployment Insurance–UI Program." *Unemployment Insurance Occasional Paper* 91-3. U.S. Department of Labor, Washington, DC.

Earle, J., and C. Pauna. 1998. "Long-Term Unemployment, Social Assistance and Labor Market Policies in Romania." *Empirical Economics* (Austria) 23 (1/2): 203–235.

Ehrenberg, R.G., and R.L. Oaxaca. 1976. "Unemployment Insurance, Duration of Unemployment, and Subsequent Wage Gain." *American Economic Review* 66 (5): 754–766.

Ehrlic, I., and G. Becker. 1972. "Market Insurance, Self-Insurance and Self-Protection." *Journal of Political Economy* 80 (4): 623–648.

Elmeskov, J., J.P. Martin, and S. Scarpetta. 1998. "Key Lessons from Labor Market Reforms: Evidence from OECD Experiences." *Swedish Economic Policy Review* 5 (2): 205–252.

Esguerra, J., M. Ogawa, and M. Vodopivec. 2001. "Options of Public Income Support for the Unemployed in the Philippines." *Philippine Review of Economics* 38 (2): 37–66.

Fafchamps, M., and S. Lund. 1997. "Risk-Sharing Networks in Rural Philippines." Mansfield College, Oxford University and Department of Economics, Stanford University, Stanford, CA.

Fallon, P.R. and R.E.B. Lucas. 1991. "The Impact of Changes in Job Security Regulations in India and Zimbabwe." *World Bank Economic Review* 5 (1): 395–413.

Fehn, R., N. Berthold, and E. Thode. 2000. "Falling Labor Share and Rising Unemployment: Long-Term Consequences of Institutional Shock." Paper presented at the EALE/SOLE conference, Milan, June 22–26.

Felderer, B., H. Hofer, R. Koman, and U. Schuh. 2003. "The Austrian Severance Payments Reform." Paper presented at the workshop "Severance Pay Reform: Toward Unemployment Savings and Retirement Accounts," Laxenberg/Vienna, November 7–8.

Feldstein, M. 1976. "Temporary Layoffs in the Theory of Unemployment." *Journal of Political Economy* 84 (5): 937–957.

———. 1978. "The Effect of Unemployment Insurance on Temporary Layoff Unemployment." *American Economic Review* 68 (5): 834–846.

Feldstein, M., and D. Altman. 1998. "Unemployment Insurance Savings Accounts." NBER Working Paper No. 6860, National Bureau of Economic Research, Cambridge, MA.

Folster, S., R. Gidehag, M. Orszag, and D. Snower. 2002. "Assessing Welfare Accounts." Discussion Paper No. 3479, Centre for Economic Policy Research, London.

Forster, M. 2000. "Trends and Driving Factors in Income Distribution and Poverty in the OECD Area." *OECD Labour Market and Social Policy Occasional Paper* No. 42.

Forteza, A., and M. Rama. 2001. "Labor Market 'Rigidity' and the Success of Economic Reforms across More than One Hundred Countries." World Bank, Development Research Group, Poverty and Human Resources, Washington, DC.

Fredriksson, P., and B. Holmlund. 2001. "Optimal Unemployment Insurance in Search Equilibrium." *Journal of Labor Economics* 19 (2): 370–399.

———. 2003. "Improving Incentives in Unemployment Insurance: A Review of Recent Research." Working Paper No. 922, Center for Economic Studies and the IFO Institute, Munich.

Freeman, R.B. 1992. "What Direction for Labor Market Institutions in Eastern and Central Europe?" NBER Working Paper No. 4209, National Bureau of Economic Research, Cambridge, MA.

Fretwell, D., J. Benus, and C.J. O'Leary. 1999. "Evaluating the Impact of Active Labor Programs: Results of Cross Country Studies in Europe and Central Asia." Social Protection Discussion Paper No. 9915, World Bank, Washington, DC.

Friedman, M. 1968. "The Role of Monetary Policy." *American Economic Review* 58 (1): 1–17.

Galasso, E., and M. Ravallion. Forthcoming. "Decentralized Targeting of an Anti-Poverty Program." *Journal of Public Economics*.

Garcia, J. 1989. "Incentive and Welfare Effects of Reforming the British Benefit System: A Simulation Study for the Wives of the Unemployed."

In *The Nature of Unemployment in Britain: Studies of the DHSS Cohort,* eds. S.J. Nickell, W. Narendranathan, J. Stern, and J. Garcia, 164–198. Oxford: Oxford University Press.

Gill, I.S., and N. Ilahi. 2000. "Economic Insecurity, Individual Behavior and Social Policy." Paper prepared for the Regional Study "Managing Economic Insecurity in Latin America and the Caribbean," World Bank, Washington, DC.

Gough, I. 2000. "Welfare Regimes in East Asia and Europe." Paper presented at the Annual Bank Conference on Development Economics, Paris, June.

Gruber, J. 1997a. "Consumption-Smoothing Effects of Unemployment Insurance." *American Economic Review* 87 (1): 192–205.

———. 1997b. "The Incidence of Payroll Taxation: Evidence from Chile." *Journal of Labor Economics* 15, Part 2 (3): S72–S101.

———. 1999. "The Wealth of the Unemployed: Adequacy and Implications for Unemployment Insurance." NBER Working Paper No. 7348, National Bureau of Economic Research, Cambridge, MA.

Gruber, J., and D. Wise. 1998. "Social Security and Retirement: An International Comparison." *American Economic Review, Papers and Proceedings* 88 (2): 158–163.

Guasch, J.L. 1999. "An Alternative to Traditional Unemployment Insurance Programs: A Liquidity-Based Approach against the Risk of Earnings Losses." World Bank, Latin America and Caribbean Region Sector, Finance, Private Sector, and Infrastructure, Washington, DC.

Haddad, L., and M. Adato. 2001. "How Efficiently Do Public Works Programs Transfer Benefits to the Poor? Evidence from South Africa." FCND DP 108. International Food Policy Research Institute, Washington, DC.

Haltiwanger, J.C., S. Scarpetta, and M. Vodopivec. 2003. "How Institutions Affect Labor Market Outcomes: Evidence from Transition Countries." Paper presented at the World Bank Economist Forum, April 10.

Haltiwanger, J.C., and M. Singh. 1999. "Cross-Country Evidence on Public Sector Retrenchment." *World Bank Economic Review* 13 (1): 23–66.

Haltiwanger, J.C., and M. Vodopivec. 2002. "Gross Worker and Job Flows in a Transition Economy: An Analysis of Estonia." *Labour Economics* 9 (5): 601–630.

Ham, J., and S. Rea. 1987. "Unemployment Insurance and Male Unemployment Duration in Canada." *Journal of Labor Economics* 5 (3): 325–353.

Ham, J., J. Svejnar, and K. Terrell. 1998. "Unemployment and the Social Safety Net During Transitions to a Market Economy: Evidence from the Czech and Slovak Republics." *American Economic Review* 88 (5): 1117–1142.

Hamermesh, D.S. 1992. "Unemployment Insurance for Developing Countries." World Bank Policy Research Working Paper No. 897. Washington, DC.

Hamermesh, D.S., and D.T. Slesnick. 1995. "Unemployment Insurance and Household Welfare: Microeconomic Evidence 1980–93." NBER Working Paper No. 5315, National Bureau of Economic Research, Cambridge, MA.

Hassler, J., F. Zilbotti, and J. Mora. 1999. "Equilibrium Unemployment Insurance." Discussion Paper No. 2126, Centre for Economic Policy Research, London.

Hazell, P., C. Pomaseda, and A. Valdez. 1986. *Crop Insurance for Agricultural Development: Issues and Experiences.* Baltimore: Johns Hopkins University Press.

Heckman, J.J., and C. Pages. 2000. "The Cost of Job Security Regulation: Evidence from Latin American Labor Markets." NBER Working Paper No. 7773, National Bureau of Economic Research, Cambridge, MA.

Heer, B. 2000. "Unemployment and Welfare Effects of a Two-Tier Unemployment Compensation System." CESifo Working Paper No. 297, Center for Economic Studies and IFO Institute for Economic Research, Munich.

Hoddinott, J., M. Adato, T. Besley, and L. Haddad. 2001. "Participation and Poverty Reduction: Issues, Theory, and New Evidence from South Africa." Food Consumption and Nutrition Division Discussion Paper 98, International Food Policy Research Institute, Washington, DC.

Holen, A. 1977. "Effects of Unemployment Insurance Entitlement on Duration and Job Search Outcome." *Industrial and Labor Relations Review* 30 (4): 445–450.

Holmlund, B. 1998. "Unemployment Insurance in Theory and Practice." *Scandinavian Journal of Economics* 100 (1): 113–152.

Holzmann, R., J. Gacs, and G.W. Georg. 1995. *Output Decline in Eastern Europe: Unavoidable, External Influence or Homemade? International Studies in Economics and Econometrics.* Dordrecht: Kluwer Academic.

Hopenhayn, H., and J.C. Hatchondo. 2002. "The Welfare Consequences of Alternative Designs of Unemployment Insurance Savings Accounts." University of Rochester, Department of Economics, Rochester, NY.

Hopenhayn, H.A., and J.P. Nicolini. 1997. "Optimal Unemployment Insurance." *Journal of Political Economy* 105 (2): 412–438.

Hopenhayn, H.A., and R. Rogerson. 1993. "Job Turnover and Policy Evaluation: A General Equilibrium Approach." *Journal of Political Economy* 101 (5): 915–938.

Horton, S., and D. Mazumdar. 2001. "Vulnerable Groups and the Labor Market: The Aftermath of the Asian Financial Crisis." In *East Asian Labor Market and the Economic Crisis: Impacts, Responses, and Lessons*, eds. G. Betcherman and R. Islam, 379–422. Washington, DC: World Bank.

Housmann, R., and M. Gavin. 1996. "Securing Stability and Growth in a Shock Prone Region: The Policy Challenge for Latin America." Working Paper 315, Inter-American Development Bank, Office of the Chief Economist, Washington, DC.

Hunt, J. 1996. "Has Work-Sharing Worked for Germany?" NBER Working Paper Series No. 5724, National Bureau for Economic Research, Cambridge, MA.

Hur, J. 2001. "Expanding the Coverage of Korea's Unemployment Insurance." In *Labor Market Reforms in Korea: Policy Options for the Future*, eds. F. Park, Y. Boom, G. Betcherman, and A. Dar, 25–45. Washington, DC: World Bank and Korea Labor Institute.

Iglesias, A., and R.J. Palacios. 2000. "Managing Public Pension Reserves." Pension Reform Primer Series. World Bank, Human Development Network, Social Protection Unit, Washington, DC.

ILO (International Labour Organization). 2000. *Key Indicators of the Labour Market*. Geneva: ILO.

———. 2001. LABORSTA. Geneva: ILO.

———. 2003. *Options for the Development of an Unemployment Protection Scheme: Sri Lanka*. Geneva: ILO.

Islam, R., G. Bhattacharya, S. Dhanani, M. Iacono, F. Mehran, S. Mukhopadhyay, and P. Thuy. 2001. "The Economic Crisis: Labor Market Challenges and Policies of Indonesia." In *East Asian Labor Markets and the Economic Crisis: Impacts, Responses, and Lessons*, eds. G. Betcherman and R. Islam, 43–96. Washington, DC: World Bank.

Jain, S. 1997. "Basic Social Security in India." In *Social Security for the Excluded Majority: Case Studies of Developing Countries*, ed. W. van Ginneken. Geneva: ILO.

Jeon, D., and J. Laffont. 1999. "The Efficient Mechanism for Public Sector Downsizing." *World Bank Economic Review* 13 (1): 67–88.

Jones, D.C., and M. Kotzeva. 1998. "Work Incentives and Other Effects of the Transition to Social Assistance in the Transition Economies:

Evidence from Bulgaria." In T. Boeri (ed.), *Lessons from Labour Market Policies in the Transition Countries*, OECD Proceedings, 255–307. Paris: OECD.

Katz, L.F., and B.D. Meyer. 1990. "The Impact of the Potential Duration of Unemployment Benefits on the Duration of Unemployment." *Journal of Public Economics* 41 (1): 45–72.

Kiefer, N.M., and G.R. Neumann. 1989. *Search Models and Applied Labor Economics*. Cambridge: Cambridge University Press.

Klassen, S., and I. Woolard. 2001. "Surviving Unemployment without State Support: Unemployment and Household Formation in South Africa." CESifo Working Paper No. 533, Center for Economic Studies and Ifo Institute for Economic Research, Munich.

Kochar, A. 1995. "Explaining Household Vulnerability to Idiosyncratic Income Shocks." *American Economic Review, Papers and Proceedings* 85 (2): 159–164.

Kotzeva, M., D. Mircheva, and A. Wörgötter. 1996. "Evaluation of Active and Passive Labour Market Policy in Bulgaria." In *Lessons from Labour Market Policies in the Transition Countries*, OECD Proceedings, 77–118. Paris: OECD.

Kugler, A. 1999. "The Impact of Firing Costs on Turnover and Unemployment: Evidence from the Colombian Labour Market Reform." *International Tax and Public Finance Journal* 6 (3): 389–410.

———. 2002. "From Severance Pay to Self-Insurance: Effects of Severance Payments Savings Accounts in Colombia." Discussion Paper No. 3197, Centre for Economic Policy Research, London.

Kugler, A., and G. Saint-Paul. 2000. "Hiring and Firing Costs, Adverse Selection and the Persistence of Unemployment." Discussion Paper No. 2410, Centre for Economic Policy Research, London.

Kwiatkowski, E. 1998. "Unemployment Benefits and Labor Market Developments in Poland in Transition." University of Lodz, Deparment of Economics.

Lal, D. 1994. "Labor Market Insurance and Social Safety Nets." Human Resource Development and Operations Policy Working Paper No. 41. World Bank, Washington, DC.

Lancaster, T. 1979. "Econometric Methods for the Duration of Unemployment." *Econometrica* 47 (4): 939–956.

Layard, R., S. Nickell, and R. Jackman. 1991. *Unemployment: Macroeconomic Performance and the Labour Market*. New York: Oxford University Press.

Lazear, E.P. 1990. "Job Security Provisions and Employment." *Quarterly Journal of Economics* 105 (3): 699–726.

Leipold, K. 2000. "Information Technology for Income Support Programs." World Bank, Human Development Network, Washington, DC.

Levine, D.I., and L.A. Tyson. 1990. "Participation, Productivity, and the Firm's Environment." In *Paying for Productivity: A Look at the Evidence,* ed. A.S. Blinder, 183–237. Washington, DC: Brookings Institution.

Lindbeck, A. 1995. "Hazardous Welfare State Dynamics." *American Economic Review, Papers and Proceedings* 85 (2): 9–15.

Lipsett, B. 1999. "Supporting Workers in Transition: Income Support Programs for the Unemployed in Brazil and Argentina." Paper prepared for the World Bank, Human Development Network, Washington, DC.

Ljungqvist, L., and T. Sargent. 1997. "Taxes and Subsidies in Swedish Unemployment." In *The Welfare State in Transition: Reforming the Swedish Model,* eds. R. Freeman, R. Topel, and B. Swedenborg, 299–314, Chicago: University of Chicago Press.

Lubyova, M., and Jan C. van Ours. 1999. "Unemployment Durations of Job Losers in a Labour Market in Transition." *Economics of Transition* 7 (3): 665–686.

Lund, F., and S. Srinivas. 2000. "Learning from Experience: A Gendered Approach to Social Protection for Workers in the Informal Economy." Turin: International Labour Organization.

Maani, S.A. 1993. "Post-Unemployment Wages, the Probability of Re-Employment, and the Unemployment Benefit." *New Zealand Economic Papers* 27 (1): 35–55.

MacIsaac, D., and M. Rama. 2000. "Mandatory Severance Pay in Peru: An Assessment of Its Coverage and Effects Using Panel Data." World Bank, Development Research Group, Public Service Delivery, Washington, DC.

Madzar, L. 2003. "Report on Claims to the Guarantee Fund of the Republic of Slovenia, 1994–2002." Guarantee Fund of the Republic of Slovenia, Ljubljana.

Mahmood, M., and G. Aryah. 2001. "The Labor Market and Labor Policy in Macroeconomic Context: Growth, Crisis, and Competitiveness in Thailand." In *East Asian Labor Market and the Economic Crisis: Impacts, Responses, and Lessons,* eds. G. Betcherman and R. Islam, 245–292. Washington, DC: World Bank.

Maloney, W.F. 2001. "Evaluating Emergency Programs: Intertemporal and Financing Considerations." World Bank, Latin America and the

Caribbean Region, Poverty Reduction and Economic Management Sector Unit, Washington, DC.

Mansor, N., T.E. Chye, A. Boehanoeddin, F. Said, and S.M. Said. 2001. "Malaysia: Protecting Workers and Fostering Growth." In *East Asian Labor Market and the Economic Crisis: Impacts, Responses, and Lessons,* eds. G. Betcherman and R. Islam, 141–194. Washington, DC: World Bank.

Marquez, G. 1999. "Labor Markets and Income Support: What Did We Learn from the Crisis?" Inter-American Development Bank, Office of the Chief Economist, Washington, DC.

Marston, S.T. 1975. "The Impact of Unemployment Insurance on Job Search." *Brookings Papers on Economic Activity* 1 (75): 13–48.

Martin, J., and D. Grubb. 2001. "What Works and for Whom: A Review of OECD Countries' Experiences with Active Labour Market Policies." Working Paper 2001/14, Institute for Labour Market Policy Evaluation (IFAU), Uppsala, Sweden.

Mazza, J. 1999. "Unemployment Insurance: Case Studies and Lessons for Latin America and the Caribbean." Technical Study RE2/SO2. Inter-American Development Bank, Washington, DC.

Meltzer, A., and S. Richard. 1983. "Tests of a Rational Theory of the Size of Government." *Public Choice* 3: 1403–1418.

Meyer, B.D. 1990. "Unemployment Insurance and Unemployment Spells." *Econometrica* 58 (4): 757–782

———. 1995. "Lessons from the U.S. Unemployment Insurance Experiments." *Journal of Economic Literature* 33 (1): 91–131.

Micklewright, J., and G. Nagy. 1994. "Flows to and from Insured Unemployment in Hungary." European University Institute Working Papers in Economics No. 94/41, Florence.

———. 1998. "The Implications of Exhausting Unemployment Entitlement in Hungary." Budapest Working Paper on the Labour Market No. 1998/2. Budapest University of Economics.

Millard, S.P. 1997. "The Cyclical Effects of Labour Market Policy." In *Business Cycles and Macroeconomic Stability: Should We Rebuild Built-In Stabilisers?* eds. J.-O. Hairault, P.-Y. Henin, and F. Portier, 211–230. Dordrecht, the Netherlands: Kluwer.

Moffitt, R. 1985. "Unemployment Insurance and the Distribution of Unemployment Spells." *Journal of Econometrics* 28 (1): 85–101.

Moffit, R., and W. Nicholson. 1982. "The Effect of Unemployment Insurance on Unemployment: The Case of Federal Supplemental Benefits." *Review of Economics and Statistics* 64 (1): 1–11.

Mortensen, D.T. 1977. "Unemployment Insurance and Job Search Decisions." *Industrial and Labor Relations Review* 30 (4): 505–517.

———. 1994. "Reducing Supply-Side Disincentives to Job Creation." In *Reducing Unemployment: Current Issues and Policy Options*, Federal Reserve Bank of Kansas City. Proceedings of a symposium held in Jackson Hole, Wyoming, August 25–27.

Mortensen, D.T., and C. Pissarides. 1999. "New Developments in Models of Search in the Labour Market." Discussion Paper No. 2053, Centre for Economic Policy Research, London.

Mroz, T.A., and T.H. Savage. 2000. "The Long-Term Effects of Youth Unemployment." University of North Carolina, Department of Economics, Chapel Hill.

Murdoch, J. 1999. "Between the State and the Market: Can Informal Insurance Patch the Safety Net?" *World Bank Research Observer* 14 (2): 187–207.

Narendranathan, W., S. Nickell, and J. Stern. 1985. "Unemployment Benefits Revisited." *Economic Journal* 95 (378): 307–329.

National Statistical Office, Republic of Korea. Various years. *Annual Report on Economically Active Population Survey*. Seoul.

Ministry of Labor, Republic of Korea. Various years. *Monthly Statistics of Employment Insurance*. Seoul.

Nickell, S. 1979. "The Effect of Unemployment and Related Benefits on the Duration of Unemployment." *Economic Journal* 89 (1): 34–49.

Nickell, S., and R. Layard. 1999. "Labor Market Institutions and Economic Performance." In *Handbook of Labor Economics*, Vol. 3, eds. Orley Ashenfelter and David Card, 3029–3083. Amsterdam: North Holland.

Nicoletti, G. R., C.G. Haffner, S. Nickell, S. Scarpetta, and G. Zoega. 2001. "European Integration, Liberalization and Labour Market Performance." In *Welfare and Employment in a United Europe*, eds. G. Bertola, T. Boeri and G. Nicoletti, 147–236. Cambridge, MA: MIT Press.

OECD (Organisation for Economic Co-operation and Development). 1994. *The OECD Jobs Study.* Paris: OECD.

———. 1995a. *Benefit Systems and Work Incentives in OECD Countries: 1995.* Available at www.oecd.org/els/socpol/BenefitsCompendium/index. htm.

———. 1995b. *Employment Outlook.* Paris: OECD.

————. 1999a. *Benefit Systems and Work Incentives 1999.* Paris: OECD.

————. 1999b. *Employment Outlook.* Paris: OECD.

————. 2000a. *Pushing Ahead with Reform in Korea: Labour Market and Social Safety Net Policies.* Paris: OECD.

————. 2000b. *Employment Outlook.* Paris: OECD.

O'Leary, C.J. 1997. "Adequacy of the Weekly Benefit Amount." In *Unemployment Insurance in the United States, Analysis of Policy Issues,* eds. C.J. O'Leary and S.A. Wandner, 163–210. Kalamazoo, MI: Upjohn Institute for Employment Research.

Orszag, J.M., P.R. Orszag, D.J. Snower, and J.E. Stiglitz. 1999. "The Impact of Individual Accounts: Piecemeal versus Comprehensive Approaches." Paper presented at the Annual Bank Conference on Development Economics, World Bank, Washington, DC, April 29.

————. 1998. "Anatomy of Policy Complementarities." CEPR Discussion Paper No. 1963. Centre for Economic Policy Research, London.

Palacios, R. 2002. "Managing Public Pension Reserves Part II: Lessons from Five Recent OECD Initiatives." Social Protection Discussion Paper Series No. 0219, World Bank, Washington, DC.

Pedersen, P.J., and N. Westergård-Nielsen. 1993. "Unemployment: A Review of Evidence form Panel Data." *OECD Economic Studies* 20 (Spring): 65–114.

Pissarides, C. 2001. "Employoment Protection." *Labour Economics* 8 (2): 131–159.

Puhani, P.A. 1996. "Poland on the Dole: Unemployment Benefits, Training and Long-Term Unemployment during the Transition." Discussion Paper No. 96-30, Zentrum for Europaishe Wirtschaftsforschung, Mannheim, Germany.

Rama, M. 1999. "Public Sector Downsizing: An Introduction." *World Bank Economic Review* 13 (1): 1–22.

Rama, M. and R. Artecona. 2000. "A Database of Labor Market Indicators across Countries." World Bank, Development Economics Department, Washington, DC.

Ravallion, M. 1991. "Reaching the Rural Poor through Public Employment: Arguments, Evidence, and Lessons from South Asia." *World Bank Research Observer* 6 (2): 153–175.

————. 1999a. "Appraising Workfare." *World Bank Research Observer* 14 (1): 31–48.

————. 1999b. "Is More Targeting Consistent with Less Spending?" Policy Research Working Paper 2079, World Bank, Washington, DC.

————. 2003. "Targeted Transfers in Poor Countries: Revisiting the Trade-offs and Policy Options." Policy Research Working Paper 3048, World Bank, Washington, DC.

Ravallion, M., E. Galazo, T. Lazo, and E. Philipp. 2001. "Do Workfare Participants Recover Quickly from Retrenchment?" *Policy Research Working Papers* No. 2672, World Bank, Washington, DC.

Ravallion, M., and M. Lokshin. 1999. "Who Wants to Redistribute? Russia's Tunnel Effect in the 1990s." Policy Research Working Paper 2150, World Bank, Washington, DC.

Rawlings, L.B., and G.M. Rubio. 2003. "Evaluating the Impact of Conditional Transfer Programs: Lessons from Latin America." World Bank, Policy Research Working Paper No. 3119, Washington, DC.

Rawlings, L., L. Sheburne-Benz, and J. Van Domelen. 2002. *Letting Communities Take the Lead: A Cross-Country Evaluation of Social Fund Performance.* World Bank, Human Development Network, Social Protection, Washington, DC.

Rodrik, D. 1999. "Why Is There So Much Income Insecurity in Latin America?," John F. Kennedy School of Government, Harvard University, Cambridge, MA.

Rosenzweig, M.R., and H.P. Binswanger. 1993. "Wealth, Weather Risk and Profitability of Agricultural Investments." *Economic Journal* 103 (416): 56–78.

Rosenzweig, M.R., and K. Wolpin. 1993. "Credit Market Constraints, Consumption Smoothing, and the Accumulation of Durable Assets in Low-Income Countries: Investments in Bullocks in India." *Journal of Political Economy* 101 (2): 223–234.

Rowe, G. 2000. *Welfare Rules Databook, State TANF Policies as of July 1999.* Washington, DC: Urban Institute.

Ruppert, E. 1999. "The Algerian Retrenchment System: A Financial and Economic Evaluation." *World Bank Economic Review* 13 (1): 155–183.

Saint-Paul, G. 1993. "On the Political Economy of Labor Market Flexibility." Discussion Paper No. 803, Centre for Economic Policy Research, London.

Scarpetta, S., and A. Reutersward. 1994. "Unemployment Benefit System and Active Labour Market Policies in Central and Eastern Europe: An Overview." *Unemployment in Transition Countries: Transient or Persistent,* 255–307. Paris: OECD.

Schoeni, R.F. 2002. "Does Unemployment Insurance Displace Familial Assistance?" *Public Choice* 110 (1): 99–119.

Schwarz, A.M., and A. Demirguc–Kunt. 1999. "Taking Stock of Pension Reforms around the World." Pension Reform Primer Series. World Bank, Human Development Network, Washington, DC.

Sethuraman, S.V. 1997. "Urban Poverty and the Informal Sector: A Critical Assessment of Current Strategies." Available at www.ilo.org/public/english/employment/recon/eiip/publ/1998/urbpover.htm.

Shavell, S., and L. Weiss. 1979. "The Optimal Payment of Unemployment Insurance Benefits." *Journal of Political Economy* 87 (6): 1347–1362.

Siegel, P., J. Alwang, and S. Canagarajah. 2001. "Viewing Microinsurance as a Social Risk Management Instrument." Social Protection Discussion Paper No. 0116, World Bank, Washington, DC.

Smetters, K. 2000. "The Design and Cost of Pension Guarantees." Brookings/SIEPR/TIAA–CREF Conference on Public Policies and Private Pensions, September 21–22.

Snower, D. 1995. "The Simple Economics of Benefit Transfers." *IMF Working Paper* 95/5. Washingon, DC.

Standing, G. 2000. "Unemployment Benefits and Income Security." ILO Discussion Paper. Geneva.

Subbarao, K. 1997. "Public Works as an Anti-Poverty Program: An Overview of Cross-Country Experience." *American Journal of Agricultural Economics* 79 (2): 678–683.

———. 2001. "Coping with Climatic and Systemic Risks: Role and Effectiveness of Public Works Programs." World Bank, Africa Region, Human Development Network, Washingon, DC.

———. 2003. "Systemic Shocks and Social Protection: Role and Effectiveness of Public Works Programs." Social Protection Discussion Paper No. 0302, World Bank, Washington, DC.

Subbarao, K., A. Bonnerjee, J. Braithwaite, S. Carvalho, K. Ezemenari, C. Graham, and A. Thompson. 1997. *Safety Nets Programs and Poverty Reduction: Lessons from Cross-Country Experience*. Washington, DC: World Bank.

Terrell, K., M. Lubyova, and M. Strapec. 1996. "Evidence on the Implementation and Effectiveness of Active and Passive Labour Market Policies in the Slovak Republic." In *Lessons from Labour Market Policies in the Transition Countries*, OECD Proceedings, 227–265. Paris: OECD.

Terrell, K., and D. Munich. 1996. "Evidence on the Implementation and Effectiveness of Active and Passive Labour Market Policies in the Czech Republic." In *Lessons from Labour Market Policies in the Transition Countries*, OECD Proceedings, 179–223. Paris: OECD.

Topel, R. 1983. "On Layoffs and Unemployment Insurance." *American Economic Review* 73 (4): 541–559.

Tzannatos, Z., and S. Roddis. 1998. "Unemployment Benefits." Social Protection Discussion Paper No. 9813, World Bank, Washington, DC.

U.S. Social Security Administration. 1999. *Social Security Programs throughout the World: 1999.* Washington, DC.

———. 2002a. *Social Security Programs throughout the World: Europe.* Washington, DC. Available at www.ssa.gov/policy/docs/progdesc/ssptw/2002-2003/europe/index.html.

———. 2002b. *Social Security Programs throughout the World: Asia and the Pacific 2002.* Washington, DC. Available at www.ssa.gov/policy/docs/progdesc/ssptw/2002-2003/asia/index.html.

van Ginneken, W. 1996. "Social Security for the Informal Sector: Issues, Options, and Tasks Ahead." Working Paper for the ILO Interdepartmental Project on the Urban Informal Sector. International Labour Organization, Geneva.

———. 1999. "Overcoming Social Exclusion." In *Social Security for the Excluded Majority: Case Studies of Developing Countries,* ed. W. van Ginneken, 1–36. Geneva: International Labour Organization.

van Ours, J.C., and M. Belot. 2000. "Does the Recent Success of Some OECD Countries in Lowering Their Unemployment Rates Lie in the Clever Design of Their Labor Market Reforms?" Discussion Paper No. 2492, Centre for Economic Policy Research, London.

Vodopivec, M. 1995. "Unemployment Insurance and Duration of Unemployment: Evidence from Slovenia." Policy Research Working Paper Series No. 1552, World Bank, Washington, DC.

———. 1999. "Does the Slovenian Public Work Program Increase Participants' Chances to Find a Job?" *Journal of Comparative Economics* 27 (1): 113–130.

Vodopivec, M., and L. Madzar. 2003. "Experience with Severance Pay in Slovenia." Paper presented at the World Bank and Ludwig Boltzmann Institute for Economic Analysis Workshop "Severance Pay Reform: Toward Unemployment Savings and Retirement Accounts," Laxenberg/Vienna, Austria, November 7–8.

Vodopivec, M., and T. Rejec. 2002. "How Viable is the System of Unemployment Insurance Savings Accounts: Simulation Results for Estonia?" World Bank, Human Development Network, Washingon, DC.

Vodopivec, M., A. Wörgötter, and D. Raju. 2003. "Unemployment Benefit Systems in Central and Eastern Europe: A Review of the 1990s."

Social Protection Discussion Paper No. 0310, World Bank, Washington, DC.

Von Braun, J., T. Teklu, and P. Webb. 1991. "Labor-Intensive Public Works for Food Security: Experience in Africa." Working Series on Food 6, International Food Policy Research Institute, Washington, DC.

von Furstenberg, G. M. 1976. "Stabilization Characteristics of Unemployment Insurance." *Industrial and Labor Relations Review* 29 (3): 363–376.

Vroman, W. 2002. "Unemployment Insurance and Unemployment Assistance: A Comparison." Social Protection Discussion Paper No. 0203, Urban Institute and World Bank, Washington, DC.

Wadsworth, J. 1991. "Unemployment Benefits and Search Effort in the UK Labour Market." *Economica* 58 (1): 17–34.

Wang, C., and S. Williamson. 1996. "Unemployment Insurance with Moral Hazard in a Dynamic Economy." *Carnegie-Rochester Conference Series on Public Policy* 44 (1): 1–41.

Welch, F. 1977. "What Have We Learned from Empirical Studies of Unemployment Insurance?" *Industrial and Labor Relations Review* 30 (4): 451–461.

Wodon, Q. 2000. *Poverty and Policy in Latin America and the Caribbean.* World Bank Technical Paper No. 467, Washington, DC.

World Bank. 1994. *Averting the Old Age Crisis.* Washington, DC: World Bank.

———. 1999. "Sri Lanka: A Fresh Look at Unemployment." Report No. 19609-CE. South Asia Region, Poverty Reduction and Economic Management Unit, Washington, DC.

———. 2000. *Philippines: Poverty Assessment. Volume I: Main Report, Volume II: Technical Chapters.* Washington, DC: World Bank.

———. 2001a. *Social Protection Sector Strategy: From Safety Net to Springboard.* Washington, DC: World Bank.

———. 2001b. *World Development Report 2000/2001: Attacking Poverty.* Washington, DC: World Bank.

———. 2002. *Bosnia and Herzegovina: Labor Market in Postwar Bosnia and Herzegovina: How to Encourage Businesses to Create Jobs and Increase Worker Mobility.* Report No. 24889–BIH. Europe and Central Asia Region, South-East Europe Country Unit, Washington, DC.

———. 2003. Statistical Information Management and Analysis (SIMA). *World Development Indicators* and *Global Development Finance* central database. Washington, DC.

Wright, R. 1986. "The Redistributive Role of Unemployment Insurance and the Dynamics of Voting." *Journal of Public Economics* 31 (3): 377–399.

Yoo, K.-S. 2001. "The Feasibility of Introducing an Employment Insurance Scheme in the Philippines." Paper prepared for the World Bank–ILO–JMOL–PDOLE seminar on "Labor Market Policies: Their Implications for East and South East Asia," Manila, March.

Yun, J. 2001. "On the Integration of Unemployment Insurance with Pension through Individual Savings Account." World Bank, Human Development Network, Washington, DC.

Index

Tables, figures, and boxes are indicated respectively by t, f, and b.

active programs, 25, 28t3.1, 29
  See also public works; training
    programs
  shocks and, 110
  use in combination with other
    programs, 174
actively seeking work, defined, 20,
  20b2.3
adequacy of support, 71–74, 79t4.3, 81
  consumption-smoothing effects,
    53t3.6, 72, 81
  as performance evaluation criteria, 15
  poverty-reducing effects, 68t4.1,
    72–74
administrative capacity for program
    implementation, 133–37,
    134b5.1, 135b5.2, 136b5.3, 148t5.2
  implications for program choice and
    design, 16, 136–37
  lack of in Latin America, 155
  unemployment insurance, 157
adverse selection problem
  conditions of, 23n6
  in public sector retrenchment
    programs, 51
  unemployment insurance and, 17,
    18, 19

Africa
  See also developing countries; *specific*
    countries
  incidence of income support
    programs, 61, 61f3.3
  informal sector in, 138
  severance pay in, 46t3.5
  unemployment assistance in, 39t3.3
  unemployment insurance in, 35t3.2
age of claimants
  See also older workers; younger
    workers
  severance pay and, 42, 98
  unemployment assistance and, 40
  unemployment insurance and, 36
agriculture
  El Niño drought and, 172b6.9
  self-insurance measures and, 143–44
Aid to Families with Dependent
    Children (AFDC) (United
    States), 49b3.1
Algeria and social insurance, 62b3.2, 64
Argentina
  informal sector in, 139
  public works program in, 47, 48, 74,
    108, 115, 173b6.10
  social insurance in, 107

Argentina (*continued*)
unemployment insurance and
monitoring in, 134, 136*b*5.3, 154
unemployment insurance savings
accounts in, 59
Asia
See also specific countries and regions
incidence of income support
programs, 61, 61*f*3.3
informal sector in, 138
severance pay in, 46*t*3.5
unemployment assistance programs
in, 39*t*3.3
unemployment insurance in, 34*t*3.2
Australia
entitlement duration in, 180
severance pay in, 44*t*3.5
unemployment assistance in, 36, 94
activation among recipients of, 95,
95*b*4.2
benefits and costs of, 157–58,
158*b*6.3
Austria and severance pay reform, 60,
170*b*6.7
automatic stabilization effects of
unemployment insurance, 22,
92–93

benefit generosity. *See* generosity of
benefits
benefit recipients
See also eligibility requirements
activation among recipients of
unemployment assistance in
Australia, 95, 95*b*4.2
disqualifying benefit recipients in
transition countries, 134*b*5.1
identifying ineligible recipients in
Argentina, 136*b*5.3
income redistribution, 74–78,
75–76*t*4.2
unemployment insurance,
determining, 19–21, 20*b*2.3
Brazil
poor people's representation among
unemployed, 137
self-employment in, 126
unemployment insurance in,
62*b*3.2, 64
coverage of, 70

effect of increase in, 89
redistribution of income and, 77
unemployment insurance savings
accounts in, 40, 59
evaluation of, 96
Fundo de Garantia do Tempo de
Servico (FGTS) program, 96,
96*b*4.3, 166–67
Britain. *See* United Kingdom

Canada
duration of benefits, effect of, 119
early retirement in, 50
mandated work-sharing programs,
50
severance pay in, 44*t*3.5, 168
short-time compensation programs
in, 51
Caribbean. *See* Latin America and
Caribbean region
Chile
political reform in, effect of, 116
public works program in, 47, 77
unemployment benefit program in,
108, 163, 164*b*6.4, 177
unemployment insurance savings
accounts in, 40, 59, 137
civil strife, effect of, 146
climate
El Niño drought, 145, 172*b*6.9
shocks due to, 145, 146. *See also*
shocks
collective bargaining
declining benefits and, 179
taxation and, 89
Colombia
consumption-smoothing effects in,
72
prefunding of severance pay in, 169,
170*b*6.8
unemployment insurance savings
accounts in, 107
coverage of, 70
evaluation of, 96
income redistribution and, 78
community-based arrangements to
assist informal sector, 181,
182*b*6.12
complementarity of income support
programs, 173–75

comprehensive insurance, theory of, 11–12, 13b2.2
construction and maintenance work. *See* public works
consumer credit, access to, 142–43
consumption patterns changed due to unemployment, 141–45, 142t5.1, 143b5.4
consumption-smoothing effects, 53t3.6, 72, 81, 156b6.2, 163
costs
  advanced technology to reduce in Poland and Germany, 135b5.2
  implications for program choice and design, 136–37
    unemployment assistance, 157–59, 158b6.3
    unemployment insurance's introduction costs, 156–57, 156b6.2
  under means-testing programs, 135
  methods to limit, 185n5
  of public works, 99–100, 173
  Sri Lanka's severance pay programs and, 169b6.6
coverage, 53t3.6, 67, 68t4.1, 78, 79t4.3, 81
  See also specific income support programs
  income protection, 70–72
  as performance evaluation criteria, 15
credit insurance, availability of, 143
Cruzado Plan (Brazil), 62b3.2
cultural factors and informal mechanisms, 146, 150t5.2, 151
Czech Republic
  duration of benefits, effect of, 119
  public works programs in, 99
  replacement ratio in, 119

declining benefits, 179
defined benefit programs, 26t3.1, 29
defined contribution programs, 27t3.1, 29
Denmark
  disability pensions and early retirement, 50
  replacement rates and entitlement duration of unemployment benefits, 71
  voluntary unemployment insurance in, 29

design and implementation criteria, 6, 131–85, 147t5.2
  administrative capacity for program implementation, 133–37, 134b5.1, 135b5.2, 136b5.3
  characteristics of unemployment, 137–38, 148t5.2
    implications for program choice and design, 138
  country-specific, 16–17, 21
  cultural and political factors, 146, 150t5.2, 151
  guiding principles, 183–84, 184b6.13
  interactions with labor market institutions and shocks, 131–32, 147t5.2
  nature of shocks and, 145–46, 150t5.2
  nonsocial insurance and self-protection, 141–45
    implications for program choice and design, 144–45, 150t5.2
  prevalence and pattern of interhousehold transfers, 139–41
    implications for program choice and design, 141, 149t5.2
  size of informal sector, 138–39
    implications for program choice and design, 139, 149t5.2
determinants of social insurance programs for unemployed, 63–64, 64tA3.1
developing countries
  administrative capacity as factor in, 133, 136
  characteristics of unemployment in, 137
  coverage in, 67, 78
  income support programs in, 30f3.1, 52, 53t3.6, 59, 60f3.2
    choice of, 15, 136, 153–77
    improving, 153–85
    types of, 52–59
  informal sector in, 138–39
  monitoring in, 134, 137
  poor people's representation among unemployed, 137
  poverty reduction in, 73
  public works in. *See* public works

developing countries (*continued*)
    replacement rates and duration of
        unemployment benefits, 71
    self-protection as main strategy in,
        14, 21
    social assistance in, 71
    underemployed persons in, 20, 138
    unemployment assistance in, 157–59,
        160t6.1
    unemployment in, compared with
        industrial countries, 14
    unemployment insurance in.
        See unemployment insurance
    unemployment insurance savings
        accounts in, 165–66
disability pensions and early
    retirement, 50
discouraged workers, 20, 21, 23n10
discrimination in employment, 70
disincentive effects
    of early retirement, 100
    of unemployment assistance, 94
    of unemployment insurance, 88,
        88b4.1, 93
disqualifying benefit recipients in
    transition countries, 134b5.1
domestic workers' eligibility for
    unemployment insurance, 29
downsizing
    experience rating and, 128n10
    in public sector, 51–52, 125
    severance pay in, 42, 51
    unemployment insurance's effect on,
        91–92, 104
duration of benefits, 71–72, 81, 129n17
    in industrial countries, 71, 81,
        119, 123
    in transition countries, 119
    unemployment assistance, 50, 59–60
    unemployment insurance, 30, 59–60,
        71–72, 82, 93, 179–80
    variation in, 179–80

early retirement, 49–50
    ability of program to confront
        different shocks, 111
    efficiency effects of, 100–101
    as income maintenance program,
        26t3.1
    in transition countries, 50, 106

East Asia
    See also specific countries
    coverage in, 67
    crisis of 1998, 108–10, 142t5.1,
        143b5.4, 144, 184b6.13
    shocks and, 108–10, 109f4.3, 158b6.3
Eastern Europe
    See also transition countries; *specific*
        countries
    coverage in, 67
    discouraged vs. unemployed
        workers in, 21
    income redistribution in, 77
    poverty reduction in, 67, 68t4.1, 73
    severance pay in, 45t3.5
    shocks and, 104–6, 105f4.1
    unemployment assistance in, 38t3.3
    unemployment insurance in, 32t3.2
econometric techniques and social
    insurance programs, 63–64
economic theory, 11, 15
efficiency effects, 81–104, 102t4.6,
    118–27, 138
    choice of program and inconclusive
        research on, 117–18
    of early retirement, 100–101
    as performance evaluation
        criteria, 15
    of public works, 99–100, 103t4.6
    of severance pay, 97–99, 103t4.6,
        104, 168
    of social assistance, 100
    types of, 128n16
    of unemployment assistance, 94,
        95b4.2, 102t4.6, 104
    of unemployment insurance, 17–18,
        82, 88–90, 101, 102t4.6, 104,
        156b6.2
        disincentive effects, 88b4.1, 93
        in OECD countries, 83t4.4
        in transition countries, 85t4.5
    of unemployment insurance savings
        accounts, 94–97, 96b4.3, 103t4.6,
        104
    of work sharing, 101
elderly persons. *See* older workers
eligibility requirements
    differences as rationale for multiple
        programs, 174
    for public works, 47

for severance pay, 42
for social assistance, 48–49
for unemployment assistance, 36
for unemployment income support,
  19–21
  monitoring issues, 22
for unemployment insurance, 30
El Niño drought, 145, 172*b*6.9
Emergency Loan Facility (Philippines),
  71, 110
employability, methods to increase, 1
employment protection
  argument against government
    involvement in, 123
  effects of unknown, 128*n*11
  legislation, 66, 70, 74, 92, 128*n*12
  severance pay and, 98, 124
entitlement effect and labor force
  participation, 122
equilibrium labor market outcomes,
  121–24
  as performance evaluation
    criteria, 15
  transferability of results, 22
equilibrium unemployment, 82, 121–23
  declining benefits and, 179
  design and implementation criteria
    and, 17, 132
Estonia
  coverage in, 67
  disqualifying benefit recipients in,
    134*b*5.1
  duration of benefits, effect of, 119
  flat-rate benefits in, 71
  generosity of benefits in, 72, 124
  income redistribution in, 77
  poverty reduction in, 73
  replacement ratio in, 119
  unemployment assistance in, 158
  women's benefits in, 65
Europe
  See also specific countries and regions
  employment protection in, 92
  mandated work-sharing programs
    in, 50
  short-time compensation programs
    in, 50–51
  variations in unemployment
    insurance in, 63
evaluation criteria, 5, 14–17

design and implementation criteria,
  16–17. *See also* design and
  implementation criteria
efficiency effects. *See* efficiency
  effects
performance evaluation criteria, 6,
  15–16
experience rating in unemployment
  insurance, 36, 92, 128*n*10

fairness and formal income support
  systems, 17
family assistance programs and
  poverty reduction, 74
family, employment of other members
  in, 125–27
  interhousehold transfers and,
    139–41, 149*t*5.2
  unemployment assistance and, 94,
    125–26
  unemployment insurance and, 125
farmers. *See* agriculture
financial markets, strengthening of, 12
first-time job seekers
  See also younger workers
  eligibility for unemployment
    insurance, 29
formal income support mechanisms
  informal vs., 9, 10*t*2.1, 17
  limitations of, 11–14, 21
France
  decision to enter regular vs. informal
    job in, 126
  pension reduction for public service
    employees, 114
fraud
  See also monitoring and sanctions
  advanced technology to fight in
    Germany and Poland, 135*b*5.2
Fundo de Garantia do Tempo de
  Servico (FGTS) program (Brazil),
  96, 96*b*4.3, 166–67

general equilibrium
  growth interactions and, 9
  output and growth and, 126–27
  theoretical predictions with, 122
  transferability of results, 22
  unemployment insurance's effect on,
    91–92, 93

generosity of benefits, 89, 113–16
  conditions of, 66
  declining over time, 179
  design and implementation criteria
    and, 16
  index of generosity, 72
  labor reallocation and, 124
  precautionary savings and, 142
  shocks and, 90, 106, 107
  susceptibility to pressures to
    increase, 113–14
  tolerance to reforms that reduce,
    114–16
geography and shocks, 145
Germany
  advanced technology to fight fraud
    and reduce costs in, 135*b*5.2
  early retirement in, 50
  entitlement duration in, 180
  short-time compensation programs
    in, 51
  unemployment insurance,
    desirability of, 156*b*6.2
  work sharing in, 101
government accounts for insurance
    programs, 112, 113*b*4.4
government backing. *See* public sector
guarantee funds in transition countries,
    106, 110

health subsidies, 175, 185*n*8
high-income countries
  See also industrial countries
  income support programs in, 30*f*3.1,
    57*t*3.6, 59–60, 60*f*3.2, 61*f*3.3,
    170*b*6.7
Hong Kong and unemployment
    assistance, 36, 158
Hungary
  coverage in, 67
  disqualifying benefit recipients in,
    134*b*5.1
  early retirement in, 106
  generosity of benefits in, 72
  income redistribution in, 77
  poverty reduction in, 73
  public works programs in, 99
  replacement ratio in, 119
  training programs in, 106

ILO. *See* International Labor
    Organization
implementation criteria. *See* design and
    implementation criteria
improving income support programs
    in developing countries, 153–85
  choosing right program, 136*b*5.3,
    153–77, 155*b*6.1, 160*t*6.1
    complementarity of programs and
      policies, 173–75
    evaluation of programs, 160*t*6.1,
      175–77
    public works, 171–73
    severance pay programs, 167–71
    unemployment assistance, 157–59,
      158*b*6.3
    unemployment insurance savings
      accounts, 159, 163–67, 164*b*6.4,
      166*b*6.5
  designing unemployment insurance,
    177–80
  improving income protection of
    informal sector, 180–83
inactive people, classification as
    unemployed, 20
incentive effects
  of reemployment bonuses, 121
  of UISAs, 96, 96*b*4.3
  of unemployment assistance, 94
  of unemployment insurance
    experiments in U.S., 119–20
    in OECD countries, 82, 83*t*4.4
    in transition countries, 82, 85*t*4.5
  unemployment insurance savings
    accounts (UISAs), 94–96
incidence of income support programs,
    25–52
  by geographic regions, 61, 61*f*3.3
  in high-income countries, 30*f*3.1,
    57*t*3.6, 59–60, 60*f*3.2, 61*f*3.3,
    170*b*6.7
  in low-income countries, 30*f*3.1, 52,
    53*t*3.6, 59, 60*f*3.2
  in middle-income countries, 30*f*3.1,
    55*t*3.6, 59, 60*f*3.2
  variations across countries, 53*t*3.6,
    61–62
income maintenance programs, 25,
    26*t*3.1, 29

income protection, 66–81, 79t4.3
  See also income redistribution
  adequacy of support. *See* adequacy
      of support
  coverage, 53t3.6, 67, 68t4.1, 70–72, 78,
      79t4.3, 81
  of informal sector, 180–83
  severance pay and, 124, 167–68
income redistribution, 74–78, 75t4.2,
      79t4.3, 81
  as performance evaluation criteria,
      15
  resistance to political risk and, 111
income support programs
  See also specific type
  choice of program in developing
      countries, 153–85
    principles for, 183–84
  complementary programs and
      policies, 173–75
  comprehensive framework for, 1, 66,
      183
  importance of, 1
  incidence of
    by regions, 61, 61f3.3
    by types of countries, 52–60, 53t3.6
  objectives of, 7–8
  performance of, 65–129
  review of, 25–64
  types of, 25–52, 26t3.1
index of generosity, 72
India
  job security regulations in, 98
  public works programs in, 42, 47, 48,
      73–74, 77, 115
  SEWA integrated social security
      program in, 182b6.12
Indonesia
  financial crisis of 1998, 109, 141
  public works programs in, 110
  subsidized credit programs in, 110
industrial countries
  See also high-income countries;
      specific countries
  coverage in, 67
  definition of unemployment slanted
      toward, 21
  early retirement in, 49–50
    social security and, 100

entitlement duration of
  unemployment benefits in, 71,
      81, 119
expenditures compared to Latin
      America, 108
guidance from, for developing and
      transition countries, 21–22
incidence of unemployment support
      programs in, 61, 61f3.3
job security and lower employment
      in, 98
self-insurance in, 142
severance pay in, 22, 43t3.5
unemployment assistance in, 37t3.3
unemployment in
  compared with developing
      countries, 14, 21–22
  replacement rate and duration of
      benefits, effect of, 123
unemployment insurance in, 15, 25,
      29, 30f3.1, 31t3.2
  incentive effects of, 82, 83t4.4
  monitoring, effectiveness of, 178
informal sector, 127n1, 138–39, 149t5.2
  coverage of, 53t3.6, 67
  decision to enter, 126
  definition of, 151n3
  implications for program choice and
      design, 17, 137, 139
  unemployment insurance, 157
  improving income protection of,
      180–83, 182b6.12
  income support programs aimed at,
      174
  pooling of community resources to
      assist, 181, 182b6.12
Integrated Unemployment Insurance
      Programs, 165, 166b6.5, 167
interactions of public income support
      programs, 8–14, 12b2.1, 21, 66
interhousehold transfers, 139–41,
      149t5.2
International Labor Organization (ILO)
  definition of underemployment,
      23n9
  definition of unemployment, 19–21,
      20b2.3
  freedom of association convention,
      ratification of, 63

Jawahar Rojgar Yojana program
    (India), 48
Job Opportunities and Basic Skills
    Training (JOBS) (United States),
    49b3.1
job release programs, 50
Job Search Allowance (Australia), 36
job-search efforts, 118–20, 129n21
    active programs used as screening
        device for, 174–75
    actively seeking work, defined, 20,
        20b2.3
    intensity
        inclusive studies on effects of, 88
        monitoring of, 66, 93
        as performance evaluation
            criteria, 15
        post-unemployment wages
            and, 121
job security, 98, 110, 124

Korea. See Republic of Korea

labor force participation
    efficiency effects of unemployment
        insurance and, 81, 82, 88–90
    disincentive effects, 88, 88b4.1
    in OECD countries, 83t4.4
    in transition countries, 85t4.5
    entitlement effect and, 122, 129n16
    severance pay's effect on, 98
labor market institutions
    benefit generosity and, 114
    equilibrium unemployment and,
        9, 132
    implications of program choice and
        design, 132
    in Latin America, 108
    persistence of unemployment
        and, 132
    political reform and, 114–15
    shocks and, 131–32
labor taxes. See taxes
Latin America and Caribbean region
    administrative capacity for
        unemployment insurance
        programs in, 155
    coverage in, 67, 78
    incidence of income support
        programs, 61, 61f3.3

job security and lower employment
    in, 98, 124
public works programs in, 48
severance pay in, 22, 45t3.5, 78, 99,
    107, 168
shocks in, 106–8, 107f4.2, 152n6
training programs in, 108
unemployed in, 1, 4n1
unemployment insurance in, 33t3.2,
    108
unemployment insurance savings
    accounts in, 40, 41t3.4, 59, 61,
    61f3.3, 70
Latvia
    coverage in, 67
    poverty reduction in, 73
layoffs. See downsizing
lost wages, replacement of, 7
low-income countries. See developing
    countries
lump-sum payments. See severance pay

macroeconomic volatility, 145
Maharashtra Employment Guarantee
    Scheme (MEGS) (India), 47, 48,
    73–74, 77, 115
market insurance, 13b2.2
Maryland Unemployment Insurance
    Work Search Demonstration,
    178b6.11
means-tested programs, 27t3.1, 29
    in Australia, 36
    desirability of, 157–59
    equilibrium model and, 122
    in United States, 49b3.1
Mediterranean countries and
        interhousehold transfers, 141
MEGS. See Maharashtra Employment
    Guarantee Scheme
Mexico
    contraction of output in, 106
    school and health subsidies in, 175
    training programs in, 71, 108
microcredit to assist informal sector,
    181
middle-income countries
    See also transition countries
    focus on, 2
    income support programs in, 30f3.1,
        55t3.6, 59, 60f3.2

minimum wage and public works programs, 47
monitoring and sanctions
  active programs used as screening device, 174–75
  administrative capacity and, 134–37
  eligibility for unemployment insurance, 22, 133, 177–78
  intensity of job search, 66, 93
  reemployment and, 22, 93, 178, 178b6.11
moral hazard problem
  conditions of, 23n6
  credit insurance and, 143
  self-insurance and, 13b2.2
  severance pay and, 99
  underemployment and, 138
  unemployment insurance and, 17, 18, 88, 119–20, 127
    correction for, 19, 178–79
  unemployment insurance savings accounts and, 95

natural disasters. *See* climate; shocks
Netherlands
  early retirement in, 50
  monitoring and sanctions in, 178b6.11
  short-time compensation programs in, 51
NewStart Allowance (Australia), 36
New Zealand and unemployment assistance, 36, 157
nongovernmental organizations to assist informal sector, 181, 183, 185n7
nonsocial insurance, 141–45, 142t5.1, 143b5.4
  implications for program choice and design, 144–45, 150t5.2

objectives of income support programs, 7–8
  differences among programs as rationale for adopting multiple programs, 173–74
OECD countries. *See* industrial countries
older workers
  See also early retirement

as beneficiaries of private transfers, 17
  reemployment likelihood of, 19
  severance costs associated with, 70, 98
output and growth, 81–82, 126–27
  as performance evaluation criteria, 15
  unemployment insurance's effect on, 91–94

pension programs
  See also early retirement
  East Asian financial crisis and use of, 109
  high administrative costs of, 185n5
  Integrated Unemployment Insurance Program and, 166b6.5
  in OECD countries, 128n15
  in public sector retrenchment programs, 51
  resistance to political risk, 114
perfect competition, 22n5
perfect information, 22n5
performance of income support programs, 65–129
  efficiency effects. *See* efficiency effects
  evaluation criteria, 6, 15–16, 21, 65
  income protection effects, 66–81, 79t4.3
  resistance to political risk, 111–17, 117t4.8, 124–25
  suitability to confront different shocks, 104–11, 105f4.1, 107f4.2, 109f4.3
persistence of unemployment, 81, 90–91, 93, 132
  choice of program affected by, 137
Peru
  consumption-smoothing effects in, 72
  interhousehold transfers in, 140
  poor people's representation among unemployed, 137
  severance pay in, 70, 114, 124
    income redistribution and, 78
  unemployment insurance savings accounts in, 107

Philippines
  consumer credit, access to, 142–43
  East Asian financial crisis, effect on,
    141
  Emergency Loan Facility in, 71, 110
  financial crisis of 1998, 109, 143b5.4
  interhousehold transfers in, 139, 140
  policy changes to deal with
    unemployment effectively in,
    12b2.1
  poor people's representation among
    unemployed, 137
  public works program in, 47
    aiding coconut farmers affected by
      drought, 172b6.9
  share-tenancy as informal insurance
    mechanism, 144
  underemployed persons in, 21, 138
  unemployment insurance
    introduction in, 155, 155b6.1
    monitoring capacity for, 135
Poland
  advanced technology to fight fraud
    and reduce costs in, 135b5.2
  coverage in, 67
  early retirement in, 106
  generosity of benefits, 72
  poverty reduction in, 73
  public works programs in, 99
  unemployed spouse, effect of, 94, 126
political factors
  as design and implementation
    criteria, 146, 150t5.2, 151
  unemployment insurance and, 155, 157
political risk, resistance to, 111–17,
    117t4.8, 124–25
  flexible income support programs
    needed due to, 115
  as performance evaluation criteria,
    15–16
  protection of benefit levels during
    downturns, 112, 113b4.4
  susceptibility to pressures to increase
    benefit generosity, 113–14
  tolerance to reforms that reduce
    benefit generosity, 114–16
pooling
  of community resources to assist
    informal sector, 181
  of risk and insurance, 18

post-unemployment wages as
    performance evaluation criteria,
    15, 104, 120–21, 129n18
poverty-reducing effects, 18, 72–74, 81,
    127n3
  complementary program use for, 175
  in high-income countries, 60
  political reform and, 116
  social assistance and, 48–49, 49b3.1
  in transition economies, 68t4.1, 73
prefunding of programs to protect
    against downturns, 112, 171
  severance pay, 168–69, 170b6.7 & 6.8
private accounts for insurance
    programs, 112, 113b4.4
private risk management mechanisms,
    9, 18, 127
  beneficiaries of, 17
  interhousehold transfers as, 139–41,
    149t5.2
Probecat program (Mexico), 108
PROGRESA program (Mexico), 175
protection effects. *See* income
    protection
public guarantee funds in transition
    countries, 106, 110
public sector
  mandated work-sharing programs
    in, 50
  pension reduction for employees, 114
  as public works provider, 48
  retrenchment programs, 42, 51–52
  as social assistance provider, 49
  as unemployment assistance
    provider, 40
  as unemployment insurance
    provider, 17–19, 36
public works
  ability of program to confront
    different shocks, 106, 108, 110,
    111, 112t4.7
  as active program, 28t3.1
  adequacy of support, 80t4.3
  administrative costs of, 136
  choice of program as best suited,
    162t6.1, 171–73, 176–77
  costs of, 99–100, 173
  coverage of, 71, 80t4.3
  design and implementation criteria
    for, 147t5.2

in developing countries, 25, 52, 53*t*3.6, 59, 71, 171–73, 172*b*6.9, 173*b*6.10
East Asian financial crisis of 1998 and, 110
efficiency effects, 99–100, 103*t*4.6
eligibility requirements, 47
evaluation of, 3, 99, 171, 176–77
features of, 42, 47–48, 171–73
incidence of
by region, 61, 61*f*3.3
by types of countries, 52, 53*t*3.6
income protection effect of, 80*t*4.3
income redistribution and, 74, 77, 80*t*4.3, 81
in middle-income countries, 55*t*3.6, 59
objectives of, 8
poverty reduction and, 73–74, 81
principles for designing programs, 173
psychological stigmatization as effect of, 8
resistance to political risk, 116, 117*b*4.8
social funds to finance, 48
strengths vs. weaknesses of, 162*t*6.1, 171–73
taxes to finance, 48
in transition countries, 106
wages in, 47

recession
protection of benefit levels during, 112
reduced government social spending and, 108
unemployment risk and, 18, 146
recipients. *See* benefit recipients
reduction of poverty. *See* poverty-reducing effects
reductions in force. *See* downsizing
reemployment
duration of benefits, effect of, 119
monitoring and sanctions. *See* monitoring and sanctions
public works and, 99
replacement rates, 71–72, 81, 119, 122, 123
Republic of Korea
coverage in, 67

financial crisis of 1998, 109
guarantee funds in, 110
health subsidies, 185*n*8
job preservation and hiring subsidies in, 110
job security regulations in, 110
public works programs in, 110
unemployment insurance introduction in, 183, 184*b*6.13
resistance to political risk. *See* political risk, resistance to
restructuring of enterprises, 124–25
severance pay's effect on, 97
unemployment insurance and, 91–92, 104
retrenchment programs, 51–52
coverage of, 71
rehiring of same workers, 125
severance pay in, 42, 51
risk management mechanisms. *See* social risk management mechanisms
risk pooling and insurance, 18
Russian Federation and government redistribution, 115

sanctions. *See* monitoring and sanctions
Scandinavian countries
See also specific countries
social assistance in, 100
school and health subsidies, 175
Self Employed Women's Association (SEWA) integrated social security program (India), 182*b*6.12
self-employment
East Asian programs to promote, 110
eligibility for unemployment insurance, 29
generosity of benefits and decision to enter, 126
self-insurance
combining with social insurance, 163, 164*b*6.4
moral hazard problem and, 13*b*2.2, 138
shadow price of, 13*b*2.2
UISA program as, 40, 42

self-insurance (*continued*)
  unemployment insurance in
    conjunction with, 177
  using "bad" instruments for, 12
self-protection, 141–45, 142*t*5.1, 143*b*5.4
  implications for program choice and
    design, 144–45, 150*t*5.2
  prevalence in developing countries,
    14, 21
  as risk management instrument,
    13*b*2.2
severance pay
  ability of program to confront
    different shocks, 111, 112*t*4.7
  adequacy of support, 80*t*4.3
  choice of program as best suited,
    161*t*6.1, 167–71, 176
  consumption-smoothing effects
    of, 72
  costs of, 136, 169*b*6.6
  coverage, 67, 70, 78, 80*t*4.3
  design and implementation criteria
    for, 147*t*5.2
  East Asian financial crisis and use of,
    109, 110
  efficiency effects, 22, 97–99, 103*t*4.6,
    104, 168
    empirical evidence, 98–99
    theoretical predictions, 97
  eligibility requirements, 42
  evaluation of, 3, 98–99, 176
  factors affecting choice of, 161*t*6.1
  features of, 42, 167–71
    by country, 42, 43*t*3.5
  incidence of
    around world, 53*t*3.6, 59
    by region, 61, 61*f*3.3
  as income maintenance program,
    26*t*3.1
  income protection effect of, 80*t*4.3,
    167–68
  income redistribution effect of,
    80*t*4.3, 81
  individually tailored and later
    rehiring, 125
  job-search efforts and, 120
  in low-income countries, 53*t*3.6, 59
  in middle-income countries, 55*t*3.6, 59
  moral hazard and, 99
  nonperformance problem of, 70

  objectives of, 8
  predicted effects on unemployment
    of, 122–23, 124
  prefunding programs, 168–69,
    170*b*6.7 & 6.8, 171
  reforming, 60, 170*b*6.7, 170*b*6.8
  resistance to political risk, 114, 116,
    117*b*4.8
  streamlining current programs, 168,
    169*b*6.6
  strengths vs. weaknesses of, 161*t*6.1,
    167–71
  in transition countries, 45*t*3.5, 106
  coverage of, 67
SEWA (Self Employed Women's
    Association) integrated social
    security program (India),
    182*b*6.12
share-tenancy as informal insurance
    mechanism, 144
shocks
  civil strife, wars, and social
    upheavals, 146
  geography and climate, 145, 146
  household as locus of distress to deal
    with, 144, 175
  implications for program choice and
    design, 146
  income support programs and,
    9, 16, 132
  interactions with labor market
    institutions and, 131–32, 147*t*5.2
  macroeconomic volatility, 145
  self-insurance and, 177
  structural and technological, 145
  suitability of programs to confront,
    104–11, 112*t*4.7, 183
    East Asia, 108–10, 109*f*4.3
    European transition economies,
      104–6, 105*f*4.1
    Latin America and Caribbean,
      106–8, 107*f*4.2
    as performance evaluation
      criteria, 15–16
    as rationale for multiple
      programs, 174
  types of, 145–46
  unemployment insurance and,
    90–91, 111, 112*t*4.7
short-time compensation, 50–51

Singapore and income support
    programs, 59
Slovak Republic
    duration of benefits, effect of, 119
    early retirement in, 106
    income redistribution in, 77
    poverty reduction in, 73
    unemployed spouse, effect of, 94,
      125–26
Slovenia
    disqualifying benefit recipients in,
      134b5.1
    early retirement in, 106
    entitlement duration in, 180
    generosity of benefits in, 72, 124
    job preservation subsidies in, 106
    monitoring of eligibility in, 133
    nonperformance problem of
      severance pay in, 70
    poverty reduction in, 73
    public works program in, 99
    replacement ratio in, 119
social assistance, 48–49, 49b3.1
    coverage, 67, 71
    efficiency effects of, 94, 100
    as income maintenance program,
      27t3.1
    unemployment insurance in
      conjunction with, 177
social funds and public works
    programs, 48
social insurance
    combining with self-insurance, 163,
      164b6.4
    determinants of programs, 63–64,
      64tA3.1
    importance of, 2
    in Latin America, 107–8
    in low-income countries, 2
    in middle-income countries,
      55t3.6, 59
    origin of, 23n8
    poverty reduction and, 74
    trade unions and, 62, 62b3.2, 64
social risk management mechanisms
    formal, 9, 10t2.1
      fairness improved under, 17
      guidelines and limitations of,
        11–14, 13b2.2, 21
      framework of, 9–11, 66

general equilibrium and growth
    interactions, 9
income support programs as subset
    of, 5
informal, 9, 10t2.1
interactions among, 8–14, 12b2.1, 66
model for utility-maximizing
    individual, 13b2.2
other policies and programs,
    interactions with, 11
private mechanisms, interactions
    with, 9, 18
social security
    effect on early retirement, 100
    effect on job creation, 152n5
    informal sector and, 181, 182
    as social contract, 114
social upheavals, effect of, 146
South Africa
    absence of unemployment benefits
      in, 151n2
    public works program in, 47, 77
Southern Europe and severance pay,
    44t3.5
Sri Lanka
    characteristics of unemployment in, 137
    severance pay programs in, 169b6.6
    unemployment insurance
      introduction in, 156
Sweden
    short-time compensation programs
      in, 51
    unemployment insurance in
      duration of benefits, effect of, 119
      trade unions and, 64n1
      voluntary nature of, 29

taxes
    financing of public works programs
      by, 48
    financing of social assistance
      programs by, 49
    labor taxes, effect of, 89, 92, 128n8, 132
    reemployment tax as penalty, 179
technology
    structural and technological shocks,
      145
    using advanced technology to fight
      fraud and reduce costs in
      Poland and Germany, 135b5.2

Temporary Assistance for Needy
    Families (TANF) (United States),
    49b3.1
Termination of Employment of
    Workman Act (TEWA) of 1971
    (Sri Lanka), 169
Thailand
    financial crisis of 1998, 109
    public works programs in, 110
    rural migrants returning to regions
        of origin, 64n3
    severance pay and guarantee funds
        in, 110
    unemployment insurance
        introduction in, 155
theoretical modeling, limitations of,
    11–14
Trabajar program (Argentina), 47, 48,
    74, 108, 115, 173b6.10
trade unions and social insurance, 62,
    62b3.2, 64, 64n1
    See also collective bargaining
training programs, 25
    as active program, 28t3.1
    income redistribution and, 74, 77
    Job Opportunities and Basic Skills
        Training (JOBS) (United States),
        49b3.1
    nongovernmental organizations
        providing, 185n7
    severance pay and, 97
    in transition countries to confront
        shocks, 106, 108
transition countries
    See also middle-income countries;
        specific countries
    disqualifying benefit recipients in,
        134, 134b5.1
    early retirement programs, 50, 106
    focus on, 2
    generosity of benefits, 72
    income redistribution in, 77, 81
    income support programs in
        choice of, 15, 153–77
        incidence of, 61, 61f3.3
    job security and lower employment
        in, 98
    poverty-reducing effects of benefits
        in, 68t4.1, 73

protection of benefit levels during
    downturns in, 112
public paternalism in, effect of, 146
public works in, 106
replacement rates and duration of
    unemployment benefits, 71, 117
restructuring of enterprises and
    overall adjustment, 124–25
severance pay in, 45t3.5, 106
    coverage of, 67
shocks and, 104–6, 105f4.1
unemployment assistance in, 157–59,
    160t6.1
unemployment insurance in. *See*
    unemployment insurance
unemployment insurance savings
    accounts simulation in, 97
types of income support programs,
    25–52, 26t3.1, 60f3.2

UISAs. *See* unemployment insurance
    savings accounts
underemployed persons, 20, 21, 23n9 &
    11, 138
unemployment
    Asian financial crisis of 1998 and, 109
    characteristics of, 137–38, 148t5.2
    consumption patterns changed due
        to, 137–38, 142t5.1, 143b5.4
    covariant, 145
    extent of, 1
    idiosyncratic, 145
    ILO definition of, 19–21, 20b2.3
    implications for program choice and
        design and, 127, 138
    monitoring. *See* monitoring and
        sanctions
    origin of, 23n7
    persistence of, 81, 90–91, 93, 132
        choice of program affected by, 137
    risk management mechanisms,
        choice of, 5
unemployment assistance
    ability of program to confront
        different shocks, 111, 112t4.7
    adequacy of support, 79t4.3
    age of claimants and, 40
    choice of program as best suited,
        157–59, 160t6.1, 176

design and implementation criteria
for, 147t5.2
disincentive problems of, 94
duration of benefits, 50, 59–60
efficiency effects and, 94, 95b4.2,
102t4.6, 104
eligibility after exhausting
unemployment insurance, 36
evaluation of, 2, 176
family members, employment of,
and, 125–26
features of, 36–40
by country, 36, 37t3.3
in high-income countries, 59–60
incidence of
around world, 52, 53t3.6
by region, 61, 61f3.3
as income maintenance program,
27t3.1
income protection effect of, 79t4.3
income redistribution and, 79t4.3, 81
income-tested targeting, 50
job-search efforts and, 118–20
means-tested targeting, 50, 122,
157–59, 158b6.3, 160–62t6.1
objectives of, 7
public sector as provider of, 40
resistance to political risk, 116,
117b4.8
strengths vs. weaknesses of, 40,
157–59, 160t6.1
in transition countries, 70–71
unemployment insurance
ability of program to confront
different shocks, 90–91, 111,
112t4.7
adequacy of support, 79t4.3
adverse selection and, 17
age of claimants and, 36
automatic stabilization effects of, 22,
92–93
choice of program as best suited,
153–57, 160t6.1, 175–77
country-specific considerations for,
154–55
coverage, 67, 79t4.3
decreasing benefits over time, 178–79
design and implementation criteria
for, 147t5.2

designing program, 164b6.4, 177–80,
178b6.11
determining benefit recipients,
19–21, 20b2.3
in developing countries, 15, 25, 30,
35t3.2, 67, 157
disqualifying benefit recipients,
134b5.1
duration of entitlement, 30, 59–60,
71–72, 82, 179–80
efficiency effects of, 82–94, 101,
102t4.6, 104, 156b6.2
disincentive effects, 88, 88b4.1, 93
on output and growth, 91–94
on persistence of unemployment,
90–91
on unemployment and labor force
participation, 82, 83t4.4, 85t4.5,
88–90
eligibility requirements for, 30
evaluation of, 2, 175–76
experience rating in, 36, 92
family members, employment of,
and, 125
features of, 17, 19, 29–36, 30f3.1
by country, 30, 31t3.2
in high-income countries, 59–60
incentive effects
in OECD countries, 82, 83t4.4
in transition countries, 82, 85t4.5
incidence of
around world, 52, 53t3.6
by region, 61, 61f3.3
as income maintenance program,
26t3.1
income protection effect of, 79t4.3
income redistribution and, 75t4.2,
77–78, 79t4.3, 81
in industrial countries, 15, 25, 29,
30f3.1
Integrated Unemployment Insurance
Program, advantages of, 166b6.5
introduction costs and benefits,
156–57, 156b6.2
job-search efforts and, 118–20
in middle-income countries, 55t3.6,
59
monitoring and sanctions, 22, 93,
177–78, 178b6.11

unemployment insurance (*continued*)
  moral hazard and. *See* moral hazard
    problem
  objectives of, 7
  premiums and contributions, 19, 36
  public sector's role in providing,
    17–19, 36
  rationale for, 6
  resistance to political risk, 112, 116,
    117*t*4.8
  self-insurance in conjunction with,
    177
  strengths vs. weaknesses of, 153–57,
    160*t*6.1
  trade unions and, 62, 62*b*3.2, 64, 89
  in transition countries, 15, 25, 32*t*3.2
    coverage of, 67
    disincentive effects of, 88, 88*b*4.1
    disqualifying benefit recipients,
      134*b*5.1
    duration of benefits, effect of, 119
    incentive effects of, 82, 85*t*4.5
  voluntary programs, 29
unemployment insurance savings
    accounts
  in developing countries, 165–66
unemployment insurance savings
    accounts (UISAs)
  ability of program to confront
    different shocks, 111, 112*t*4.7
  adequacy of support, 79*t*4.3
  administrative costs of, 136
  based on lifetime income, 185*n*3
  choice of program as best suited, 159,
    161*t*6.1, 163–67, 176
  coverage, 79*t*4.3
  cum-borrowing program, 42, 163,
    164, 165, 167, 176
  design and implementation criteria
    for, 147*t*5.2
  efficiency effects, 94–97, 103*t*4.6, 104
    empirical evidence, 96–97, 96*b*4.3
    theoretical predictions, 94–96
  evaluation of, 2–3, 96–97, 176
  features of, 40–42, 159, 163–67,
    164*b*6.4, 166*b*6.5
    by country, 40, 41*t*3.4
  high-income countries, not used by,
    60

  incentive issues with, 94–96, 96*b*4.3
    design and implementation
      criteria and, 16
  incidence of
    around world, 52, 53*t*3.6
    by region, 61, 61*f*3.3
    as income maintenance program,
      27*t*3.1
  income protection effect of, 79*t*4.3
  income redistribution and, 76*t*4.2, 78,
    79*t*4.3, 81
  job-search efforts and, 120
  in middle-income countries, 55*t*3.6,
    59
  objectives of, 8
  resistance to political risk, 114, 116,
    117*b*4.8
  strengths vs. weaknesses of, 95–96,
    159, 161*t*6.1, 163–67
  types of, 42
unions. *See* trade unions and social
    insurance
United Kingdom
  administrative costs of programs in,
    135
  job-search practices in, 120
  monitoring and sanctions in,
    178*b*6.11
  short-time compensation programs
    in, 51
  unemployment insurance in
    conjunction with social
    assistance, 177
United States
  consumption-smoothing effects in,
    72, 156*b*6.2
  early retirement in, 50
  interhousehold transfers in, 140
  replacement rates and entitlement
    duration of benefits, 71, 72, 126
  severance pay in, 44*t*3.5
  short-time compensation programs
    in, 51
  temporary aid to needy families in,
    49*b*3.1
  Temporary Assistance for Needy
    Families (TANF), 49*b*3.1
  unemployment insurance in
    desirability of, 156*b*6.2

duration of benefits, effect of, 119
experience rating and, 92
government vs. private accounts
    for, 113*b*4.4
moral hazard and, 88, 119–20
variations from European
    programs, 63
unemployment insurance savings
    accounts simulation in, 97

wages
in East Asian financial crisis,
    143*b*5.4
in public works programs, 47
wage-setting institutions and
        interaction with income support
        programs, 66, 89, 132

wage subsidies
    as active program, 28*t*3.1
    to confront shocks, 108
war, effect of, 146
women
    benefits for child raising, 65
    Philippines financial crisis, effect on,
        144
    severance pay and, 98
workfare. *See* public works
work sharing, 50, 101

younger workers
    in East Asian financial crisis, 144
    replacing older retirees with, 50
    severance pay and, 98
    in transition countries, 106